The Ethics and Politics of Pornography

Also by David Edward Rose

FREE WILL AND CONTINENTAL PHILOSOPHY: The Death without Meaning

HEGEL'S 'PHILOSOPHY OF RIGHT': A Reader's Guide

The Ethics and Politics of Pornography

David Edward Rose
Newcastle University, UK

palgrave
macmillan

First published 2013 by
PALGRAVE MACMILLAN

Palgrave Macmillan in the UK is an imprint of Macmillan Publishers Limited, registered in England, company number 785998, of Houndmills, Basingstoke, Hampshire RG21 6XS.

Palgrave Macmillan in the US is a division of St Martin's Press LLC, 175 Fifth Avenue, New York, NY 10010.

Palgrave Macmillan is the global academic imprint of the above companies and has companies and representatives throughout the world.

Palgrave® and Macmillan® are registered trademarks in the United States, the United Kingdom, Europe and other countries

ISBN: 978–0–230–37111–8

This book is printed on paper suitable for recycling and made from fully managed and sustained forest sources. Logging, pulping and manufacturing processes are expected to conform to the environmental regulations of the country of origin.

A catalogue record for this book is available from the British Library.

A catalog record for this book is available from the Library of Congress.

Contents

Acknowledgements

Most references in the following pages follow standard practice except for certain digital editions of books whereby, *in lieu* of any agreed convention, I have used the location (loc.) marker as one would normally use the page number. Some historical texts use paragraph numbers (¶) and some use section numbers (§) rather than page numbers, but this is clearly indicated with the appropriate symbol. Following standard practice, references to the giants of the canon (notably Aristotle and Kant here) usually use the expected citation which is common to all (or most) editions and can be found in the margin. It is, mostly, self-explanatory when you pick up the edition to search out the original quotation. Concerning references, the only other note to make is the Dworkin problem. There are two Dworkins, Andrea and Ronald, but I very often just refer to Dworkin. I do not feel that it is easy to confuse their respective positions; basically Andrea really does not like pornography. If the reader bears that in mind, confusion should be avoided. The Dworkins are not related.

The present work has been written over a period of intense teaching and on the back of certain conference papers and subsequent articles. These activities have all had an influence on the final content of the book and I thank all those who have made comments, reviewed and asked questions during those activities. The actual writing of the book benefited immensely from two anonymous referees who cast an eye over it at different stages of its completion. The actual manuscript has also been the subject of comments by and discussions with Dudley Knowles and Eleni Leontsini who have both made invaluable contributions. It has also been very much helped by the dedication of the editorial team at Palgrave Macmillan: Melanie Blair, Brendan George and Priyanka Gibbons.

On a personal note, my family and friends all had to put up with having to discuss or, at times, being too enthusiastic about having to discuss the subject matter of this book. It was one of those topics that, after a glass of red wine, everyone seems to have an opinion about. The sort of opinions that require a glass of red wine to surface. This wasn't that odd were it not for the fact that my eldest is preparing for his first communion.

Above all, then, thanks to Laura, Nicholas and Jeremy for continuing to put up with me and making every day worth it.

That is the nearest thing to a dedication as I'm not sure how a person might feel about having a book about pornography dedicated to them. I also think, after this, I'll have to promise Laura that I won't write a book about philosophy and Japanese horror films ... Ever.

1
Risky Business

When I was eighteen, I manipulated two male friends into coming to the cinema with me to watch *Betty Blue,* informing them it was a French film with an 18 certificate and letting their own imaginations do the rest. Copious amounts of beer helped my machinations and we went to the late showing in Norwich's Picturehouse. This was to prove to be a mistake. If you are not familiar with the film, my mates would probably recount it thus: 'French bird gets her kit off a lot, is quite mad and pokes her eye out before dying'. There is much more to the film than that. It is a very fine film that, now comfortably in my middle age, I would recommend to most people. The film, though, opens with a very well shot and, in relation to most other films, rather long sex scene. Between my mates' giggling and the furtive looks of those more mature than us, I had an excruciatingly embarrassing experience. The reason I am recollecting this now is that I remember several cinema-goers walking out of the film during the opening scene, as though the offence caused by the representation was so shocking it was better not to experience it. The scene is explicit, but it is not hard pornography nor truly soft pornography, if that distinction makes any sense at all. It occurs to me now that if those persons who left were asked then their reasons for leaving, they would have responded that they would rather not watch pornography and that the scene was pornographic.

Let me continue with a further piece of odd personal information. And here, as in so much of this book, I am taking a risk; uncomfortably lying down on a rather comfortable leather, Le Corbusier chaise longue and beginning to ramble. I confess that I used to know far too much about French cinema (hence my desire to see *Betty Blue*) when I was an adolescent and the cause of such knowledge was BBC2's late night Film Club series, which I used to watch in my room on an old, flickery black and white set. I had mixed motivations for watching such films, but one definite motivation was that it was one of the few places to consume representations of sexual activity. There were, as I have said, other motivations for watching the best of continental European cinema, but it would be disingenuous to deny that my perseverance through some of the more boring French offerings was the hope of a flash of breast or an image of copulation.

Such perseverance was due to the fact that, when I was very young, there were only three television channels in Britain (becoming four when I was nine years old) and, besides the ubiquitous and largely unerotic presence of Page Three in *The Sun*, pornographic or erotic imagery was not easily available. Things soon changed. First, Channel Four, with its pretension to some imagined right of expression of aesthetic value, then more unashamedly, Channel Five, with its seasons dedicated to such great actresses as Shannon Tweed and its 'penetrating' documentary series about the porn industry, soon meant that sexual imagery became almost commonplace. However, it was the internet explosion that changed the whole nature of the game, making sexual imagery easily available and widely consumed. One study reveals that the third most common term to be typed into an internet search engine is 'sex'; coming before 'the' and behind only 'of' and 'and' (Spink et al., 2000: 231).

It would be naïve and hasty to deny that the consumption of pornographic objects has been a constant throughout history, although in the next chapter I shall dismiss such a claim. It is in the era of mass production and pornography's increased consumption in line with other goods that it truly presents itself as an urgent ethical issue (Traeen et al., 2010). If you want to be titillated or excited by sexual imagery, there is no longer any need to labour through the existential angst of French cinema or the excessive aestheticism of Italian films. The images and representations are already there, prepared for use. One could argue that this is akin to everything in late capitalism: if you want a luxury vegetable to eat, you no longer need to toil to produce it but will find it readily available, lying before one and ready for consumption. And there is sufficient surplus wealth and leisure time to make such consumption a possibility. The relationship between capitalism and pornography is, perhaps, not a trivial one and is in need of interrogation.

But later, not yet.

So, you may ask, why on Earth one would write a book about pornography and, specifically, in a philosophical idiom. It would seem, in the field for which such a book is primarily proposed, that such an endeavour may well invite ridicule. Philosophy ought to concern itself with loftier objects of reflection. And, yet, such a risk is perhaps akin to a film director seeking to make a serious film about sexual relations. There is a long list of such films that testify to such absurdity and self-indulgence: Kubrick's *Eyes Wide Shut* and Bertolucci's *The Dreamers* immediately jump to mind. The possibility of ridicule rather than the more normal rational rejection ('his ideas are wrong', 'there is no logical connection between the premises and the conclusion', or 'the film is an artistic failure') may well reveal something of interest, like the embarrassed giggle of a schoolboy at the back of the class (or the cinema!) during a sex education lesson, even if such a lesson is handled with the utmost professionalism and delivered in an informative, entertaining and appropriate manner. One can imagine when women first began to wear trousers, there would have been red cheeks, averted eyes and childish giggles and, to accompany such adolescent responses, there may well have been ideological expressions of reasons why such wearing of trousers is an abomination, why it should be stopped and why it is immoral. To believe that thinking alone is enough to overcome conventional prejudice is naïve. If there had not been women brave enough to invite ridicule, the *status quo* of inequality might well have remained unbroken.

And, of course, even if Bertolucci failed with *The Dreamers*, he did make the far more elegant and profound *Last Tango in Paris*. Other successes do of course exist, Medem's *Sex and Lucía* being foremost amongst them and perhaps also Ferrario's *Guardami*. And just as it is possible to make a serious film about human sexuality, so it ought to be possible to talk seriously and reflectively about the representations of sexual activity. Such activity is, after all, a staple of human action and a central, even if a silent, constituent of human culture. Just as we turn sustenance into complicated rituals of social play and regulated desire, so too does sexual activity institutionalize a physical need into a social code of meanings and behaviours. Meanings and behaviours we must somehow learn, incorporate into our behaviours and modify when the circumstances demand it. Just as we learn to hold the fork in our left hand, but as we develop, we learn that it is acceptable to move it to the right if we are eating pasta, so our behaviours are judged as appropriate or not in a social milieu.

My interest in the subject of pornography is neither an aesthetic one nor directly a cultural one; it is an ethical (and consequently) a political interest. A constellation of ethical issues attach themselves to the production, exchange and consumption of pornographic objects, be they films, photographs, novels, poems, computer games, lithographs, or whatever. We most naturally concentrate on examples of mpegs and jpegs but any evaluative moral judgements, made (irrespective of any aesthetic evaluative judgements) on the basis of the pornographic nature of such objects, ought to apply equally to Sade's and Bataille's novels, to Crowley's poems and to ancient Indian and Japanese drawings. If *Debbie Does Dallas* or *120 Days of Sodom* is morally problematic, and are so because of their sexual content, then there is also at least a query to be raised about texts such as Lawrence's *Lady Chatterley's Lover*. One cannot believe that there is a class of individuals with the requisite aesthetic sense to appreciate sexual representation, and that they alone can decide what is or is not a valuable representation without inviting the charge of elitism. Our intuitions concerning pornography are either the expression of a brute, emotional response such as disgust (or unease) or they are statements which are rationally defensible (and hence defeasible). Such responses or statements apply equally to Lawrence's work, as history testifies. Such intuitions are moral in nature.

So, one might hold that pornography is offensive, a worthless pursuit, aesthetically without value, or that it harms specific individuals or groups. Such judgements correspond to well-defined moral positions: emotivism; conservatism; utilitarianism; and Kantianism. Politically, one might argue that pornography ought to be tolerated as a consequence of the right to freedom of expression and autonomy. It might well be a worthless pursuit, but it is not the business of individuals or groups to dictate to others how they should spend their time or money. Alternatively, feminists may well argue that the production, exchange and consumption of pornography violate the rights of individuals or the group of women as a whole because it sustains and reinforces a state of inequality. It is obvious that the ethical and political dimensions of pornography are not that easily disentangled. More controversially, I shall attempt to argue that the simplistic modern approach to applied ethics actually collaborates with the maintenance and reproduction of unequal sexual relationships precisely because it fails to consider that pornography properly conceived and executed may well overcome such inegalitarian relationships and have a positive moral value. And such a refusal to think through the basic axiology of pornography may well be based in the same immaturity as the schoolboy's giggling at the back of the class.

So, my risk has doubled. Not only do I intend to direct philosophical thinking to the most unserious of subjects, sexual representation, but also to argue that the proper representation of sexual activity is morally worthwhile and to be encouraged. I am sure that Bertolucci squirmed in his director's chair when delivering instructions to Brando (especially concerning the use of the butter), but did so because he was aware of the potential prying eyes of the faux puritanical media. Similarly, when the feminists slipped into their trousers for the first time, there may well have been apprehension. Risks can lead to success as well as failure. And failure as well as success.

The existence of pornographic objects is itself a moral issue and the limits of censorship and toleration are political consequences of such moral discussions, but the risk is worth taking for a second reason. When I boldly state that a puritanical immaturity resides at the bottom of the (seemingly) most rigorous reflections on the philosophy of pornography, such immaturity is pathological to much applied ethical thinking. Pornography is to be prohibited because it has a negative effect on individual welfare or because it violates rights. Or, it is to be tolerated because it is expressive of a right to personal autonomy or because personal choice is constitutive of individual welfare. I said that most immediate intuitions concerning pornography corresponded to established moral positions, and the debate concerning the production, exchange and consumption of pornography was located in a familiar landscape. Many issues in applied ethics share a similar fate: abortion is basically about the philosophical rights of the person and what is ontologically a person (Kantianism) or the welfare of a mother (never, oddly, fathers!) versus the child (utilitarianism); euthanasia is about the welfare of individuals and suffering (utilitarianism) or the secularization of the sanctity of life principle (Kantianism); and the morality of behaviour in warfare is about means to ends cost–benefit analysis (utilitarianism) or about the deontological limits of action even in life and death situations (Kantianism). Two points of view dominate modern moral discourse: Kantianism and utilitarianism. (Every so often, it is true, the dominant schools of thought allow the virtue ethicists to chime in with acceptable if, for the other two, quaint and idiosyncratic comments.) Because of this, the modern moral landscape displays an undeniable paucity, if not full bankruptcy. And the immature, puritanical ground of our more sophisticated moral judgements is perhaps symptomatic of this comfortable dichotomy. Discussing pornography may well allow us to begin to think more subtly about a whole range of ethical issues and ethical judgements in general.

Utilitarian and Kantian vocabularies dominate moral thinking about contemporary issues to such an extent that their polar framing of all issues determines the conditions and limits of any rational discourse. There should, though, be an alternative. Virtue ethics has for a while been touted as just such an alternative, even if its treatment in most moral discourse is equivalent to an old spinster aunt at Christmas, whose opinions are listened to in a patronizing manner because it is better not to encourage her to continue. Such an attitude is a shame, but it is grounded in the fact that Kantian ethics and utilitarianism both seek to rationalize moral problems by identifying those features which are transcendental to a specific culture and can be applied universally across history. Such thinking may well corrupt what is actually important. Euthanasia, for example, was not a real moral problem for the Ancient Greeks since they knew that when you were seriously ill or wounded, you were probably going to die anyway. Making such a death as humane as possible was obviously the right ethical path. Modern medical technology changes the debate because life can be preserved at the cost of human dignity and with an increase, rather than an alleviation of suffering. Or a life can be preserved but such preservation will also raise the question about what a 'life' actually is and what is worth preserving. Technology, not thinking, raises such questions. Add in a cultural heritage that has a real, central commitment to the principle of the sanctity of life and we can see why the problem of euthanasia is a specific, cultural problem in the here and now. Attempting to find a solution solely in ahistorical utilitarian and Kantian responses, may well obscure the very problem that one is seeking to investigate.

Technology and heritage play an equal role in determining our intuitions concerning pornography. When the perception of sexual activity as a base pleasure that rather unfortunately accompanied the religious obligation to reproduce was dominant, the representation of such activities was predominantly morally wrong. When the representation of sexual activity was the exclusive pursuit of the rich and of the few who had the means to defy conventional normative systems, there was no real urgency in discussing the value of such images and their consumption. Society can tolerate the few idiosyncratic perverts such as D'Annuzio or Crowley, so long as it is just a few. However, the internet and generalized media coupled with the secularization of society have changed the terms of the debate. Everyone is at it; or so it seems. Pornography is a problem of the here and now, demanding a culturally sensitive ethical response. A grown up response free of schoolboy tittering, one might say.

The separation of ethical and political judgements, the simple belief in a positive or negative moral value to be attached to a set of objects, and the belief in the identification of universal properties that distinguish one set of objects (pornography) from another (literature, art, erotica) are all comfortable ways of thinking that are supported by our usual moral positions. But, perhaps there is a need to think in uncomfortable ways, to take some risks, in order to advance our general responses to those moral problems most urgently in need of discussion. But, let us start with pornography in order to attempt maturity in discussing a problem which most obviously encourages immaturity.

The present book, then, has two interrelated objectives. First, and most substantively, pornography itself is an ethical issue which still requires appropriate discussion because it is politically subject to sanction and morally subject to disapproval. The argument will dialectically proceed through the moral and political arguments in support of and against the production, exchange and consumption of pornography: offence; aesthetic disapproval; harm; toleration; exploitation; feminism; and equality. The aim of challenging the traditional framework is to argue that pornography may have a positive moral value but only if we can see through the immaturity of the more common arguments. Of course, the word 'immaturity' is at this point mere rhetoric and I plead for patience before dismissing it as *merely* so. The nature of the immaturity is, although this needs to be shown in some depth, a non-philosophical tendency to beg the question in a normatively silly way when defining what pornography actually is, as well as an inability to acknowledge a puritanical cultural heritage that sees sexual activity as worthless because it belongs to the so-believed baser side of human nature, probably an Enlightenment secularization of specific religious themes. Again, to reiterate, such a claim needs a more subtle presentation and that will follow.

More importantly, and the argument will hinge upon this, the immaturity that obstructs thinking through a proper rationalization of sexual identity and its representation centres upon the notion of objectification. By far the most sophisticated argument against the existence of pornography is that it objectifies individuals or a certain group, thus denying these individuals or groups recognition or treatment as equal subjects in society. Pornography fosters attitudes inhibiting equality. Objectification, though, adequately comprehended is a necessary part of human relationships and there is nothing necessarily coercive about the objectification of groups. A proper understanding of objectification, alienation and power should reveal the intimate connection between contemporary pornography and our own social reality, that is capitalism. Pornography and pornographic objects may be valuable. The conditional nature of that sentence, though, is very crucial, as most contemporary examples of the genre do not exhibit any moral value – often the opposite – but such empirical contingencies lead many thinkers to assume that there is a necessary relationship between pornography and moral wrongness, whether it be in instances of harm, objectification, or the reproduction of institutional inequality.

The other aim of the argument is to demonstrate that Hegelian social ethics is a viable alternative to the dominance of utilitarian and Kantian thinking on issues of interest to contemporary moral, political and legal debates. I shall use the moral problem of pornography to show that a sea change is required in our moral thinking to move away from a moral sphere insulated from social and political concerns. Hegelian social ethics engages with the substantial norms and values implicit in a society and discovered through hermeneutic interpretation of one's cultural fabric (the realm of 'right'). It is an ethical method that attempts to rationalize these values and norms with respect to two standards: one, coherence with the central axiomatic values of that culture (for example, liberty and equality); and, two, whether or not these central values and their concomitant institutions and policies (for example, capitalism) actually promote autonomous self-determination or inhibit it. The radical conclusion of this work will suggest that pornography, like other aesthetic objects, has a determinant role to play in the individual's self-understanding of her or his identity. Pornography as a representation of sexual mores and practices can be didactic, like the other arts, and also can be a form of emancipation. Appropriate pornography can liberate human beings from immediate desires; allow agents to rationalize the sexual libido; demonstrate how to reconcile agents' natural egoism with the roles required of sexual behaviour and, most importantly, allow agents to articulate particular preferences in a socially coherent manner. Of course, such a defence of pornography rests on a distinction between progressive and regressive forms of the discourse and one of the objectives of the argument is to demonstrate what a progressive pornography would actually be. Pornography is an aesthetic production and, like other aesthetic productions, constitutive of an agent's self-understanding and a rational element of full social existence. It will argue that there can, and normatively should, exist progressive pornographic objects, and that such objects, like works of art, are valuable to culture because they promote autonomous self-determination for a specific culture.

There is perhaps just a slight need to say something about the style and the title. First, between the chapters, the reader will find critical interludes which ruminate on examples of sexual representation. These interludes are in no way a complete or full treatment of the aesthetic objects in question but they do set the scene or relate to the content of the preceding and succeeding chapters. They are an invitation to think through the actual nature of sexual representation beyond the simple characterizations of pornography as commonly understood, but my interpretation of them rests on actually consuming the objects in question. I do not offer a full reading of the texts. Without the reader engaging with the texts themselves, it will be difficult to properly question what I say. Second, I have tried to write this book as I teach, with the aim of engaging whomever happens across it by using techniques of rhetoric and polemics. These should not be taken too seriously, only insofar as they initiate thinking. No matter the playful nature of some of the text, I have also tried to be transparent in the revelation of foundations and metaphysical assumptions. And that, in part, begins to explain the title of this book. Let's be honest, a book called drily *The Ethics and Politics of Pornography* is not, to excuse the frighteningly obvious pun, sexy enough for either publisher or booksellers. One would think that to sell a book, a better title was required, which spoke of 'sex', 'emancipation', 'alienation' or 'domination'. However, such a title would, in California (and possibly Milton Keynes), attract the tag of 'guru' literature and this is something I truly wish to avoid from the outset. There is no advice here about how to have sex (let alone good sex), nor the spiritual benefits of sex. The only advice I could offer would merely extend, much like my navigation skills, to: 'Stick that in there, jiggle it about and then ask for directions'. (Often realizing that I should have asked for directions much earlier, but pride is such a terrible thing!) This is not what this book is about at all. I have tried to avoid discussions of the psychology of sex and the metaphysics of sexual activity as much as possible. The book is interested in the representation of it above all else and not what the purpose, or the nature, of such activity is.

Yet, there is a difference between emancipation and liberation, which grounds much of my rejection of the feminists' mainly contra-pornography positions that perhaps should have been acknowledged in the title. You can liberate slaves by breaking their chains and you can liberate women by allowing them to vote. In both cases, you restore a freedom to the members of a specific group. But, unless such political policies are supported by an economic and cultural base, then such legislation is a castle built on sand. Emancipation requires independence: the slave must be economically and ethically free: that is, not bound to the master's order because he must of necessity work for him or because there exists some putative religious or ethical obligation to his master that negates the law that made him free. Similarly, a women must be economically and ethically free of her father and husband to vote as she would wish. I hope that the word 'emancipation' communicates both the liberation and independence that may be brought about by worthwhile representations of sexual activity. The successive pages should also support this and make more robust the meaning of emancipation. Only subtly thinking through the value of sexual representation and its role in our conception of ourselves as sexual beings will make emancipation possible. You can liberate a slave by outlawing the institution and extending the possession of rights to him, but when the chains are broken, very often that slave will 'consent' to unfairly paid positions and bondship to his economic superior. Names change, but positions do not. Emancipation requires more subtle, cultural transformations: the recognition of oneself as a subject with particular aspirations, the conception of oneself as equal to others, the education to articulate these conceptions and the material possibility to fulfil them.

First and foremost, though, we need a definition of the word 'pornography' and to ascertain what sorts of phenomena belong to the set of pornographic objects because we need to know which objects we are going to assign moral value to, which we are going to prohibit, and so on. That is where we shall start.

Interlude 1 Sex and Lucía

Sex and Lucía is an adult version of *Alice in Wonderland*. Just as Alice falls down the hole of her imagination to protect her from the dullness of the adult world, so the characters in the film all fall down their own holes to protect themselves from the cruel happenstance of life. We are told very early on that Lucía trusts people who tell good stories, thus excluding those who tell poor ones and those, if they can even exist, who tell the truth. Stories protected her from the grief of losing her family when she was young. When she believes she has also lost her boyfriend, Lorenzo, and there is no one left to tell her stories, she flees to the imagination itself, the island, which is not attached to the ground but floats on the ocean without anchorage and is described as holes within holes, hollowed out by holes. The plot itself is a amalgamation of the real and the fictional in an attempt to deconstruct the very difference because when the real is real we suffer loss. Lorenzo discovers he has a daughter from a one night stand and seeks to access her through courting her babysitter, Belen, only to suffer the death of his child as a result of his actions and to become himself lost to Lucía. Stories are what Hume once called necessary fictions, ways for us as human beings to make sense of things that are largely senseless, but require to be believed. In a secular world, in a largely individualistic world and one with no shared storybook, we tell ourselves our own stories in order to keep on going, to make sense of the senseless.

Medem's film, like much of his oeuvre, is aesthetically impressive. The story-telling device is, like *Alice in Wonderland*, the metaphor of falling through holes into parallel worlds where life is better (or worse). Names are symbols, the lighting and colour washes are expressive of emotion and the director continually plays with viewer expectations through the subversion of genre. Holes are mistakes into which we tumble in our lives, but they are also changes of course and the merging of reality and fantasy. The island, the centre of the film, where Lorenzo's romantic tryst, the event, which sets the story in motion occurs, is itself mythical, unattached to reality, floating free of material reality. A wonderland. The whole film is then a fantasy, a story which is wound upon itself so tightly that stories are revealed as that peculiarly human power to make sense of what cannot have sense, to such an extent that the child's death at the heart of the film can only be confronted through its reinvention in a story. To such an extent that, by the end of the film, it is hard to know where fantasy begins and reality ends, where truth is actually to be found – such an obfuscation of harsh reality is necessary for the human being. Stories are our new necessary fictions. Of interest, though, is the fact that a film as impressive and as artistic as this contains several sexually explicit scenes. Scenes that involve fellatio, penetration and erect phalluses. Some, it is true, could be justified because one of the characters, Belen's mother, is an actress in pornographic films, and so they are shown in an informative way, much like a television documentary about the sex industry. Yet, not all are like this. It is not all representations of Belen's mother, but there is Belen's own reproduction of her mother's acting for the purposes of telling a story to excite Lorenzo. There is the highly charged and erotic activity between Lorenzo and Lucía, amongst other scenes. The sex is extremely erotic because it is very human. By my definition to follow, and by most definitions, the film is pornographic. Human beings are reduced to sexual body parts, characters objectify their gender, there is explicit sexual activity that is not simulated by the actors, and there are games of subordination and desire. The sex does not, contra Scruton (2006: 154), concentrate solely on the face and yet it is sublimely erotic. The film remains beautiful and aesthetically valuable. Yet, if one objects to pornography and seeks to censure or prohibit it, the same judgement must apply to this film.

One might say that the actual sexual representation is not necessary to the film and the offensive scenes could simply be edited out. The scenes, though, are necessary to the film because it is about human existence and it requires the oscillation, like the island itself swaying and making all the characters seasick, between reality and irreality. We need to believe that the characters are real humans in order to doubt their stories properly. Cutting the scenes would do aesthetic damage to the film itself.

One may want to defend the film as eroticism, as not pornography, but what does such a defence amount to? Just the claim that those films which we like, which we want to be distributed, are eroticism and those that are trash are pornography. But even if one could make such a move, it would still not cover over the real problem. If one, as an individual, has the desire to be aroused, like the desire to be scared or thrilled, one would watch a certain genre of film. By choice, one would like to have the time to devote to *Sex and Lucía* for the purposes of arousal, but such time would be seen as wasted, as indulgence and as wrong. You must admire the film in spite of its propensity to arouse. You can watch the film as an aesthetic embodiment of value, but not as a simple tool for arousal. If one must do that, it is better to look at trash, to do it quickly with direct pornography and do it seedily and hidden from view. When one wanders around a gallery and chances upon Rodin's *Kiss*, we apprehend it mostly intellectually, divorced from our emotions, denying the arousal it causes. We lose something, just as we lose something when we deny that *Sex and Lucía* is arousing for us.

Such a puritanical drive to force the films of arousal (unlike the films of fear and violence) off the stage, seems to play into the hands of the cheap, trashy pornographic producers because theirs is the only product in town. If one were not pushed off stage in this fashion, who knows what representations of sexual activity would actually find value in our culture? It may even be possible to separate the nature of arousal from its supposed necessary culmination; after all, when we watch horror films we never actually flee.

2
The Mull of Kintyre Is Not in Naples: The Definition of Pornography

2.1 Naples

Inside the quite magnificent *Museo di Archeologico Nazionale* in Naples, just behind some of the most spectacular mosaics saved by the lava of Vesuvius, is a small room entitled the *Gabinetto Segreto* displaying objects which putative moral authorities have decided should not be for public consumption. The collection is now open to the general public. It is much like Naples itself – loud, gauche, obscure, dangerous, dilapidated and in need of serious attention – but, above all, if one takes the time to truly look – beautiful and sensual. Most of the objects date from the eruption in 79 AD that covered Pompeii and Herculaneum and consist of an odd mixture of amulets, charms, ornate mosaics, mythical and realist mosaics, and sculptures. Their discovery embarrassed many in the educated classes, who had long held the Roman republic to be a paradigm of moral virtue. Nor does the room contain the most explicit of the art works. Anyone who believes that modern images are distinguished by the degree of their explicitness should look at the scenes of penetration found in the *apodyterium* of the suburban thermal baths at Pompeii.

The question to be considered is whether such objects should be considered pornography. My simple answer to that is a rather categorical negative. Of all the objects in the *Gabinetto Segreto,* those that could most easily be considered pornography are those which are supposed to be wall mosaics from a brothel. They depict couples involved in lovemaking and would no doubt have acted as guides ('I want to try that', says the Roman client pointing at the mosaic). They are realist in nature and explicit. The little fauns sitting astride the huge phalluses who bring luck to a house that displays them are not, in any simple sense, pornographic. Much of what was discovered in Pompeii and Herculaneum was public, adorning dining room and hall walls where guests, children and slaves would pass, or on outside walls and embedded into public pathways and pavements. The representations were very, very public.

Etymologically, the word 'pornography' is constructed from Ancient Greek syllables referring to writing or, more generally, representations of prostitutes or prostitution. It might also be interpreted as the writings *of* prostitutes: the emperor Tiberius was alleged to have devoted much of his retirement to the study of the concubine Elephantis's sexual manuals and the courtesan Philaenis's explicit writings were also widely read at the time. However, what is most interesting is that there is very little evidence that the word itself was a Greek or Roman word: it was probably first used in earnest in 1857 (Kendrick, 1987). The fact that the word 'pornography' did not enter modern European languages until the nineteenth century is not accidental, coinciding as it does with the maturation of the modern subject, of industrialization, and of privacy. Let me make a bold historical claim – all the bolder because I do not even pretend to be an historian – that prior to industrialization there was no such thing as pornography.

2.2 A historical metaphysics of pornography

My claim is that pornography did not exist until the age of privacy, industrialization and capitalism. What is intended by that playful statement is that the concept of pornography and its correlates could not sensibly be used or applied prior to industrialization. I shall not trace the historical genesis, nor point to the temporal beginnings of pornography, instead I shall attempt a rather haphazard metaphysics of pornography – that is, delineate the conditions necessary for the modern phenomenon of pornography to actually exist. The private space and atomism of the modern subject determine a sphere where pursuits of an individual and not a communal nature can be realized. The technology of industrial production makes possible the reproduction of art works such that they can be more widely distributed and capitalism equates value with consumption. All these historical features of our time cohere to make the modern phenomenon of pornography possible. For such a radical claim, a little more historical elaboration is required.

First, the necessary distinction between public and private space, whether this refers, metaphorically, to the individual use of the mind free from conventional ways of thinking or, literally, to the possibility of a room to oneself away from others, is a prerequisite for the consumption of pornography. The birth of the word in 'writing' ('graph') rather than in the visual sustains this supposition. Reading is the creation of a private space for thinking away from the interference and observation of others. Pornography can only be predominant in a literate culture because it is private: no one can know what you're reading, or thinking, or imagining, but you. Reading creates the space for you as an individual to exist in some way separate from the social fact that you exist amongst others. In the same way that reading opens a private space in the mind, so the architecture of modern living arrangements and the surplus wealth of late capitalism make it possible to have physical spaces to oneself to watch images and peruse the internet. Private rooms, private terminals and private space are only imaginable for an individual who sees himself or herself as the negation of his or her social self and the conventions that rule such a social self. Individuals of this type – what Hegel refers to as 'persons' – only come into being as a majority in late capitalism and when literacy reaches a civilized level (Hegel, 1991). The 'person' is, for Hegel, a precursor of the modern self, emerging with the nascent idea of private property in Rome and working itself out through history until he or she becomes the rights-bearer of Lockean social contract theory. The 'person' is that individual atom who has desires, needs, wants and preferences that are individual to that subject and which identify them as an individual within a community. It opens the space for the individual to say, 'I want this or that' whether or not the community as a whole approves of it, because I have the right to liberty and property independent of the demands and obligations of my social group. The subject makes claim to a 'space' that is very much his or her own in negation of the social identity and obligations. Such individualization is only possible given the opportunity of privacy in physical space and a widespread literacy such that an inner life can exist, private from the observation of one's peers.

For pornography, more than most other pursuits, the ideas of personal choice and privacy are more central. If it were a genre (an idea we shall entertain below), pornography may have started as an uncomfortable, almost public, experience (stag films, adult cinemas), but it works best in literature, home video or on the internet because the consumer has total control (to move it forward, to cut and paste, to skip) and not in public where expectations of a narrative need to be shared. In Ancient Rome, the representations of sexual activity were public objects adorning walls like our own Ikea prints, expressing something about the wealth or tastes of the family group or the class to which they belong, whereas in the contemporary world pornography exists for a single consumer on his or her own, coinciding with his or her own private tastes and preferences.[1]

One can well imagine that the regulatory and social frameworks required to divide culture into the public and the private (what is mine separate from what is held in common in terms of values and projects) is intimately linked to private property and only fulfilled in the modern age. As the secret museum created a physical space for the 'obscene' objects (that is, what is 'off the stage' and hence designating what should be out of view), so modern life creates the space of transgression, the desire for what should not be desired. In the pre-modern period, one's life was divided between the public world of the home and the public world of work (or the state) and there was no space for the private. Pornography as pleasure has no place in one or the other. It does not belong to the family (it is individual and not part of the economics of the home) or the workplace, thus it has to be kept hidden. Only when there is a private space, can the individual take out what is hidden and use it.

Second, the technology of modern industrial production has fundamentally altered the nature of artistic objects (Benjamin, 2008). Lawrence (1997) related industrialization to pornography and nature to eroticism; he disapproved of the former because of his normative commitment to the superiority and domination of nature by human spirit. The actual technology changed the nature of consumption. In 1839 Daguerre demonstrated his first process for capturing images and within fifteen years there were nudes appearing and one feels it would have been sooner had it not taken half an hour to take the picture – requiring a very still and disciplined model. It is no coincidence that it was in the nineteenth century that the female nude became, for the first time, scandalous after years of existing at the centre of the Western aesthetic tradition. Material technological acceleration (a representational version of Moore's law) is directly linked to the production of pornographic objects: Gutenberg's first printing press was made in 1450 and by 1527, Pietro Aretino's lewd sonnets were married with Giulio Romano's explicit drawings, known as the *Postures*, and published. When we come to the internet, pornography was available in the late eighties prior to the commercialization of the web (partly in 1991 and fully by 1995).

Both Benjamin and Lawrence make a deeper point, though, reflecting the assertion of Heidegger that technology is more than the machines and instruments for the realization of human desires, but rather a way of thinking.[2] The essence of our view of nature and our environment is derived from the essence of technology; and the way in which our environment is revealed through modern technology has the characteristic of a 'setting-upon' and a 'challenging-forth':

> What kind of unconcealment is it, then, that is peculiar to that which results from this setting-upon that challenges? Everywhere everything is ordered to stand by, to be immediately on hand, indeed to stand there just so that it may be on call for a further ordering. We call it the standing-reserve ... Whatever stands by in the sense of standing-reserve no longer stands over against us as object. (Heidegger, 1993: 322)

And art is no different. As we reproduce aesthetic objects, they are stored and await our demands: to entertain, to improve us, to titillate and to arouse. They no longer exist as a form of truth or representation in itself. The nature of aesthetic objects are ordered as a waiting to be used. Such an attitudinal engagement with objects in our environment has three main material consequences. One, reproduction processes have brought down costs such that more and more individuals can privately own aesthetic objects and not merely encounter them in public spaces such as the gallery. Two, given the burgeoning technologies of late capitalism and the privacy established in that epoch, the consumer can remain anonymous and objects can evade moral censorship from putative authorities. Objects, given this technology, become harder to censor or hide. From the erotic novel in the aristocrat's library, to the private video in an unmarked box. Most objects now exist in webspace as a collection of 0s and 1s. Three, given that objects are now bought, the reason behind aesthetic production is no longer a religious value system, an aesthetic or excellence value system but, simply and without judgement, a market logic whereby what is produced is a response to the desires of the consumer. Objects are reduced to the simple exchange value of the market.

Following on from the first two claims, the mass production of objects and the possibility of consuming them in excessive proportions is made possible by the surplus wealth of capitalism (only when we have sufficient surplus wealth to be secure and safe in our purchases do we begin to consume objects that are not necessary and begin the cycle of what Debord (1983) calls 'pseudo-needs'). Couple such factors with the accessibility of these images due to their industrial reproduction and the rising literacy of the population, and the idea that only the educated have the moral discernment to be able to encounter such works disappears and they become objects on the market available to all. The problem of political exclusion disappears only to be replaced by one of inclusion: normal rules do not apply because we can all be trusted, we are all educated.

The medium determines who sees the object and how it is to be seen (museum artefact, high culture, low culture and so on) and, at base, late modernity and its drive for equality (both moral and material) make the consumption of pornography as pornography possible. Historically, pornography as pornography (and not as sexual imagery) cannot exist until these conditions of late modernity are realized.

2.3 The need for a definition

Histories and etymologies are fascinating but they cannot tell us what is or what is not pornography. The word designates a set of objects and when we assert that 'X is pornographic', we state a belief that the object before us – whatever it may be – belongs to that set. Such an assertion can be true or false but its truth cannot be gauged by its coherence with the component parts of a word or its consistency with an historical narrative. The reasons are simple: on the one hand, the component parts of words and their historical meanings have no necessary relationship with the contemporary usage of a specific word. If one were to look to the etymological origins of the word 'comfortable' and break it down into the atoms that construct it ('with strength') one would find it very difficult to arrive at its current day usage. The Hebrew origins of the word 'jubilee' are almost opposite to its contemporary meaning: 'ram's horn' which would have been blown to denote the beginning of a period of rest and reflection. It does not mean that etymology is not useful, but it is often abused. Similarly, the history of an object or discourse can only be written if one has in mind what the set of objects are that belong to that history. Implicitly one has already decided what is and what is not pornography (and one can see clearly from my connection between capitalism and pornography above that I too have made such a decision). No matter how interesting the history or etymology of a word, such investigations have no necessary relationship with what a contemporary public will understand by the use of that word. And if we are to discuss whether pornography is to be prohibited or not, it is the current usage of the word that we must understand.

Many writers on pornography share the putative stance of the American judge who pronounced that 'I can't define pornography, but I know it when I see it' and sidestep the problem of the definition.[3] Of course, we do know that *Debbie Does Dallas* is pornographic and that *Shrek* is not, but we also know that a Spaniel is a dog and a Persian is not (and we know that both are mammals). That knowledge in the latter case does not stop us offering definitions of dog and cat respectively, and such definitions are required. So, for example, I know that the following paragraph is pornographic (which at this point means nothing more than a consensus of persons would agree that the following passage exhibits aspects that are characteristic of pornographic writing):

> All at once, I halted, out of breath: I had reached the bushes where the shadow had disappeared. Excited by my revolver, I began looking about, when suddenly it seemed as if all reality were tearing apart: a hand, moistened by saliva, had grabbed my cock and was rubbing it, a slobbering, burning kiss was planted on the root of my arse, the naked chest and legs of a woman pressed against my legs with an orgasmic jolt. I scarcely had time to spin around when my come burst in the face of my wonderful Simone: clutching my revolver, I was swept up by a thrill as violent as the storm, my teeth chattered and my lips foamed, with twisted arms I gripped my gun convulsively, and, willy-nilly, three blind, horrifying shots were fired in the direction of the château. (Bataille, 1977: 25–6)

Such a reliance on intuition is inadequate as pornography occupies both a legal and moral place in the public sphere. Legally, it is subject to censure and to discussions of whether or not it should be prohibited or distributed and to whom. Morally, it is subject to debate over whether or not it is a worthwhile use of time and, more significantly, whether participating in the making or consumption of pornography constitutes wrongdoing. Knowing that the above example is pornographic will not help me in problematic cases such as *Last Tango in Paris*. And if the conclusion of our argument is that pornographic objects must be restricted, prohibited, or more mildly morally disapproved of, then whether we describe the film as pornographic or not determines whether or not it should be censored, banned or disapproved of. Knowing what is actually being discussed would, then, seem to be quite important. And it is so even for the critics of pornographic material.

Critics of pornography will, at some point in their reasoning, assert the principle that 'Pornography should be prohibited or subject to legal redress' and what they mean is that '*All* pornography should be prohibited or subject to legal redress'. If they do not include the 'all' and wish to discuss a case by case censorship of objects, then it is not the pornographic aspect of these objects that leads to their prohibition, but some other property: a production involved exploitation, for example. But, if that is the case, then it is exploitation which ought to be outlawed (and is, in fact). Critics would usually hold that the production of pornography necessarily harms a specific group of individuals and so long as pornography is produced, exchanged and consumed, then these individuals will be harmed. The only way to protect them is to prohibit the production, exchange and consumption of pornography.

However, what if one were to hold that some of or some parts of D. H. Lawrence's novels are pornographic. It is one thing to prohibit *Debbie Does Dallas*, there will be no great cultural loss if such an object were erased from our aesthetic history, but the loss of even a part of Lawrence's novels would be a reason for remorse. Normally, the critic of pornography would state that Lawrence's novels are not pornographic and so the problem is avoided. But that is inadequate as a reply because their defence of Lawrence rests on a belief that it does not harm individuals (or some other criterion). But that means pornography is those objects which harm individuals or, to put it more obviously, those objects which should be censored.

Putting aside the tautological approach, there is a further point implicit in a very English attitude: radical empiricism. Lawrence's novel was tried for obscenity, so some people obviously held it to be worthy of censure, whereas some individuals may find my willingness to cast *Debbie Does Dallas* into the cultural bin rather too elitist. (Although such plebeians would be wrong!) Who is to decide whether something is pornography and, further, whether it is worthy of censure? The basic problem is that one can discuss, in the abstract, the wrongs of pornography but when one sits down to decide whether such and such a film or novel is to be banned or restricted, without a prior working idea of what is or what is not pornography, for the most part we will call it pornography if we decide to ban it and that is just the wrong way round. For these reasons alone a working definition is required.

2.4 Working out a definition

So, of all things in Heaven and Earth, what are the sort of things that we can describe as pornographic? One can describe a chair as Baroque or red, but not pornographic. My wife has a lovely way of describing certain chocolate desserts – those 'gangbanged' with toppings and oozing viscous cream – as 'pornographic'. But that is a metaphorical use, even if it does seem to tap into something that critics of pornography would want to assert. It might be because the cake is about excess and excess is offensive (we decry the rich for their gauche expressions of wealth, after all). And many would claim that pornography is offensive, but does that mean that pornography is offensive material (RCOFC, 1979)?[4] The dessert could quite as easily be described as 'offensive', but such a definition cannot be sufficient, or in the least necessary. There are obvious instances of obscenity that are not pornographic, especially when considering it as a form of offence: passing wind and swearing jump to mind. So, if pornography is to be defined by being offensive, it is at best a subset of all offensive objects. Our first intuition might quite sensibly be that pornography is sexually explicit material. The cake, for example, is and could not conceivably be a sexually explicit object.[5] Pornographic objects are sexually explicit and it might be that the sexually explicit nature of these objects is the cause of offence.

The answer to that must be no because there are sexually explicit materials that are not pornography: the textbooks that a medical student may carry under his or her arm, or the *Bible* passages read out in church (one thinks of the treatment of Tamar by her brother-in-law in Genesis 38), or the photographs in this month's *National Geographic*, for example. One might claim that these are not pornography, even though they are sexually explicit material, because they are not offensive. The problem is that if one were to ask why these are not obscene, the answer will be something along the lines of 'it is not pornography'. Obscenity or offence without a pre-understanding of a distinction between pornographic and non-pornographic objects will do no work whatsoever as it remains painfully circular.

Moreover, the actual designation of what is or is not sexually explicit is not, nor can it be, an objective description in any robust sense; it must remain a socially contextual one. Rea (2001) illustrate this with an hypothetical example: the 'Shoe Fetishist Island' describes a community in which, for some reason, images of shoes are sexually arousing for most members.[6] A normal shoe catalogue is then sold to the island and is bought for the purpose of aiding sexual gratification whilst protest groups demand its prohibition because of a supposed harm to the community. The shoe catalogue illustrates that what we take to be pornographic may not be in other cultures and that some objects we would see as non-pornographic would be so in other cultures. However, where Rea perhaps oversteps his own example is in the claim that the images are not sexually explicit. Such a claim would only be true if 'sexually explicit' were an objective rather than a relative description. It is the latter and, in this aspect, it is similar to the property of being offensive and this might be one of the reasons that they are so quickly and reasonably connected. When we use the phrase 'sexually explicit' it must mean 'sexually explicit for a specific community'. The shoe catalogue is sexually explicit for the islanders but not for us.

Famously, and perhaps not actually, British Film Censors once applied the 'Mull of Kintyre rule' which held that if a shot of a man's penis in a film featured a member more elevated than the Scottish peninsula, then it had to be cut (the shot, not the member, I ought to make clear). Pictures that now appear in men's magazines within easy reach of children in most supermarkets would have once been hidden behind the counter. A flash of an ankle would have once been considered beyond the pale and many cultures would consider the exposure of a woman's hair to be provocative. The description of what is or is not sexually explicit is a relative one between the knower of a specific community and the object. Just as the colour blue exists only when there is a relationship between specific perceptive faculties and a particular frequency of light waves, so the designation of 'sexually explicit' exists only between a particular set of social mores and values and particular materials. But, whereas the former example of colour has some sort of relationship to a world independent of the observer (oscillation of light waves and molecular bonds), the latter is social through and through: between a socially constructed set of values and a socially received and interpreted material or text. Pornography, because of its sexually explicit content, is a relative, irreal object.

Let us not take this too seriously, though. Pornography is an irreal object, but so too are knives, tables, chairs or any thing that is a cultural artefact (broadly conceived). Pornography belongs to a set of objects which are cultural. If there were not such things as minds, the object could continue to exist but it would do so quite differently. A knife, for example, exists because there are minds which want to cut things. If there were no intentions to cut, nor anything that could have aims to cut, then the object would not really be a knife but instead a mixture of metal and wood in the same way that some rocks are a mix of quartz and granite. Artificial objects in general and communicative material in particular are always cultural because they are artefacts of minds for minds and they require a community of knowers (or attendants) to recognize the object as a certain thing that it would not be if that community did not exist. Music, for example, exists because there are human beings. The category music cannot exist independently of a random collection of sounds unless there are minds pre-prepared, educated and expectant ready to receive certain collections of sounds as music and others as not.

The nature of cultural objects can explain the historical and cultural differences in the reception of images which are now commonplace in music videos and men's magazines, which not even sixty years ago would have been considered sexually explicit or pornographic. And it can also explain how the exact same images can change designation: a calendar featuring photographs of Marilyn Monroe in the late 1940s was considered pornographic whereas the self same photographs in *Life* magazine in 1996 were not (Rea, 2001). A cultural artefact is an historical object and the community which understands it can be very temporary, almost permanent or something in between. Identical images of Marilyn Monroe exist for two different communities over a very brief time: circa fifty years. The quality 'pornographic' exists as long as the community can 'reasonably' expect agents to attend to the object in a specific way. One could, for example, imagine a collection of *Playboy* magazines being used as evidence in a trial (Rea, 2001). Unlike historical change (the photographs of Marilyn Monroe were pornographic but are no longer so), here it seems that an object which would normally be understood as pornographic, because it is sexually explicit, is not being understood as pornography. Beethoven's *Ode to Joy* could be played to scare crows away from a field and the farmer might say that it does a quite excellent object of scaring crows. But it remains a piece of music, it is just being attended to from a special point of view.

And the phrase 'a special point of view' is significant here. It seems to entail a reasonable or conventional point of view with which one attends to cultural objects (although some, like an item of furniture which is both pragmatic and ornate, may quite reasonably have more than one). Cultural artefacts are objects that would normally be understood one way or another by a given community; and that understanding determines their nature. Unique cases will be possible but will not determine the nature of the communicative content: objects used as evidence in trials, Beethoven used to scare crows, shoe catalogues used by foot fetishists, and so on. All these remain exceptional uses. Inversely, Marilyn Monroe's images cease to be pornographic as the attitudes of the community change and these attitudes *do* determine the nature of the object because the way in which one attends to an object is not a special point of view but a transformation in the accepted point of view. (One thinks too of religious icons in a secular world which become solely objects of aesthetic devotion.)

Desserts can no more be pornographic than dogs can be philosophical. We can say it but we do not mean it. Similarly, medical text books, the *National Geographic* and the *Bible* cannot be pornographic (although campaigners may well use the term rhetorically about some materials in the same way an owner may poetically describe their dog as philosophical). And individuals can also attend to such objects in a special way (the teenager using *National Geographic*), but such cases are like using pornographic material as evidence in a trial or Beethoven to scare crows. We use the term pornographic to describe a film, or a novel, or a photograph, and so on. We can readily describe a show in a theatre as pornographic and that includes both narrative plays and simple dance routines. Etchings, drawings and sculptures can also be readily described as pornographic. All of these are 'texts' or socially constructed objects: without a community of knowers, there is no difference between a Pollock painting and a weather beaten, quartz-lined rock face. So, it seems, that pornographic objects are at least expressed in an aesthetic medium, be it narrative, film, pictorial representation, and so on. Film, literature, dance, photography are all art forms. So, our first claim would perhaps be to say that for something to be pornography it must be an aesthetic object (but not claim that this is sufficient: the Mona Lisa, as we all know, is *not* pornography).

However, whereas medical books can reasonably be discounted as aesthetic material, such a dismissal is not so easy with either the *Bible* or the *National Geographic*'s photographs. So, we have so far considered pornography to be culturally constructed (an irreal object) and to be sexually explicit. Would it not be simpler to state that pornography is the sexually explicit subset of those cultural objects generally referred to as art?

So our initial intuition may be tweaked a little into: pornography is a set of sexually explicit aesthetic objects. However, just because pornographic objects are films, novels, photographs and so on, it would be too simple to immediately state that they are aesthetic objects. Photographs of people's faces on passports are not art; instruction manuals of mp3 players are not novels; public information films are not movies and so on. To treat pornography as art is mistaken, one might claim. Just because pornography is expressed in a medium that can also be used to express aesthetic objects, it does not make it an aesthetic object: if the baby moulds clay, the latter does not – one may assume – immediately become a statue.

The first point to make is that much of the material which is the target of the critics of pornography involves some narrative, plotting and characterization. Even some of the shortest mpegs contain some of these elements and the simplest photographs involve a choice of lighting and *mise en scene* that implies a characterization and narrative. Pornographic novels are, by definition, novels. It seems that at least some of the objects which would be considered pornographic are also aesthetic objects. Striptease is, after all, a form of dance and the quotation from Bataille above comes from a novel which should not be put alongside instruction manuals or recipe books in the bookshop.

Perhaps this counter argument misses the point, though. Pornography is not art because it primarily has a use value and one cannot adopt the attitude of the disinterested observer that is central to the Western aesthetic tradition.[7] Pornographic images and novels are produced in order for consumers to arouse themselves, like manuals tell us how to use our mp3 player, and that means we have an interest in the object besides its aesthetic features. An instruction manual is consumed when I need to learn how to use my mp3 player and a public information film is to be consumed when I need to be reminded of the dangers of drink driving. They can be well written and filmed, but such judgements are merely incidental. These only have value to me when I have an interest invested in them (when I want to listen to music, or am going out for the evening, or wish to be aroused). If I do not have that interest I do not attend to these objects and that is what marks them out as not art.[8] Pornography is designed for consumption: it consists of small snippets like morsels and so it is, at best, a matter of taste and not aesthetic judgement. I have no interest in art, except insofar as it is art.

However, such a distinction is not easy to either identify or delineate. Many Hollywood films are designed specifically for consumption and are disposable. Take an analogy with horror films. These have the function of eliciting fear and other similar emotions in the audience. That is what makes them belong to a specific genre. One could, no doubt, if one wanted a quick 'fear fix', watch a five minute clip from these films. Similarly, romantic comedies elicit feelings of hope and *joie de vivre* and fulfil a need for escapism. The aesthetic objects do not exist independently from the elicitation of these feelings and to say that we would attend to such objects if we had no need for the experience of these feelings is so, well, *Kantian*. We watch these films and invest in such art when we have the need for such things and even going to the art gallery satisfies some sort of need and is appropriate to certain moods and not others. Again, if it were possible, one could design a five minute fix for the need for such emotions. That we do not need this sort of fix, or cannot satisfy it so readily, says something about human needs and desires, and the priorities of our culture more than the nature of the emotions involved. Polemically, one could ask whether the contemporary experience of art galleries is consistent with the five minute fix as we flap from painting to painting like some sort of aesthetic, art-consuming butterfly. (I personally 'did' the Kyoto Museum of Modern Art in eleven minutes flat. I am claiming this as a world record.) One would not want to reduce all of the films and novels, which have been written in order to satisfy a specific human need, to the status of non-art, akin to the instruction manual of the mp3 player. It seems that they all satisfy a need or interest in the human spirit and can, therefore, be defined as functional objects like pornography. Such judgements reflect the equivocal nature of the word 'art'. When we say these are not art, we mean that they are aesthetic objects, but not good ones. The term 'art' can descriptively mean aesthetic, in the way that both Beethoven and Britney Spears (or fill in your favourite pop star) are musicians and therefore produce art. However, it can also be used normatively, meaning an aesthetic object deserving of attention: Beethoven is art, whereas Britney is not. To reduce pornography to non-art appears to set the bar too high because it rules out too many objects on the basis of controversial evaluative judgements of aesthetic value.

So, we might want to say that pornography is an aesthetic object in a very minimal sense, but that pornography cannot have the requisite aesthetic value to be considered 'art'. In other words, pornography is necessarily bad art (Berger, 1977). Such a claim, one feels, is made to protect Goya's paintings and Michelangelo's statues from charges of obscenity. Furthermore, pornography must be sexually explicit bad art at the very least, but that again is problematic. Some pornographic objects may well exhibit characteristics typical of good art: Bataille (1977), Réage (1972), Medem (2001), and Ferrario (1999) are obvious contenders. The quotation from Bataille illustrates writing technique and the novel as a whole, even if not a resounding success, is worthy of aesthetic attention. In the passage cited, there is an ironic play with the concept of *jouissance* as death using the oft used Shakespearean technique of juxtaposing traditional and hackneyed imagery (compare the Dionysian dance to exhaustion with the simple shooting of the gun) as well as the linking of the intimacy between violence and sex and the idea of transgression, which are all familiar themes from Bataille. In fact, there is often a latent poetry in much pornographic discourse. The simple phrase 'a pearl necklace' does actually embody several layers of poetic craft: the very good visual description of what the metaphor represents coupled with the ironic idea of a conventional gift for a certain type of woman. Pornography can satisfy many of the requirements of good art, but the claim that pornography is art is not actually required. All one needs to show is that some pornography can be in part appreciated for its aesthetic value.

It might be objected that the examples chosen are not pornography. Yet, it is difficult to understand the difference between these examples and those that are pornography except aesthetic quality and, as the definition asserts, pornography is bad art. So if something is good art, it cannot be pornography. Surely, though, this is a case of begging the question. For the argument to work, all that needs to be proven is there are some objects one would term pornographic that exhibit aesthetic characteristics (Kieran, 2001). Bataille's passage is one.

Akin to this definition, and almost as obviously normative, is the claim that pornography is sexually explicit material produced for profit (Huer, 1987). Given that I have made the assertion (yet to be justified) that there is an intimate connection between capitalist production and pornography, one might be forgiven for believing I have some sympathy for such a definition. And one can see how the minimally aesthetic conditions of bad art are therefore present: the storyline, characterizations, and so on are nothing more than mere clothes-horses for the carrying of the sexually explicit material that can be sold as a product for profit. However, imagine an amateur short film involving sexually explicit acts uploaded to *youporn.com* by a consenting couple. The film is not produced for profit but does satisfy some exhibitionist urge. It is still, though, surely pornography. One might want to say that the couple 'profit' from the exposure as it satisfies their exhibitionist tendencies. That is surely to empty the definition's use of 'profit' of any substantial content.

However, such a brief consideration of Huer's definition is not merely passing rhetorical time. There is an intimate connection between exchange and pornography as I have indicated above (although not yet argued). When a person performs a striptease for his or her partner, such a performance, although identical in most respects to a striptease performed in a club, is not pornography. Not even when the person is an exotic dancer and performs nightly in a club. Neither is the sexual act between two (or more) adults pornography. Not even when both participants are actors in adult films by day. Yet, if performed on film or in a theatre, it is. It seems that an aspect of pornography must be that it is a possible object of exchange. In short, what distinguishes a performance of sexual activity in the theatre from those privately performed at home (even if such a performance is a possible object of a voyeur's gaze as the curtains are open), is that there is no conscious intention for the performance to be viewed, exchanged, sold, or so on. In those circumstances it is not pornography. Private performances and texts are not pornography unless they are put into a situation in which, consciously or unconsciously, they are possible public objects of attention (stolen home videos then are pornography even if never sincerely intended to be made public). If one is to be strict here, once a performance or an activity is recorded, it becomes a possible public object. If I secretly have a film of my partner on my mobile phone, even if I never intend to show it to anyone else except her or me, it is arguably pornography because it exists as a possible object for public exchange (loan, theft, accidental possession and so on). Pornography is a public object, text or representation of sexual activity.

So, we can, first, agree that pornographic objects are, in a minimal sense at least, aesthetic objects. Pornography as a set includes stage performances, dances, drawing, photographs, films, poems, novels, computer games, and all of these are examples of objects belonging generally to the realm of aesthetic discourse. These representations and performances are possible objects of exchange. And because pornography belongs to the set of aesthetic objects it accords with the former characterization of it as a set of irreal objects governed by a relation to a given community of knowers. Just as the distinction between a cacophony of sounds and music requires a substratum of social meanings, values and expectations, so too does the designation of an object as pornographic require a shared set of cultural values, expectations and norms.

One might want to offer a common way of dividing up aesthetic objects as the way forward. Aesthetic objects belong to constellations or groups reasonably referred to as genres. Now, I do not wish at this juncture to offer a hostage to fortune, but it strikes me that there is at least an intuitive plausibility in the suggestion that pornography is a genre. A comparison with the genre of 'horror' reveals three features of a genre that seem to support the claim. First, one thinks of a horror novel, a horror film, a play, paintings such as Goya's dark period, and horror video games. All of these seem to belong to the genre of horror. A genre can include diverse art forms, so as a classificatory concept it is transcendental to the art form which is necessary for the term 'pornography'. Second, a film can be a paradigm example of a horror film just as a film can be a pornographic film, but some films have scenes which are examples of the horror genre (so a horror scene) without actually belonging to the horror genre. Such a recognition seems commonplace in the way that film censors have the choice to prohibit a film outright or, more ordinarily, demand changes and cuts (although the rationality of this will be discussed later). Similarly, some films have pornographic scenes (*Sex and Lucia* jumps to mind) without being easily identifiable as pornography. Such films are said to borrow from a genre. Three, fusion is possible. Just as you can have comedy-horrors, so you can have porno-horrors and so on.

What this tells us about the concept of genre is that it is not rigidly defined. It can, on the one hand, be understood as a structural paradigm (action films must narrate the redemption of a fallen hero, romantic comedies must be initiated by a comedy of errors or principal character blindness), yet, on the other hand, the concept of genre may indicate the inclusion of some specific, necessary content (horror films must have gore, romantic comedies must have love rivals). McElroy (1997) suggest that pornography may well be aesthetic objects that are characterized by the portrayal of subjects as mere sex objects, obviously defining the genre by the content of the representations. Whatever this may mean, it is simply not true (nor if it is, is it limited to pornographic films). Characters in pornography films are not mere objects any more than any other type of film: they are business women, housewives, babysitters, teachers, exotic dancers, timid, exhibitionist, sly, innocent and so on. The characterizations are often not at the level of an Oscar-winning film, but the basics are at least present. Even Page Three in *The Sun* attempts to tell us about the likes, hobbies and political views (usually right-wing!) of Sharon, aged 20, from Essex. Moreover, fashion models and catwalk models are mere clothes-horses: their bodies are used merely to show the form and shape of the clothes. That such models are mere clothes-horses is only worse than adult film stars being mere sex objects if one thinks there is something bad about sex independently of its representation.

Cultural objects are historical and relative, as we have seen, and as such they are subject to change. In the end, if I am to offer a definition, it should not rest on terms that themselves are controversial definitions. Neither do I have the time in this book to think through what exactly a genre is. For these reasons, it is best to avoid the use of the word genre, but equally to recognize that it does allow us to look at what may be certain threads which bind the family of pornographic objects together. The reason for raising the issue of genre, however, rests on a way such family resemblances can be bound together (and I stress there is no claim here about the proper definition of genre) by the emotional function of a genre.[9]

The emotional function of pornography is therefore a more obvious relationship between the members of the set than shared content or structure. Most viewers, readers and consumers of pornography attend to it in order to be aroused and, in most cases, to aid masturbation. Pornography might be understood as that subset of aesthetic objects intended to arouse (Levinson, 2005; Narveson, 1993). As a definition, it has an obvious advantage over the designation 'sexually explicit' because it can avoid any problems with the examples of the *National Geographic* and the medical student's handbook. Such objects, even if sexually explicit, are not intended to arouse. Similarly a lingerie catalogue in the possession of a teenager, even if arousing, is not pornography because it was not intended to be used in this way.

There are, though, two obvious problems with the intentional nature of this definition. First, it does not seem to be a necessary and sufficient condition of pornography. As an eight year old – and here, I feel as vulnerable as a stand-up because I shall reveal something hitherto known only to my wife and one of the horn players in the Hallé – I was aroused by the scene in *Flash Gordon* when Princess Aura (Ornella Muti) is bound to a table and whipped. Such a scene is arousing and minimally sexually explicit (her back is bared and the dialogue is more than suggestive). Further, I would claim the scene was intentionally arousing, put in by the director, yet to describe either that scene or the film as pornographic seems flatly absurd. Second, Rea (2001) offers us another of his examples to illustrate this point: the 'profit machine' describes an investor who sets up a computer to observe a market and to produce a commodity that will be a success in that arena. The computer produces and distributes a magazine much like *Playboy*. The investor knows nothing about what has been produced but happily takes the money. What he produces, Rea sensibly assumes, is pornographic material. The profit machine describes the production of pornographic material without the intention of producing material that has the effect of sexual arousal (the investor knows nothing nor cares about what his product is). The idea is that a director may earnestly make a film with aesthetic intentions, but it is received as pornography despite his own sincere intentions. The director does not wish to arouse his audience but the film is consumed for the gratification of its viewers. The nearest equivalent I can think of is the play within Mel Brook's film *The Producers* where the playwrite's intention (though, not the producers' of course!) is to make a serious drama but the play is a success because the audience receive it as a comedy, The intentions of the author or director do not decide whether an object is pornographic or not. The intention of the producer is superfluous to the reception of the object. Reciprocally, the director of *Flash Gordon* does want to intentionally arouse his audience, but he is not making pornography.

To reject the idea of intentional determination is, though, problematic as it raises an obvious problem: it lets an awful lot of subjectivism into the definition. After all, the intention of the producer was important to rule out lingerie catalogues, medical books and the *Bible* because such objects, even if arousing for some agents, are not pornography because it was not intended for them to be used in such and such a way. If we jettison the reference to the intention behind their production, we gain less than we lose. Yet, the nature of cultural objects outlined above makes the reference to an intention rather superfluous anyway. Cultural objects are about consumption more than they are about production. As the painter produces a work of art, his or her production process is informed by what Hegel would call 'an essential relation to the will of others' (Hegel, 1991: §113). Such a relation is also present in most of our actions: when we act, we do so according to the norms and expectations of others and produce an object which exists for the consciousness of an other. So, if I were to come to your house and throw a brick through the window in order to, as I would assert, 'see if you were in', there would be righteous mistrust of my explanation. The correct expected action to reflect my will would be ringing a doorbell or knocking on the door. Similarly, the artist must begin from the tradition from within which he or she works, even if ultimately to subvert it, otherwise others would not understand it as art and – to put it more strongly – it would not be art because of this miscomprehension.

Remember that we had said above that the quality 'pornographic' exists as long as the community can 'reasonably' expect agents to attend to the object in that way, even if a 'special point of view' is currently occurring. I can imagine a doctoral student reading in French literature who devotes part of his or her thesis to *Story of O* (Réage, 1972). Even if the novel is being read for its representation of women in early twentieth century France, it remains an example of pornography. Reference to an intention to arouse would explain it, but so would the new way that refers to attending to the essential will of others. Cultural artefacts are heterogeneous objects open to interpretation but a standard collection of categories will determine their expected use or meaning because they are public and produced for consumption by the general population. Something cannot be pornography at one moment and not at the next, because the way in which it should be understood is determined by the community of attendants and not its use in that instant for a particular subject. The doctoral student has a 'special point of view' in relation to the object but that special point of view is more than probably determined by the expected point of view (the interest of the novel lies in the fact that it is a pornographic representation of woman from a female writer).

So, even if we ignore the intention to arouse, could it not be that the collection of objects to be identified as pornographic are arousing, whether this is intended or not. Horror objects elicit fear, anxiety and terror; comedy objects elicit mirth; and pornographic objects elicit sexual arousal. To put it more distinctly, it could be reasonably expected that a member of a specific community would find the object arousing, all things being equal. Of course, as a necessary and sufficient condition this again does not rule out the scene from *Flash Gordon*. Nor does it rule out the music video for 50 Cent's song, 'P.I.M.P.' (2005). Both are sexually arousing and one would assume that it is reasonable to expect most members of society (or a specific group in society) to find them so. (That is, after all, what makes them marketable!)

However, and here one should be careful, it is possible to assert that the arousal in both of these cases, although intended and deliberate, is contingent and accidental. If one were to seek sexual gratification exclusively, one would not attend to either of these objects, or only if there were a scarcity of possible objects or a subjective predilection. Given a variety of products and conventional preferences, one would choose to gratify oneself through other films, photographs, and so on. Those objects which are pornographic are those which, one feels, a subject would have no reason to attend to if he or she did not seek sexual arousal. Samuel Pepys, for one, saw no worth in *L'Ecole des Filles* and, having read and 'used' it, he cast it onto the fire (Pepys, 1893: loc. 38736-9).[10] I can watch the 50 Cent video to listen to the music and appreciate the visual interpretation of it. I can watch *Flash Gordon* to enjoy the story and marvel at the special effects. Objects which are properly pornographic (paradigm examples of the set) propose very few aspects which would demand attention other than their capacity to arouse. It seems we return to a variation of our starting point: we need to revise the idea of a disinterested – or interest-qualified – observer and ask whether one could have an interest in *Flash Gordon* if one had a disinterest in being aroused. The answer seems to be, 'Yes'. If we apply the same criterion of the interest-qualified observer to most pornographic material (would I attend to this object if I were disinterested in being aroused) then the answer would be, 'No' (Bartel, 2010).

Of course, *Story of O* and Bataille's work do possess properties that can be of interest to an attendant (their literary worth, for example), but they can also be imagined as possible objects of choice when one seeks sexual gratification. It seems that the interest-qualified criterion determines that such objects are not pornography in that, if I were disinterested in arousal, I would still have reason to attend to them. One could bite the bullet here and merely assert that they are not pornography but, perhaps, we could invert the criterion of the interest-qualified observer into an attendant who actually seeks not to be aroused. So, if such an attendant were actually interested in not being aroused, yet experienced other feelings, could he or she attend to the object? It strikes me that the answer is definitely, 'Yes', to *Flash Gordon*, more than probably, 'Yes', to 50 Cent's music video and, 'No', to both *Story of O* and Bataille. In cases of pornography, the feelings of arousal are as necessary as the feelings of fear in a horror film (could one, for example, imagine being able to attend to the horror film without experiencing feelings of fear?). Of course, there are always special cases but, whereas one can attend to *Flash Gordon* with the desired wish not be aroused and lose next to nothing of the film, attending to Bataille or Réage with the self-same desire would involve obscuring the proper reception of the aesthetic object.

If pushed on this point, one could talk of a *narrow* and a *broad* definition of pornography. *Narrowly*, one could say that an aesthetic object is pornographic if a subject would have no reason to attend to it if he or she did not seek sexual arousal. Thus, *Debbie does Dallas* and all the clips on *youporn.com* are pornography but *Story of O* is not, as it has features which might invite attention in spite of its capacity to arouse. More *broadly*, though, one could say that an aesthetic object is pornographic if a subject cannot attend to it without being aroused (all things being equal, such as not viewing it as evidence in a trial, discussing it in a university seminar and so on). *Story of O* is, therefore, broadly speaking, pornography as, under normal circumstances, one cannot read it without being aroused. However, it would be reasonable to accuse the broad definition of being too broad, in that *Flash Gordon*, a lingerie catalogue and 50 Cent's video all seem to fit the criterion. But that is where the will of others and the reference to a community and reasonableness comes in. The lingerie catalogue, like *Flash Gordon*, may well be pornography for the community of adolescents growing up in the eighties (but not for their parents) and, oddly, 50 Cent's video may well be pornography for the community of (male) philosophy professors, but not for the intended audience.

The definition of pornography makes reference to a community and not an individual subject. To make reference to an individual is to allow anything to be pornography if it is used by at least one individual for the purpose of sexual gratification and fetishist objects are fetishist because they are not normal objects of sexual interest. Say someone likes people wearing yellow wellies so much that they can be sexually aroused by it. Just because this one person exists does not mean the catalogue of wellies and galoshes becomes pornography. Particular tastes and desires (including those listed under the category of extreme) cannot determine the content of the set pornography. One can talk of communities (age, class, regional, shared interests) with specific pornographies, but such individual consumers have a special or exceptional relationship to the object which – though possibly intelligible to the community (one finds the sexual interest in shoe magazines by a fetishist intelligible, even if one does not share it) – is recognized as exceptional due to circumstances. The judgement of whether something is to be treated as pornography is removed from the individual so that special cases no longer pose a problem. It removes the assumption of an 'ideal' audience implied in the assertion that it is reasonable to believe that 'most of the audience' will use an object in a certain way, and it admits that there are mixed motivations in the production of and heterogeneous uses of cultural objects, but that a certain community will still be able to designate it as something: so evidence in a trial is still pornography; *Story of O*, studied by the doctoral student, is still pornography; and Beethoven's *Ode to Joy* used to scare crows is still music.

Yet, the distinction between the broad and narrow definition of pornography, although perhaps descriptively appropriate, has no bearing on the political and moral questions to be raised later in this book. Take the scenes in *Sex and Lucia*, for example, where a woman's hand is placed on an engorged penis and a young woman masturbates with a dildo. Even if such a film is only broadly pornographic, in that, as a whole and in context, there are reasons other than the interest to be aroused to attend to it, one can imagine these clips being cut and pasted on to a website in isolation (or, in the olden days, the viewer fast forwarding to them in isolation). These clips would then become narrowly pornographic. And, whatever may be wrong with the narrow examples of pornography, will also be wrong with such scenes in isolation, and any prohibition and censure should also be applied to them (and the specific passages from *Lady Chatterley's Lover*). So, if something is broadly pornographic, it too must be susceptible to sanction (and this agrees with the lobby groups who want pop videos, teen magazines, and so on, all subject to the same legal prohibition as more obvious forms of pornography). So, if one is to discuss the politics and morality of pornography, it is the broad definition that ought to be invoked otherwise we are playing sleight of hand tricks.

So, it seems that any definition, after this process of reflective equilibrium, has to pay heed to the public nature of an object and its primary existence as a product for consumption. Like art, it is determined by its audience and its market as much as by its producer. It also has to make reference to the nature of that consumption as sexual arousal and how, in certain objects, such consumption is the primary or possibly the exclusive reason for their consumption.

2.5 The definition

Here, then, is a tentative definition of those objects which are pornographic. *An object is pornographic for a specific community if it is (i) a cultural object that (ii) exists in the public domain as a possible object of exchange; and (iii) it is reasonably expected by that specific community that it would be impossible for most subjects with the preference not to be aroused to attend to the object.* As we have explained above, for a thing to be pornography it should be an aesthetic object. This means that the turnip shaped like a penis is not pornography although it can be obscene. Second, because it is a cultural object. the designation of 'pornographic' will always be relative to a specific community or age, so the statement, 'Marilyn Monroe's photographs for her calendar were pornographic in 1945 in the USA but not in 1995 in the USA but were in 1996 in India', is not controversial and every time the description 'pornographic' is used, it must be shorthand for a phrase 'at time *t* in place *p*'. (In this book from now on it may be assumed when I say pornographic I mean in the 'here and now'.)

Why accept such a definition? First, it is descriptive and not normative and I shall say a little more about that below. Second, it easily identifies non-controversial pornographic objects: *Playboy*, *Debbie Does Dallas* and strip performances in a theatre. Third, it excludes sexually explicit material that is non-controversially not pornography: a private strip show for a partner (as it is not a possible object of exchange); Goya's *Las Maja Desnuda*; pictures in the *National Geographic*; a medical text book; and the *Bible* (as these last three are possible objects of attention even if one has the preference not to be aroused). Fourth, it explains how certain objects can move from belonging to the set to being excluded from the set. Naked pictures of Marilyn Monroe are pornographic in 1940, but not in 1996, and they are pornographic for the thirteen year old, but not for the adult. Lastly, it does some real work with problematic cases. A lingerie catalogue is not pornography because one can imagine a man attending to it to look for a present for his wife with the preference of not being aroused. A private striptease by a partner recorded on a mobile phone is pornography even if never intended to become public because it could be stolen.

Two further problematic cases illustrate the worth of the definition: Medem's *Sex and Lucia* and the educational film *The Lover's* (Sic.) *Guide* (1991).[11] A definition ought to be able to allow us to assign the descriptor 'pornographic', or not, to these objects. Our first intuition is that a definition ought to be binary: an object is or is not pornography. *Sex and Lucia* is pornography, but remember that this is not evaluative; it is descriptive. It says nothing about the worth of the film, only that it meets the requirements of the definition. But, like *Story of O*, just because it is pornography, its aesthetic value is not negated because one can still have desires to attend to the object that are not sexual. Again, though, it differs from *Flash Gordon* in that it is reasonable to assume one could not attend to Medem's film with the preference of not being aroused.

The educational film is similar. The object is both pornographic and educational, and is equally both because both audiences are reasonably expected by our community. There are non-sexual desires to attend to it (to be educated), but that aim is not exclusive of, nor possible, without being aroused (unlike choosing a bra for one's wife from a catalogue). So, it seems the definition does do some work when our intuitions are confused in that it helps to sort out our thinking in borderline cases. And, at this point, we are happy to settle with the broad set of pornographic objects.

There are, of course, a few obvious objections to consider. The first is the male bias in my definition. Images in *Playboy* may or may not be arousing for most female attendants and this can only be answered by sociological investigation or, even better, psychological research that connects the brain up to an ECG to see the effects on women in the target community. Traditionally, pornography has been produced by heterosexual men for consumption by heterosexual men and, although that is changing, I cannot understand how the majority of pornography could be arousing for women or homosexuals. The full consideration of this objection constitutes a large part of the following text and it is perhaps worth mentioning at this point that the definition, for our culture, could have been changed to make reference to the community of heterosexual males based on empirical factors. There exists, however, homosexual pornography and female pornography. It would be amiss (if not an error) for a definition to conceptually rule these out and we can make reference to a community within a community (so *Debbie Does Dallas* is pornography for male heterosexuals at such and such a time).

The second objection concerns the use of the quantifier 'most' in clause (iii). Logically, it entails that communicative content can be pornography only if more than half the subjects with the preference not to be aroused within the community can reasonably be expected not to attend to the object. Just as the range of sexual preferences is vast and, at times, particularly idiosyncratic, so are the capacities of human beings not to be aroused by the content of aesthetic objects. No doubt there exists a cultural theorist who is able to attend to *Debbie Does Dallas,* as a representation of male domination, without once succumbing to a sexual impulse. Or a lawyer who surveys the evidence in a particular trial, including photographs from an adult magazine, without finding the least sexual interest. But both are cases of the 'special point of view' turned on its head. It would obviously be impossible to expect that 'all subjects' in a community would form the same attitudes to a particular object. 'Most' falls between 'one' and 'all'. The actual empirical objects that fit the clause would be found out through hermeneutic endeavour by the sociologist who defines the particular community in question (and certain particular puritan communities may push the 'most' down to a 'some', but then the question becomes, if very few experience arousal, whether we can still talk of a pornography in such a community). The hermeneutic endeavour may well be as simple as asking a section of the community what it believes is pornography, or as difficult as interpreting the artistic production of a culture.

And that leads on to a further objection: the capacity for a thing to be both pornography and not pornography at the same time. The point is not truly a problem if one admits that cultural objects are very often conditional in just this very sense. If one thinks of 'Inuit art', the objects that constitute such a group would not normally be art if they were produced in one's own community. However, 'Inuit art' like 'children's art' identifies a set of objects that one comprehends as 'art' for a particular community. Terms such as 'art' and 'pornography' implicitly possess the condition 'for us' if never stated and that 'us' identifies a relevant community; one can sensibly talk about 'Victorian pornography', 'Islamic pornography', 'male heterosexual pornography' and so on.

The conditional nature of the concept entails judgements that may well differ within a society which will almost inevitably be made up of distinct communities. What may be not pornography for me, could plausibly be so for Islamic or Christian communities. Again, though, this is not truly problematic. Films in the United Kingdom are evaluated by the Film Classification Board and given age restrictions. Such evaluations say that the film is appropriate for certain groups. At present, such judgements concern only age but it is not implausible to assume that a multi-cultural society may feel it necessary to offer advice on which films are inadvisable for which religions (but they must, as we shall see in a later chapter, remain advisory if this is the case). 'Pornographic' may well work in this way. As such, the concept is open and flexible. What may be pornography for a fourteen-year-old may not be for an adult. What is not pornography for a thirty-year-old may well be pornography for an adult over sixty-five years of age.

But, of course, that opens up the definition to the most problematic objection: who are the 'us'? What is the community? Communities are geographical and historical objects and an agent can belong to more than one. The problem is to identify the borders of such communities: where do they end and new ones begin? Such a metaphysics of communities is beyond the scope of this book, but one can talk of Victorian England

and England in 2013 as two different communities and Muslims and Christians as two different communities because the values and topics of reasoning are different and available to hermeneutic investigation. Such difference is all the definition needs to be plausible.

2.6 Postscript: avoiding a confusion

It might be mentioned that clause (iii) of this definition makes the set of objects that are pornography very broad, including aesthetic objects that one might want to exclude. However, it is important to note that the definition makes no normative judgement and those who feel uncomfortable about including such objects in the set of pornography are guilty of an assumption that pornography is morally wrong. That assumption has not been discussed here and the definition deliberately says nothing that may make one hold such an assumption (or its opposite). One of the advantages of the above definition is that it avoids a mistake (and most times a deliberate one) in the literature. If one is going to make moral judgements or political judgements about pornography, then one identifies something that is pornographic (*Debbie Does Dallas*) and says that it is morally bad or demands that legislation be invoked against it.

Such arguments are commonplace in moral and political philosophy. Court cases seek to establish whether a murder has or has not occurred in order to distribute blame. One identifies an event (a killing) and demands that the legislation be applied. But, murder is a normative, moral concept. It means 'unlawful killing', so if a murder has occurred (and this is what the court case has to establish), then it is necessarily wrong (both morally and legally). Many definitions of pornography are normative in the same way. the Obscene Publications Act (1959) defines pornography as that which has a tendency to deprave and corrupt. Under the Act, it is necessarily the case that pornography is bad because depravity and corruption are morally bad. MacKinnon, whose work we shall consider later, defines pornography as 'the graphic sexually explicit subordination of women' and if this is the case and we think equality to be a good thing, then pornography is morally wrong and should be subject to legal sanction (1993: 121). Longino (1980: 31) defines pornography as 'material that explicitly represents or describes degrading and abusive sexual behaviours so as to endorse and/or recommend the behaviour as described'. Not only do Mackinnon's and Longino's definitions describe a much narrower set of objects than my own, but such normative definitions also seem to beg the question.

Pornography can be (and has been) described either as 'sexually explicit material' or as 'offensively sexually explicit material'. Neither is adequate, as we have seen above, but here they illustrate the conceptual confusion. The first is a description, it identifies a set of objects. The second is a normative judgement, it evaluates a set of objects. If we use the first definition, it is a further question whether sexually explicit material is bad or not (that is, should be publicly available). If we use the second definition, this question is rather empty (if we accept that to offend is bad). Take the analogy with murder: murder is unlawful killing, so it is a priori wrong. Killing on the other hand is not a priori wrong and we have to ask which instances of killing are unlawful (hence murder) and, more importantly, why. Most definitions of pornography confuse the conceptual distinction between the descriptive and the normative.

The word 'pornography' and its associated adjective are both immediately descriptive and normative. They are much like the word 'slavery' and its adjective in that respect. Descriptively, 'pornography' identifies a set of literary, photographic and cinematic objects and also some social practices such as strip shows, peep shows and live theatre performances. Normatively, the judgement of something as pornographic is usually intended to be negative: that it is offensive or should be considered offensive, that it is aesthetically worthless, a representation of inequality, and so on. Yet, as with the word 'slavery' one can easily separate the descriptive meaning of the word from its negative connotations: descriptively, slavery is a form of labour relations whereby the worker cannot own private property; and normatively such a relationship is only possible through the violation of an individual's autonomy made possible by economic power. So what is wrong with slavery is not implicit in its definition, but for the institution to exist at all, it requires the violation of personal autonomy and is hence (arguably) wrong (whether one proposes that the violation is conceptually entailed or empirically unavoidable). If slavery had been defined as a form of coercion, then the descriptive and normative aspects would have been combined and it would have been a tautology that slavery is an immoral practice. What is odd about most philosophical discussions of pornography is that they conflate the definition and the normative evaluation of pornography. By beginning with a descriptive definition, we have before us a set of objects which are pornographic and we can now ask why they should be subject to moral judgement and legal sanction, if they should be.

Such a discussion constitutes the rest of the book.

Interlude 2 Crepax and Manara

In Italy, one can visit the kiosks at the corners of most streets and buy newspapers, magazines, books and selected videos. The kiosks also sell bus tickets. Like newsagents in the United Kingdom, they are also a distributor of pornographic materials, but the variety and sophistication of what is available is broader and far deeper. They also sell comics for adults. Not exactly graphic novels, but full of characters such as Dylan Dog (who offers a very strange fairground reflection of what Italians actually believe living is London is like), Nathan Never and Diabolik. And amongst these adult comics are very adult comics, written by the likes of Crepax (who is most famous for his heroine Valentina and his reworkings of classic pornography novels) and Milo Manara (Crepax, 1992, 1994; Manara, 2001, 2002).

The comic books, like pornographic literature, do not involve any participants. No one is harmed in their production, except perhaps the artist's finger, and they are not prepared solely for the generation of capital. Next to the comic books are magazines and videos of adult material, yet customers prefer to purchase the comic books over and above more conventional pornographic materials. Like most comic books, they involve aesthetic production: both in the art and in the narrative plotting and characterization. Some of the work is greatly to be admired.

Yet, they also contain scenes that reduce men and women to their body parts, scenes of humiliation and bondage, themes of subordination and domination, and explicit imagery and language. They are pornography but they exist in an odd limbo: literary pornography is never truly seen as a problem because one can pretend that one is more concerned with the literary aspects, whereas the immediacy of the graphic arts undoes such a pretence. But these comics are simultaneously literary and also immediate. And they are bought for the purposes of arousal. I repeat, consumers choose them over and above other materials.

The question, then, one would need to ask is whether such comic books, their production, their exchange and/or their consumption, are instances of wrongdoing. There is no direct harm in their production, their consumption appears to be more reflective and thoughtful than the consumption of simple pornography, but they do not pretend to be anything but pornography and are ultimately for the purpose of arousal.

3
Oblique Suggestions, Polarized Pumpkin Eaters and Women Haters: The Morality of Pornography

3.1 Necessary and contingent wrongdoing

We have now a working, descriptive definition of pornography. *An object is pornographic for a specific community if it is a cultural object that exists in the public domain as a possible object of exchange; and it is reasonably expected by that community that it would be impossible for most subjects with the preference not to be aroused to attend to the object.* The claim of the following pages is that the wrongness of pornography has to be a wrongness with the consumption of pornography and not its production. There is nothing unique about the production of pornography that marks it out as different from other media goods or cultural objects. The present chapter will consider whether or not the existence, production, exchange or consumption of pornography is immoral and whether that requires that pornography should not exist, be produced, exchanged or consumed because these processes *necessarily* involve moral wrongdoing. First, it will be demonstrated that, even if pornography did involve wrongdoing, this is no *prima facie* reason to censure or prohibit it. Censure or prohibition of a whole subset of aesthetic objects (say, all painting, or all examples of gothic horror) can only be justified if its production *necessarily* involves serious wrongdoing. Two, the argument will then demonstrate that there is no necessary reason for the production of pornography to involve serious wrongdoing (contra MacKinnon), so there can be no general reason to prohibit or censure the *production* of pornography. Of course, this does not affect the claim that the consumption of pornography is a wrong, but it will reveal the morality of pornography cannot be insulated from the political aspect, the topic of the succeeding chapter.

Wrongdoing in pornographic practices can occur in one (or more) of its three aspects: production; exchange; and consumption. Considering exchange, one can steal a motor car or one can avoid paying tax on it when it is purchased. There is no reason to suppose the case of pornography is different from this: as long as it is exchanged legally, then there can be no wrongdoing in these transactions.[1] If we take it for granted that pornography is only possible in a society with property relations (and, given the intimate relationship between capitalism and property, private property relations), then wrongness in exchange will occur when pornography is exchanged against the rules of those property relations: theft, fraud, coercion, and so on. But since any good that is exchanged in such a way would also be an instance of wrongdoing, there is nothing about pornography in itself that requires special elucidation. If pornography in itself should not be exchanged, it would be due to it being an illegal or immoral object. Such objects are illegal or immoral because they should not be produced as their production includes illegal or immoral practices (snuff movies, counterfeit goods); or should not be consumed because their consumption is wrong whether for prudential (cigarettes), moral (panda burgers) or legal reasons (cocaine). It is pertinent, then, to consider in depth first the production and second the consumption of pornography.

3.2 Gauguin and his family

Let me first introduce a character called Gauguin who – a bit like the real Gauguin and a lot like Williams' (1976) Gauguin – is an artist. He is also a very good artist, destined to take a rightful place in the canon. His art employs expressivist techniques, but requires the colour and light of Tahiti to be fully realized. Unfortunately, Gauguin has a family and his choice to pursue his art (and consequently to progress the canon) requires that he travel alone from Europe to Tahiti. This comes at the cost of breaking his promises to, not fulfilling his voluntary obligations to, and disregarding the needs of his family. Our Gauguin (possibly unlike the real Gauguin) recognizes the value of family and burdens and responsibilities that his original promise in the registry office entailed, but still he chooses his art.

What interests me about the story is that, had Gauguin abandoned his family in order to count blades of grass or to discover the world's best beer, his course of action would not justify – never mind how successful he was – the moral wrongdoing. However, there exists a very plausible intuition that his talent and success as an artist exonerates (although such a word may be a little strong, as we shall later see) his morally bad treatment of his family or, to put it more colloquially, he is 'let off' because he is a great artist. In short, the worth of the art justifies the moral wrongdoing that occurred in its making. If he had been a blade-counter or a beer-seeker, Gauguin would have been purely and simply self-indulgent. Similarly, had he produced bad art or just banal art, he would have been judged negatively.

There is something about the production of works of art and their value which differentiates the creative pursuit from other arbitrary courses of action: it is a worthwhile pursuit and involves the creation of value. The activity of artistic creation is a special case whereby normal moral judgements are rendered, somehow, 'softer'.[2] If we were to concede provisionally that the production of pornography involves moral wrongdoing, it would not, if it is aesthetic production, in and of itself, necessarily entail prohibition and censure. If it did, many aesthetic objects including 'Gauguin's', would also have to be prohibited and censured and that, one feels, is intuitively far from acceptable (otherwise the film director who shouts at her actors has to ensure that the film she produces is appropriately worthwhile).

Given these plausible intuitions, here is a formal argument about the production of aesthetic objects:

1. Morally undesirable behaviour was necessary for the production of Gauguin's art.
2. The value of Gauguin's artistic production exonerates his morally undesirable behaviour.

And such an argument can be transposed to the current debate thus:

1a. Morally undesirable behaviour is necessary for the production of pornography.
2a. The aesthetic value of a particular pornographic object exonerates the morally undesirable behaviour involved in its production.[3]

One might want to assert that the analogy is not valid because Gauguin's wrongdoing is incidental to his art whereas pornographic production is necessarily an exercise of wrongdoing. You can paint pictures such as Gauguin's without abandoning your family, whereas you cannot produce pornography without (for example) objectifying or exploiting the participants or instigating gang rape. Gauguin just happened to behave badly, but to produce pornography you *must* behave badly. However, given that our example is fictional, let us make it the case that Gauguin's work involved necessary wrongdoing for its production: his art flourished in Tahiti and used the islanders and landscape as aesthetic material. He could not but abandon his family in order to achieve his aesthetic success. At least, that is the story we should tell. And still, given these facts, we would treat an artist-Gauguin differently from a beer-seeking-Gauguin. The structure of this argument is interesting because if the aesthetic worth of Gauguin's art negates or excuses his morally bad behaviour, then the aesthetic worth of a pornographic object (if meritorious to the sufficient degree) can negate or excuse undesirable behaviour involved in its production.

The point of this example is to propose the idea that the constellations of arguments caught in the description of 'critics' of pornography may be inconsequential if this argument is valid because it need not deny that the production of pornography involves moral wrongdoing. Let us then initially assume that the critics of pornography are correct in their assertion that the production of pornography harms individuals or groups, but that this consideration – as in the case of other aesthetic objects – does not trump the aesthetic value of the object and so cannot, *tout court*, lead to its prohibition or criminalization. Just as Gauguin's wrongdoing is weighed against his artistic production, so too may pornographic productions. One must first gauge the aesthetic worth of an object and only then, if required, the moral status of its production.

But let us return to the above comment that 'the aesthetic worth of a pornographic object (if *meritorious to the sufficient degree*) can negate or excuse undesirable behaviour involved in its production.' The objection is obvious: pornography may well be an aesthetic object in the manner which *I* have chosen to talk about such things, but Picasso it ain't! More significantly, it could never be so, because pornography just cannot have the requisite aesthetic value. One may want to admit that pornography is art, but insist that it is necessarily bad art (Berger, 1977). If such a claim is correct, then pornography is, by definition, bad art and even if the formal validity of the argument could be defended, it is immaterial because pornography could never have the requisite aesthetic value; there could never be a case in which pornography would be preferred to moral value, no matter how minimal the latter is. (So not even being mean or snappy with one's actors is to be tolerated in the production of pornography!)

Again, in the previous chapter, it has been established that many objects which fit the definition offered have minimal aesthetic value. However, for the present argument to work, more than minimal aesthetic value is required to justify the wrongdoing in its production. It strikes me, if we are faithful to my working definition of pornography, then Bertolucci, Medem, Bataille and Réage are pornographic objects with arguably a level of aesthetic value to allow them into the canon. Of course, the critic of pornography might object that such examples are not pornography. They might want to offer some sort of distinction between pornography and eroticism, or they might want to subdivide pornography itself into soft and hard core, the non-aesthetic equivalent of the pornographic/erotic dichotomy (Levinson, 2005; cf. Kieran, 2001). MacKinnon, for example, is only interested in pornography defined as 'graphic sexually explicit subordination of women' (1993: 121), proposing that the graphic sexual explicit material which does not subordinate women is eroticism (although, I doubt for her such a thing exists). We shall consider MacKinnon's full position below and in succeeding chapters, but she identifies a supposed wrong in the production of pornography that fuels much of her argument and which far outweighs obscenity: 'In pornography, women are gang raped so they can be filmed ... Only for pornography are women killed to make a sex movie ... It *is* essential to do them to make pornography' (1993: 15).[4] Pornography is then material that embodies moral and legal wrongdoing, whereas eroticism is sexually explicit material that embodies no such thing. Of course, the real question is then whether eroticism is possible. Lawrence (1997) believed that pornography is aligned with the industrial and eroticism with the natural; and Scruton bases his distinction explicitly on how pornography makes the sexual object a transferable good, unlike eroticism which makes the object a good in itself (2006: 103–107). Pornography is like a glass of water: any glass will do, and if one is denied, another can replace it. But sexual arousal should not be like this and, like anger, is aimed at a particular person and not a person with certain characteristics in general. Sexual arousal, for Scruton, must be for a person who is not transferable, and eroticism somehow captures this: 'In true erotic art it is usually the face and not the sexual organ that provides the focus of attention' (2006: 154). So, if we were to ask why my examples are not pornography (and are perhaps eroticism or literature instead), the answer would probably be that they exhibit the requisite aesthetic value whereas *mere* pornography does not. It does not, one might hold, because it *presents* sexual activity (aesthetic realism) rather than *represents* the experience of it through simulation and aesthetic technique.

Such a preoccupation with realism in representation and the need to differentiate between the 'veracity' of pornography and the 'art' of eroticism may well map onto a moral debate, though. Simulation or representation is acceptable whereas presentation is somehow vulgar and obscene. The obscene is what, very literally, should be kept off stage and hidden, only hinted at for the viewer to understand and not see. Pornography breaks this quaint rule of sensibility. So, the wrongness involved in the production of pornography is turning what should not be an object of exchange into an object of exchange by recording, filming, or writing it down. Obscene images cause offence. Offence is, of course, justified (or excused) in art if the object in question expresses some sort of aesthetic value; many canonical works of art, and here I think most notably of Dali's *The Christ of St. John of the Cross* (1951) in Glasgow, have caused offence, but are to be defended (literally in the case of Dali from a knife attack) because of their aesthetic merit. Similarly, Medem's *Sex and Lucía* definitely has aesthetic worth, *Baise-moi* arguably has aesthetic worth, whereas *Debbie Does Dallas* does not. Bataille's *Story of the Eye* and de Sade's *The One Hundred and Twenty Days of Sodom* would be controversial. Such grey areas concerning the worth of the aesthetic object often lead to discussions of what is and what is not pornography (RCOFC, 1979: ¶1.7).

Obscenity can pre-reflectively centre on the concern whether the object in question is a 'simulation' of an act or a record of a 'real' act. There seems to be an intuitive need to distinguish between 'real' and 'simulated' acts, since this often, pre-reflectively, tracks the distinction between 'soft' and 'hard' core pornography. More significantly, it has some moral bite because 'snuff' movies are immoral because the killing constituent of them is real and not simulated. Snuff movies are a matter of legal sanction because the 'actors' actually die rather than pretend to die. For MacKinnon pornography is explicitly immoral as 'women's body parts – including but not limited to vaginas, breasts, or buttocks – are exhibited such that women are reduced to those parts'. Once these are on show simulation is no longer possible. Once we see penetration on screen, we are witnessing an actual rape for her. But, though murder is wrong and rape is wrong, consensual sex is not. We sanction agents for murder but not for having sex. However, we do sanction sex in public places because it is obscene and so there might be more to this than we first thought. Now, it is sometimes difficult to make the judgement that actors did or did not actually have sex in a specific film (Bertolucci's *Last Tango in Paris* and Moretti's *Caos Calmo* jump to mind), but that need not concern us here. Let us imagine an obvious case of real as opposed to simulated sex. Such films are obscene because they revel in their veracity: we see the penetration close up and the cum-shot, arguably in order to 'prove' that the sex being observed is real. Eroticism has the requisite aesthetic value but pornography, by definition, cannot because it is obscene.

Even with an uncontroversial paradigmatic case in mind, the claim that the obscenity of the actual making of pornographic films is wrong does not hold up to reflection. Actors in mainstream cinema kiss and they actually kiss, they do not pretend to kiss. And in soft core films they kiss, lick, bite nipples and so on. Actors in hard core films penetrate and fellate. There is no simulation in these acts. What changes is that certain practices are deemed offensive when they are not simulated: actual penetration, the tongue on the labia, the penis in the mouth and so on. What is the true difference between soft and hard core pornography? Asking oneself that question is to reveal cultural arbitrariness: compare what is taboo in the West and the East and then compare their respective pornographies. Scruton (2006) explicitly relates pornography to realism (but also elsewhere to fantasy!), as though the representation of penetration rather than the allusion to it destroys imagined reciprocity. Sex for him is worthless unless there is a practice of reciprocity and communication at its heart. This is probably true for sexual relations and the representation of sexual relations, but if one enjoys *King Lear*, it does not exclude one taking enjoyment from trash TV series and if one eats at Noma, it does not stop KFC from being tasty to one's palate and still a pleasure! The arousal from Bertolucci may be a purer, more aesthetic arousal than that from *Debbie Does Dallas*, but the latter is still arousal and neither good or bad arousal in itself. What *Debbie Does Dallas*, KFC and trash TV share is a simplicity and immediacy that appeal to the lowest common denominator: watch or eat this, and gratification will be quick and almost guaranteed. There is no complexity to the experience, but that is an aesthetic and not a moral judgement.

So, it is not the distinction between simulation and reality which matters but what actions are being filmed. Of course, some might say, 'One can kiss, but not mean it, whereas one cannot fuck and not mean it'. But on what basis can they hold such a claim? Both are simple, physical actions that have emotional connotations. And those connotations will transform from person to person, from historical age to age, and, more importantly, from culture to culture. As far as prescribing what should be presented in words or images, penetration must involve an actor penetrating another, but then kissing must involve one actor kissing another and the latter events are commonplace in most films. To say that one is an act of intimacy that cannot be simulated whereas the other is not (as both MacKinnon and Scruton seem to do) is disingenuous: people still get divorced because one has kissed another or fondled another and I have yet to hear the defence that such acts do not merit divorce proceedings because they are not intimate.

Whatever the merits of delineating between eroticism and pornography, one feels that at base it is a reflection of bourgeois sensibility centred around the erroneous distinction of soft versus hard core pornography. Snuff movies are not allowed to be produced because we cannot believe that the actors have freely participated in filming their own death, or have not done so when of sound mind. The producer will have forced them and violated their right to decide whether or not they want to participate or not. If MacKinnon is right and every filming of sex is rape, then it is obvious that the actor is in the same position as the participant in the snuff movie and would not *in their right mind* have agreed to participate. But agents enjoy having sex and some agents enjoy people watching them have sex. When we say snuff movies are immoral, implicit in what we say is that the actors would not – if they were not coerced or manipulated or simply not irrational – have agreed to act in the film. We might want to say that the intimacy of sex is such that no actor – unless they are coerced, manipulated or irrational – would consent to perform actual sex for others. As a critical distinction it is either banal, as is the case with a *lazy* reading of MacKinnon (one I hope to remedy in later chapters), where the message seems to be that we shouldn't watch films that involve serious wrongdoing (rape) in production because our consumption is complicit in this wrongdoing. Or it is puritanical: any and all representations of sexual activity in images involve rape. (And nonsensical, if one includes verbal pornographic literature.)[5]

3.3 Moral severity and pluralism

Putting aside such distractions for now, let us move to the heart of what is at stake here. The difference, it might quite reasonably be held, between Gauguin's production and pornographic production is a matter of the gravity of the wrongdoing involved. In other words, one could object that the analogy between the two arguments is misplaced. Gauguin's wrongdoing is reprehensible and caddish behaviour, but it is not actually illegal. Neither is it seriously wrong behaviour. Here one has to weigh the moral values and aesthetic values against one another and judge what is a great wrong and, for that matter, what is great art. Such judgements involve a great deal of cultural sensibility and raise the need for substantial ethical (and one feels aesthetic) theories in order to value acts and products in a way that can engage with the agent's practical reasoning. It is easy to imagine cultures in which the abandonment of one's family is a much greater wrong than it is in a late modern, capitalist epoch. The critics of pornography would, however, assert that the production of pornography involves a severity of wrongness that makes it not analogous to Gauguin's story.

One can imagine a 'snuff movie' which involved the actual killing of one or more human beings. No matter how well made, and hence the value of its aesthetic representation, such values can never excuse the moral wrongdoing at its heart. Yet, there is seemingly no formal difference here: artistic creation requires moral wrongdoing otherwise the artistic work will not have sufficient artistic merit. Had Gauguin stayed with his family, he may still have painted but he would not have painted as well or to the standard that he did. Similarly, had the snuff movie director chosen to simulate the murder rather than film the murder, then the film may well have been lacking in aesthetic merit that it would otherwise have had. The critics of pornography (and one thinks most obviously of MacKinnon) would assert that the production of pornography is more akin to a 'snuff movie' than it is analogous to Gauguin's story. No matter the aesthetic worth of the production of the resulting film, it is categorically wrong to kill for the purposes of aesthetic value.

It is obvious that such an argument is best supported by a deontological framework, but even a consequentialist would be able to argue that the cost–benefit analysis could never (normally) support the good produced by pornography outweighing the good destroyed by moral badness. However, if the question is whether the severity of wrongdoing affects our attitude towards a work of art, then the answer seems to be a mixture of 'Yes' and 'No'. If Gauguin's art was created using the death of a human being and that death was intrinsically crucial for the creation of that art, on the surface we would disapprove of that art, but would the resulting product have no value because of the process of its production? The answer seems to be, 'No' and that it would still have value *in spite of* the process of its production. The value of art and its production seem to be separate issues. I personally was awestruck by the decoration of Moscow's metro stations, for example. To be dreadfully rhetorical: should we tear them down due to the production process involved?

Before introducing some substantial theories to help us rationalize our judgements, let us begin as usual by considering a few commonplace intuitions. That the severity of the moral wrongness committed in the production process plays a role is undeniable, but a distinction between criminal and immoral behaviour may be of some initial use here. Art that is produced through the transgression of uncontroversial legal statutes (rape, killing, exploitation) is obviously an object of moral disapproval and subject to punitive measures. (The word 'uncontroversial' has been added here as I am primarily concerned with legal statutes based on sound rational moral law, such as killing, rape and violent coercion. The qualification merely recognizes that cases where art could transgress legal statutes as a form of protest in order to bring into focus the irrationality of such legal statutes may well be possible.) Not all pornographic objects involve such practices. And the wrongness of rape, killing or exploitation is wrong whether the artistic production is pornography, mainstream cinema, painting or even children's books. If this is the sort of wrongness that is involved in the production of *all* objects of pornography, then it would be irrational not to agree to its prohibition, just as if this wrongness were involved in cockle picking, farming or factory work. So, if MacKinnon is serious in her claim that all sexual representation is representation of real rape, then her argument is undeniable, but if all the critics of pornography want to do is merely to stop practices that involve illegal activities, then their argument, although obviously correct and important on one level, is, on another level, banal. Significantly, if the argument is correct, then there is no need to discuss 'pornography' as a separate issue in ethical and legal philosophy at all. Mackinnon (1993) holds that all pornographic production is coercion and violence, and that these are serious wrongs. If she is right, then my argument fails unless, as we will see in the next section, the severity of the wrongness can be counterbalanced by the value of the aesthetic production. We shall also look more deeply at MacKinnon in later chapters because her aim – as is obvious from her definition – is not philosophical, but political.[6]

One might, on the other hand, reject the truth of premises 2 and 2a above. It is not that we exonerate Gauguin, we just conveniently forget, or dismiss, Gauguin's wrongdoing because that is a fault of his character. We make two judgements: one about his moral behaviour and the other about his art. To put it more strongly, one can apply a categorical approach to wrongdoing: it does not matter what you bring about if your intentions or actions were wrong. So, Gauguin's paintings are valuable, but he has still done wrong and should be held responsible as such. It seems that this is perhaps a better description of our attitude to artists and artistic production. Moral wrongdoing is not exonerated, but is 'put up with' or 'conveniently ignored'. Moral wrongdoing is treated in this way *in this instance* because of the value of what is produced. Of course, though, what the argument does not need to say is that Gauguin is exonerated, only that his moral wrongdoing has to be balanced against the existence of his art. Implicit in such an answer is a commitment to ontological pluralism: there is more than one good in this world but given the social and ethical space it is impossible to substantiate all goods harmoniously or at one time.[7]

Moral value is a good, but so is aesthetic value. We tend to think, theoretically, that the former is somehow more valuable or matters more than the latter and when push comes to shove in serious cases, this may well be true. But it is not so simple. We may not kill or let someone die in order to save the *Mona Lisa*, but most of us would – I would contend – deceive, break promises and possibly harm to save it. And, more importantly, ontological pluralism does not require validation through action: it is enough that the agent who saves the child from the burning Louvre rather than *La Gioconda* admits that what he has done was right, but still feels *remorse* for not having the opportunity to rescue the painting. He might play various 'what if' scenarios through his head in the aftermath. As long as the moral wrongness involved in the production is akin to Gauguin's wrongness, then there seem to be good reasons to both morally disapprove and aesthetically approve simultaneously. Like decisions made when faced with a moral dilemma, one must act, and in doing so choose one value over another, but the feeling of remorse for not being able to do the other (even if it were impossible) is enough to testify to its value. Aesthetic value may just come into conflict with moral value even if they both ought to be rationally supported. Sometimes we side with one, sometimes with the other. The problem does not reside with values as such, but the shape of the world in which one tries to substantiate these values.

To support this claim, imagine a counter-factual: would we prefer Gauguin had acted morally and his art had never been created? Put like this, we can see how the severity of the moral wrongdoing plays a role in the consideration above. We can imagine possible worlds where specific moral wrongdoing is required for the production of specific aesthetic values, and no doubt severe moral wrongdoing (murder, for example) would require the production of aesthetic ideals (Dante or Shakespeare, for example). However, lying, deception and so on can easily be counterbalanced by greatness in art and being mean-spirited could probably be accepted even if the outcome is the most banal of art. Value judgements involve subtle comparisons and evaluations that are grounded in our social existence: the idea that the world can actually support categorical morality of the sort demanded by this objection is at the heart of Hegel's revision of Kantian moral philosophy and this intuition forms the beginning point of our revision of the moral positions in the chapters below (Hegel, 1975). There are many considerations, values and preferences at play in our day-to-day existence that require the use of a developed and mature practical wisdom to balance them out.

To be consistent with these reflections, it seems we would have to change premises 2 and 2a to:

Premise 2: The value of Gauguin's artistic production may matter more than his morally undesirable behaviour.
Premise 2a: The aesthetic value of a particular pornographic object may matter more than the morally undesirable behaviour involved in its production.

But that means the moral severity is still pertinent because the putative pluralism of values is not going to be an adequate defence against the perfectly aesthetic snuff movie. And that means that even if we can appreciate the value of aesthetic production and it can counterbalance the weight of moral values, if the wrongdoing is too serious, then the aesthetic value is simply trumped (yet it does remain valuable). The perfectly aesthetic snuff movie could never be acceptable and the production of pornographic objects may well be as seriously immoral. Gauguin's activity probably involved deception and deception is wrong. It is a moral wrong but not always subject to legal sanction nor even strong moral disapproval (although the context may sometimes demand either or both of these, and remember that Kant would categorically disagree). The production of most pornographic objects would involve wrongdoing akin to Gauguin's, otherwise the production activity, like exploitation in industrial production, would be subject to legal intervention and strong moral disapproval. So, it seems that wrongdoing involved in the production process must be serious for it to demand a prohibition of the practice. What type of wrongdoing that is should be articulated in terms of a robust ethical theory.

3.4 Standard moral theories, monism and pluralism

Intuitively, and by that I suppose I mean uncontroversially, although there will always be one or two voices which will dissent, paid labour is not a serious wrong (although, I bite my lip as I say that and we shall return to this in a later chapter), nor is deceiving actors about the balance between the aesthetic quality and the commercial attraction of a proposed film. The sort of things that constitute what I would call serious wrongs in film production are: actual harm to actors (including, but not exclusively, killing (snuff movies), rape, physical abuse, psychological torment, privation of basic needs); stealing of ideas (intellectual theft and copyright issues); use of private property without permission; filming of persons surreptitiously (voyeurism films); non-fulfilment of legal contracts (not paying the actors and workers); and exploitation of the workers involved in the production process (non-payment or unfair payment for labour).[8] Coercion is not explicitly named here simply because the stage at which the director's role in coaxing performances out of his actors constitutes coercion implies a question only an actor can answer; and I believe serious cases will be covered by rape and exploitation above. Coercion is uncontroversially manifest when actors engage in activities which are counter to their obvious interests. Remember that, here, we are only concerned with wrongdoing in the production of pornography and, it strikes me at least, this list exhausts the possible wrongs that could occur in that part of the process. Before discussing whether or not such serious wrongs are endemic to the production of pornography, let us first say a little about moral theory and how a serious wrong is then to be characterized,

In contemporary normative ethics, two groups of theories dominate the debate. To call them groups is perhaps to overstate their variety, in that there is an almost unanimous agreement that an ethical problem is to be resolved using exclusively the framework of one of these two positions. What is interesting is that both types of theory are in fact universal in nature and, hence, most discussions of a particular ethical issue will often descend into a theoretical justification of a position held by the writer. There is also a third, the poor cousin if you will, which exists in the shadow of the two behemoths of moral thinking and arose from a palpable dissatisfaction with these approaches (Anscombe, 1958; Williams, 1972). But, here is an odd (given the theoretical commitments to universalism) but highly plausible claim: having good intentions, being virtuous and maximizing the welfare of others are all instances of good behaviour. There is nothing actually contradictory in acting on good intentions in one minute and then trying to increase someone else's well-being in the next, unless one believes that the one must be reducible to the other. Welfare is a good (but not the only one) and more of it is better than less of it, but it is not the only good. Agents should be respected as autonomous, but not at the cost of their own welfare or that of others. Behaving virtuously is admirable, but not at the cost of ignoring the collective good. That there will be conflicts between these competing prescriptions of moral behaviour is almost as obvious as that there will be conflicts between aesthetic value and moral value and even liberty and equality. There is only so much social space in which value can be realized.

Yet, it is the tenor of our times that only one of these three theories can be true. That there is one theory to explain them all seems to be a monism borne from an too much respect for the natural sciences. Methodologically, such a model is not a bad thing but it may not be the best model to follow for ethics. Monism is the commitment to one theory for all, but in day-to-day ethical and rational reasoning, an agent is at one moment consequential in his or her reasoning, at another deontological and at times will take a virtue approach to behaviour. So, I might argue that I should tell a small lie if the result of that lie is to protect the person I have deceived (as I have been known to do with my children). I might stand by a promise even if to do so results in burdens on me and my family and reduces our welfare. I may, at times, prescribe acting in a way that is gregarious (but not too much) when hosting a social event. I see no reason why such different forms of reasons should not motivate the same agent at different times and even play a role as considerations at the same moment. To assume that an agent will find it impossible to subscribe to the pre-Copernican view of the universe on weekdays and the post-Copernican model at weekends is highly plausible: the commitment to one theory excludes the commitment to the other. But, it does not seem to be the same in ethics: I find that at times, as a moral agent, the pull of considering others' welfare, the pull of doing the right thing for the right reasons and the pull of being virtuous, stretch me in three different directions, but most of the time, and ethical theorists always play this down, they simply cohere. Some ethical thinkers believe such fragmentary and pluralistic accounts of moral motivation make rational deliberation impossible and are a specific symptom of contemporary existence (MacIntyre, 2007). However, there is no obvious reason why one agent cannot reason in a number of ways and offer courses of action that are contradictory. In fact it strikes me as a more plausible account of moral behaviour and in no way particular to contemporary existence (one need only look at the complexity of Creon in *Antigone* whose conflicted character is often brushed over by concentrating on the tragic heroine). Throughout the history of ethics, the advocates of ends over means, purity of intention, rightness of acts and paradigms of character have been in constant conversation, even if the idioms and vocabulary have varied. Moral theories are not, and should not aspire to be scientific, that is perhaps the bane of our age. And the three-way pull I have indicated, like conflicts between moral and other values, happens less often than need generate such philosophical hand-wringing or hair-pulling. Often it is forced in order to instigate the necessity of a decision between theories that aspire to universality. Most of the time, in our day-to-day moral existence, I know when welfare is to be considered, when equality demands to be respected, and when I ought to exhibit the right sort of characteristics demanded by the situation. Most of the time, there is an appropriate moral theory to guide me – almost pre-reflectively – through my moral action. Moral theories can similarly be understood as idioms more or less appropriate to the problem in hand. Let us then begin with the appropriateness question and claim that the appropriate moral idiom is, and here there is no great surprise, Kantian ethics because, as I have intimated, all problems in the *production* of pornography orbit around coercion. This need not necessarily be true of the *consumption* of pornography.

So, the three theories I have been hinting at are obviously: consequentialist or teleological theories, intrinsicalist or deontological theories and the pre-modern alternative, virtue ethics. The first two theories are, of course, most readily identified by the proper names which tend to stand in for them in their most resistant historical form: Mill and Kant. I am minded to sidestep revising, rehashing and reverting to discussions of ethical theories and their merits. The aim of such a discussion should never be the resolution of which theory, or type of theory, is true or, more weakly, the best. The question I want to ask, and given the putative (although I shall argue for it later on) commitment to pluralism in values, which is the most *appropriate* theory to allow us to progress the debate and to gain most ground in offering an answer to the ethical problems brought about by the existence of pornography. The justification of such value pluralism will, unfortunately, have to wait for a later chapter, but even methodologically it strikes me as quite reasonable to pass over substantial and meta-ethical debates in both the metaphysics of morals and the substantive nature of values in order to say some commonsensical things about pornography. So, let me just indulge in a little justification of my criterion of *appropriateness*. If one were to use an analogy, I live in a bilingual house with languages that do not compete but fulfil rather different functions. These functions are often determined by the appropriateness of the language to the aim of the discussion. It does not mean that the other language cannot fulfil this function, only that it is more 'natural' or, as I want to term it, appropriate to the subject matter and the mode of expression. For arguing or discussing food, Italian is predominantly used. When it comes to legal and tax issues, English tends to assert itself. World Cups are best avoided in my house.

Virtue theory identifies certain characteristics of persons which, when exhibited, fulfil a way of living that is to be admired or has value. As a theory, it holds that what one should do is what a morally ideal agent would do in the same situation, so to behave exhibiting characteristics that are admirable: being brave (but not rash) in war, being witty (but not foolish) in social gatherings, and being generous (but not to the point of self-harm) with others less fortunate, are examples of such behaviour. So, if one were to identify the religious life as a valuable one, then the required exhibition of piety, modesty and humility would seemingly rule out the life of the adult film star. The real problem with virtue theory is the justification of which comprehensive, metaphysical good life is to be advocated. But, avoiding problems of the metaphysical justification of which type of life is of value and *who* is to decide which type of life is valuable, we can say that whatever type of life we should aspire to, if participating in the production of pornography makes this impossible, then the agent would only participate through mistaken beliefs (deception) or through a lack of alternative options (coercion). So, if we were to cede that participating in the production of pornography is contrary to the fulfilment of the good life (whatever that may be), then the problem is one of agents being forced to do something they would not have otherwise done if it were not for mistaken beliefs or the presence of other agents. That agent is then, not able to act in a way he or she would have wished, so in this case virtue ethics (whatever its metaphysics may well be) resolves itself into a Kantian idiom for the purposes of this problem.

Similarly, turning to those moral theories which identify one (or more goods) and see the right action (or duty) of the agent as the maximization of these goods, whether this be for the agent him or herself (egoism) or for as many agents as possible (universalism), and taking utilitarianism in its welfarist form as the most diffuse contemporary form, the problem resolves itself once more into a Kantian idiom.[9] An action or practice is the right course of action if it benefits a maximal number of individuals. It is wrong if the consequences of that action harm the welfare of a majority of those involved. At this point, remember that we are only concerned with the agents involved in the *production* of pornography and the harm they may well suffer (the actors are raped, the production assistants suffer harm to the health of their own sex life and so on). We cannot ask, since we are concerned solely with production, whether the actors have an obligation to the consumers (although a utilitarian could not easily isolate the two aspects as we have done). So, imagine a room in which we have two actors, a director, a cameraman, a lighting engineer and a sound engineer. How are such agents harmed in the production of the film? The technical staff may well suffer harm to their ability to enjoy a proper sex life, but only in the same way as a kitchen assistant would suffer harm to his appetites and tastes from working in the production of food. And of course, in both cases, they may well benefit from participation. The harm to the technical staff, if there is any, is akin to the consumer of pornography in that there is some sort of causal impact on their welfare. We shall return to this below.

What, though, of the actors? Their harm is more direct because it is overtly physical: muscle fatigue, chafing, exertion. Of course, if we are hedonists, such pains should be balanced against the pleasure enjoyed by actors. Actors in war films will suffer similar pains, if not centred on the same parts of the body, so they are only harms if the actors have not agreed to them. There is also, one might add, the possibility of psychological damage, trauma and damage to the possibility of a healthy life. Participating in sexual actively for the purposes of representation is harmful to the interests of the participants involved. Yet, talk of interest is always – even in utilitarian theory – to bring in rights and the right of the agent to determine whether or not the agent does what they do because they want to and hence benefit from it (Mill, 1962: ch. 5). And if they have not agreed, or freely agreed, or their participation has been brought about by coercion (and is not therefore consent), then MacKinnon is right and we have an instance of rape (non-consensual sex). Of course, if you were to ask whether the actors were happy to perform, they most often answer, 'Yes' (Monroe, 2010). If harm is committed in the production of pornography, one feels it is in the complicit behaviour of the actors who would not, in their right mind, ever do what they do. They allow the harm because they are coerced and so the utilitarian position must first establish the Kantian claim that harm occurs because the actors are coerced.[10]

To avoid falling into the mire of interpretative debate and giving hostages to fortune, I hope the reader will permit me to use a deontological framework consistent with Kant's second formulation of the categorical imperative without any claim to it being a faithful or even reconstructed Kantianism. What is basically at stake in the second formulation is the freedom of the agent to participate or not in the projects, plans and policies of others, coupled with the universality of moral reasons. Interestingly, if the ideal of a victim is upheld, then it seems that pornographic literature is not the subject of moral judgement at all because it does not involve any actors at all. Both Arsan (1980) and Réage (1972) should rightly be considered pornographic and Lawrence (1997) was famously, of course, once described this way. Verbal pornography involves an author and a reader and no one else.

The media which carry sexually explicit ideas or representations are verbal (literature and live chat), film, dance, photographs, paintings, etchings, drawings, virtual computer generated images and animated cartoons. The medium is often supposed to be the deciding factor, some sort of McLuhan echo, in order to defend the reading of erotic literature but the prohibition of images, simply because the activity is more cerebral. Of course, the immediacy of the visual over the textual is arguably a more affective medium, but the point is misplaced. What matters is whether there are participants or not, so live chat and a written monologue that is never read out are the same medium (words), but there can be Kantian wrongdoing in the production of one but not the other (unless we move towards a fuller account of power as we shall in this book). Media ought to be grouped in terms of those that involve participants and those which do not because this distinction matters morally. What is wrong with the production of child pornography (coercion and harm) cannot be wrong with the production of animated cartoon child pornography. The internet is not a medium, at least not in any interesting sense. It carries film, chat, photos and verbal pornography and minimally influences their content (although this is a contentious claim). The internet is more akin to ink: ink is a medium but words, printed words, newspaper words, magazine words and book words differ not because of the ink but because of the formats of the newspaper, book and so on.

However, a Kantian approach still seems appropriate to the matter in hand, and to the specific nature of the production of pornography, because actors are being asked to participate in the cooperative activity of film-makers. In fact, putting aside the status of literary or verbal pornography, the notion of agency involved in the production of pornography is salient because it makes reference to the subject, the model or the actor, in a way that painting does not make reference to the model. The model is rendered as an ideal by the painter, whereas the body of the actor remains present and is indistinguishable from the artefact. The lived consciousness of the pornographic actor remains embodied in the film or the photograph and these lived consciousnesses are not incidental to the production of the artefact. They participate in it in a way very different from the painter's model or the poet's inspiration. To put it as simply and unphilosophically as we can, the actor can never say, 'That was not me,' or, 'That was how the artist saw me, but it is not me', because their existence is laid bare and recorded rather than interpreted. The participation of actors and photograph models is then permissible, required or forbidden depending on the motivation on which the agent *should* act. (As such, it returns to MacKinnon's (1993: 60–61) understanding of why pornography is different from racism, because basically it is intimately individual.)

Kant informs us that moral action is distinguished from other actions by the nature of its determination. Human beings act on a myriad of motivations: unconscious desires, a-rational desires, immediate emotional responses, pre-reflective intentions and reflective intentions (reasons good and proper). Desires, preferences, inclinations are all to be viewed as considerations when we act, in the same way that the words of another may be a consideration when we act, but such considerations only become motivations when we choose them as subjective principles of volition or, more simply, intentions. An intention is a reason which is internalized by being endorsed by the agent as not just a reason, but a reason that applies to him or her. So, action is identified by agents who act on reasons that they themselves recognize as legitimate. When considerations are internalized it is done so according to the structures of rational psychology. The agent represents the motivation to him or herself as a law that would govern behaviour in accordance with rational action. Rational action need not be moral action: it can be prudential, the furtherance of the individual's own interests, or it can simply be instrumental, so that if I want X, and Y is necessary for me to achieve that, I will Y as well. But moral reasons are categorical, in that they are privileged because they do not make reference to the particularity of the agent or the circumstances of the situation. They are categorical when they fit the formal nature of law exactly, when they can be universalized. In short, a reason is a moral reason when it fits this formula: I should do X, not because I want to, not because it allows me to achieve what I ultimately want, but simply because I should (it is unconditional) because everyone, if they are rational, should act on such a reason. It is what being rational requires of the agent and if an agent acts from the recognition that the reasons by which he or she is motivated are right reasons for all, then his or her action has moral worth.

Moral actions, then, are characterized by what Kant calls the good will, or basically by doing the right thing for the right reason. One can do the wrong thing for the right reason (lie to protect someone's feelings) and one can do the right thing for the wrong reason (tell the truth in order to secure a promotion), but only when we do the right thing, motivated by the right reason do we have moral agency. Right reasons are those which are, for Kant, practically necessary, mimicking in practical reason the logical necessity of theoretical reason. As an epistemological agent, if I know that a square has four sides and I know that the table in the dining room is square, I could only declare that it did not have four sides *at the cost of my rationality*. If I want to remain in a conversation with other epistemological agents, then I could not declare such a thing.

Motivations which are particular to a specific agent (unconscious desires, a-rational desires, emotional responses) are just not the sort of entities that can constitute right reasons because they cannot be, by their very nature, universal. Motivations remain at the level of 'mere' considerations unless endorsed and given rational form. A law is an objective representation of an intention whereby the 'I intend to X in order to Y', becomes 'In order to Y, one should X'. In other words, the intention is given a rational structure and no universality can come from rational structures that make reference to a particular agent or circumstances. Those intentions which have rational form can be of three forms: self-interested; means to an end; and practically necessary. It is obvious that one can rationally further one's ends, but such reasons cannot be without reference to a practical agent, that is the I. Hypothetical reasons of the form if X, then Y are again rational, but depend on the particularity of having a specific end in view and that, again, will belong to a particular agent. Such reasons motivate permissible forms of action so long as they do not contradict duties, and duties are those requirements which rule out a priori certain actions. Right reasons are duties which are structured around the claim 'A rational being must necessarily do X and does not do so at the cost of his or her own rationality'. If I want to be accepted as a moral agent, then if I cognize right reasons – or duties – I must act upon them and others must recognize that they, too, would have acted upon the same reasons. If I do not, I do so at the cost of my rationality and can no longer participate in conversations with moral agents because they will recognize that I do not play by the rules. More than this, if I am rational, I do not play by the rules in order to further my own interests:

> If we now attend to ourselves in every transgression of a duty, we find that we actually do not will that our maxim should become a universal law, since that is impossible for us, but that its opposite should rather generally remain a law; we just take the liberty of making an *exception* to it for ourselves, or (just for this once) to the advantage of our inclination. (Kant, 2012: 4:424)

When we queue on the motorway, we curse the driver who jumps the line by zooming down the hard shoulder. We curse her because her action is only possible if she takes for granted the rule-abiding nature of her fellow drivers. She needs us to obey the rule, so she simply assumes it is a rule for rational beings in order to profit from it. We want to know why she thinks she is a special case, what is special about her. (Imagine the conversation: 'Would you all mind queuing in an orderly fashion according to the rules of the road so I can zoom down the hard shoulder without obstruction?' 'Only if you tell me, what is so special about you?') For this reason, moral intentions are unconditional and categorical: practical reason seeks to impose laws on itself; and any intention, which makes reference to the particularity of the agent or the situation, does not hold for whomever, wherever and whenever. In short, it is not a law. But since I recognize all rational beings as being ruled by law, I could not expect them to do what is rational just in order to further my own interests. The sort of reasons which are duties are universal because reason is universal amongst moral agents, and those reasons which are right are those which all agents, no matter who, where, or when they are, would see as practically necessary:

> Reason must view herself as the authoress of her principles, independently of alien influences, and must consequently, as practical reason, or as the will of a rational being, by herself be viewed as free; i.e. its will can be such a will of its own only under the idea of freedom, and must thus for practical purposes be ascribed to all rational beings. (Kant, 2012: 4:448)

The epistemological agent cannot deny the logical necessity of the law of the excluded middle. To be a thinking thing, I must obey the laws of logic. Similarly, to be a moral thing, I must obey the laws of practical reason (I could not deny very easily without further elucidation that he who desires the ends must also desire the means). And the basic stipulation of universality means that any intention I formulate speaks to me as a rational agent and not a particular agent and so it is rationality itself which has value:

> *a rational nature exists as an end in itself.* That is how a human being by necessity represents his own existence; to that extent it is thus a *subjective* principle of human actions. But every other rational being also represents its existence in this way, as a consequence of just the same rational ground that also holds for me; thus it is at the same

> time an *objective* principle from which, as a supreme practical ground, it must be possible to derive all laws of the will. The practical imperative will thus be the following: *So act that you use humanity, in your own person or in the person of any other, always at the same time as an end never, merely as a means*. (Kant, 2012: 4:429)

Or, as Kant, formulates it elsewhere: 'For all rational beings stand under the *law* that each of them is to treat itself and all others *never merely as a means* but always *at the same time as an end in itself*' (2012: 4:433). The reasons I give for my own behaviour must be as acceptable to other agents as they are to myself. A course of action which furthers my own interest is permissible so long as the reasons which motivate it would be possible objects of endorsement by other agents. If I ask you to act in concert with me, to cooperate with me, then I recognize that you are governed by the representation of law and are rational. So, your actions can only follow on from motivations which you see as legitimate. To make you do things that you would not agree to (such as no one should zoom down the hard shoulder except Sharon) is to negate your rationality and could be executed only through an appeal to causal influence: physical force, violence, deception or the psychological motivation of threats. I would then treat you are a mere tool for my projects, no better than the relationship between cameraman and his camera.

So, let us once more list the wrongs that can occur in the production of pornography: actual harm to actors; theft; filming of persons surreptitiously; non-fulfilment of legal contracts; and exploitation. All of these violate Kant's second formulation of the categorical imperative: '*act that you use humanity, in your own person as well as in the person of any other, always at the same time as an end, never merely as a means*' (Kant, 2012: 4:429). If an agent agrees to be (excessively) harmed in film making, they can do so only at the cost of their own rationality. One would do such things only if one has been deceived, exploited or coerced into participating. Stealing of intellectual and abuse of private property again rely on not asking (deceiving) or forcing the owner to allow his or her rights to be violated. Exploitation is using a human being as a tool in that you force them (through economic violence or direct threat) to do what he or she would not otherwise have done. So, taking advantage of an actor's poverty in order to make them do things that they would not otherwise do and where no other alternatives exist, is to treat them as a means-merely. All these wrongs are wrongs because the free, rational consent of the agents is absent.

3.5 The victims

Imagine a professionally produced and marketed seven minute scene available for legal exchange which involves explicit scenes of fellatio, cunnilingus and penetrative sex. There is a little bondage, but nothing too extreme that would raise questions of possible consent, and many close ups. There is no plot or characterization. Furthermore, there is no evidence of what we would normally understand to be violence, the presence of which would make the moral discussion more complicated. Violence, at least as we normally use the word, is normally wrong and it is not intrinsic to pornographic material. (Although there is obviously a very intimate relationship because the sexual relationship is, like a conversation, a reciprocal activity and in such activities the play of power is very easily present. We shall return to this below.) The issue is whether or not this short film is immoral or necessarily involves severe immoral practices. Severe moral practices have been defined as those which involve treating other agents in ways that we ourselves would not wish to be treated. If there is anything necessarily wrong with pornography, then such a scene ought to express, embody or communicate that wrongness. Basically, the question is whether or not a person would in his or her right mind agree to act in such a film.

Pornography is often cited as a case of exploitation of the women who are coerced into performing:

> Empirically, all pornography is made under conditions of inequality based on sex, overwhelmingly by poor desperate, homeless, pimped women who were sexually abused as children. The industry's profits exploit, and are an incentive to maintain, these conditions. These conditions constrain choice rather than offering freedom. (MacKinnon, 1993: 20)

Often, little is said of the male actors. Even though it might be controversial, let us take as an axiomatic starting-point that there can be no moral wrongdoing unless one can identify a victim and such thinking is consistent with the Kantian idiom adopted.[11] There can be no wrongdoing, whether moral or legal, unless there is someone who has been wronged and such wronging will take the form of treating them in such a way that they are determined to act in a way that, if they were treated as self-determining, they would not. Exploitation is a wrong because it violates the individual agent's right to liberty: 'I would not have starred in this pornographic film had it not been for the presence of another agent who coerced me into doing as I do. If they had not been present, I would have done otherwise and their presence results in treating me as a means-merely'.

If this is the case, why then do actors (and other workers) 'agree' to participate in the production of such films? The first answer is that they are not rational, that they suffer from the incapacity to deliberate in accordance with their own interests and values, or are too easily swayed from such deliberations, and are hence open to coercion by other wills that see them as malleable. The group of participants susceptible to this sort of coercion are the mentally disadvantaged, the poorly educated and children. The group is constituted by those that are not able to clearly articulate their own wants independently of others. Some (though not all) children would fit into this group and as such the requirement for the consent of actors can form the basis of an argument against pornography involving child actors. Some children are not able to know what they want clearly and, as we have no test to reveal whether this particular child knows what he or she wants, we need to choose an age at which we are sure *all* individuals are able to determine their own course of action. The age of eighteen (or twenty one, or sixteen) will be adopted as the mark when a legal culture is satisfied that the agent can negotiate freely about what he or she wants with others. The actual age will, within limits, differ from culture to culture, but will need to be set as a 'bright line' in order for a clearly set age requirement to stand in for a woolly moral requirement that participants must have reached the age of consent. At eighteen (or sixteen or twenty one) the culture in question has decided that all agents are in the position of knowing what is best for them. Pornography that involves the participation of such agents is immoral, but so too is any labour or use of such agents that does not take into account what they may or may not want.

The second answer is that, even though they know what their interests are and are able to deliberate freely, the presence of another agent makes the desire for another's interest more pertinent. So, for example, the mugger asks me kindly for my wallet, but I refuse to participate in his project. On revealing his gun, though, my interests suddenly coincide with his own: I want to give him my wallet (despite my own interests of which I remain clearly aware) because I do not want to be shot. Threats of violence play a role in our deliberative process. The threat of death may be enough to compel me to hand over money, but not enough to compel me to betray or harm my family.

The third answer is that the agent has been deceived. The actor believes that he is to participate in a normal film, but the director has planned his death. Had he asked the actor whether he would agree to participate in the recording of his own death, he knows the answer would have been 'No', so he omits to tell him or lies to him. In all three cases, we have an instance of treating an agent as a means-merely because the agent is not allowed to decide for him or herself whether to participate or not.

Exploitation is a wrong and a form of coercion: a producer may exercise power over an actor because he possesses money. The promise of money, like the threat of harm, changes the deliberation process of the agent. However, the offer of money, all things being equal, cannot be coercion. Neither can the combination of money and some sort of distorted web-celebrity as sites such as *moneytalks.com* (if real!) seem to present, where members of the public are offered money to perform sexual acts for webcasts. Otherwise, that would rule out any agent's working for another or exchanging goods with another: practices that we implicitly consent to day in day out. If I agree to exchange my labour for a monetary value, I must be able to weigh the money against the cost of my labour. I can freely consent to such arrangements because, although I become a means for another, if he or she has dealt with me fairly and I have freely agreed, then I am not *merely* a means.

It can, of course, be exploitation when the actor is in extreme poverty and the producer knows this, or when they need the money because they suffer from some chemical addiction that requires funds to satisfy. Similarly, if the actors have been brought from their own country on false pretences and their passports have been confiscated, or they are forced to perform by the simple threat of violence, then such films are immoral. But, none of these conditions need necessarily be the case in the making of a pornographic film or image. There is no reason to suppose it impossible that, in my paradigmatic example, the actors were paid a fair wage for their time and performance and that they would prefer earn their money doing this than earn an equal amount of money in an office or teaching, for example (Monroe, 2010). Exploitation is wrong and it is the subject of legal sanction. If exploitation occurs in the production of pornography it ought to be punished as it ought to be if it occurs in the picking of cockles or the manufacture of clothes, but the crime here is exploitation and not making pornography. The actual industry is incidental to the moral wrongness.

Let us once more return to the snuff movie. An agent would agree to act in a snuff movie only at the cost of their own rationality. Without wanting to be too controversial, any agent who voluntarily agrees to act in a snuff movie in which they play the part of the victim does not view their own self-preservation as valuable. One can assert that the value of one's self-preservation is not as valuable as say the equality of one's fellow man (the political activist) or the salvation of God's chosen few (the religious martyr), but weighing the value of one's life against the value of a film – no matter how good it is – is simply not rational in our everyday meaning of the word. Similarly, a film that involves the humiliation of the actor through physical or psychological torment or through the relationship between character and a person's reputation (and here we see why the actor is different from the model of the painter), would only be agreed to at the cost of the actor's rationality, all things being equal. To meet the Kantian constraint all we need to ask is, 'Would you, had you been me, have participated?' It seems that critics of pornographic production believe that engaging in actual and not simulated sexual activity is akin to public humiliation and that an agent would agree to act in such a film only at the cost of his or her own rationality whether due to incapacity to reason, threats of violence or deception. With a snuff film, we can – by proxy – assume that if one has agreed to participate, then one is not rational or free to reason. The critics of pornography make a similar assumption, but why? The only reason I can seem to offer is a latent puritanism: sexual activity is not the sort of thing one ought to engage in for money, if one is rational. If a religious leader were to make such a claim, we would not be surprised, but for such claims to come from liberal feminists, is astonishing. It seems a putative, comprehensive moral value system has invaded our reasoning. The arguments proposed by traditional moral theories to discuss the issue of pornography are inherently conservative and reproduce unreflective cultural attitudes that are puritanical in nature. I ought to stress that this chapter is concerned only with the formal nature of coercion and consent, not the actual practice of it. Dines (2010) reduces pornography to a specific subset of pornography, namely 'gonzo' or humiliation pornography that does seem to always involve harm or humiliation of the women involved. What is more, as a sociologically empirical thesis, she claims that such pornography and its inherent violence is becoming the norm. I deal with the problem of violence in the penultimate chapter, but as concerns the conceptual wrongness of pornography, I reiterate that there is no need for violence in the material, this is a question of 'taste' and cultural expectations. These expectations can be wrong without pornography wholesale being the subject of prohibition or legal recourse.

As a free agent, I own my body and can use it as I see fit within the restraint of coexisting with others. If I can produce, or service, or facilitate through my body, I can also sell these talents and can do so freely.

Such is the basis of our economic system and labour relations. Such ownership of the body separates labour-exchange from slavery. We see clearly now the irrationality of snuff movies because I would agree to negate or annihilate the very thing which facilitates my position of being an equal partner. Yet, sexual activity is not so. One can imagine an agent (male or female) who is culturally attractive, enjoys sexual activity, is good at it and develops his or her skills through participation in it, and also takes pleasure from exhibiting his or her skills. Such a talented individual should be able to earn a living from being so endowed, as the footballer does from playing football. There seems to be no basis for the critic's assumption that any agent who participates in the presentation of sexual activity, must have been forced to do so.

MacKinnon certainly offers a version of this argument. She claims that the production of pornography necessarily violates the physical integrity of the (female) participants. But this is of no surprise if one bears in mind her definition of pornography:

> 'the graphic sexually explicit subordination of women through pictures and/or words that also includes one or more of the following: (a) women are presented dehumanized as sexual objects, things, or commodities; or (b) women are presented as sexual objects who enjoy humiliation or pain; or (c) women are presented as sexual objects experiencing sexual pleasure in rape, incest, or other sexual assault; or (d) women are presented as sexual objects tied up or cut up or mutilated or bruised or physically hurt; or (e) women are presented as in postures or positions of sexual submission; (f) women's body parts – including but not limited to vaginas, breasts, or buttocks – are exhibited such that women are reduced to those parts; or (g) women are presented being penetrated by objects or animals; or (h) women are presented in scenarios of degradation, humiliation, injury, torture, shown as filthy or inferior, bleeding, bruised, or hurt in a context that makes these conditions sexual.' In this definition, the use of 'men, children, or transsexuals in the place of women' is also pornography. (MacKinnon, 1993: 121-2; see also MacKinnon & Dworkin, 1997)

Given her definition, no woman (or man, child or transsexual) – at the cost of her own rationality – would agree to participate in such practices. When they do, we have an instance of coercion. But, the film example alluded to above need not fit this definition. The woman can be presented as a character, hence an embodied subjectivity, there is no violence and the actress may have agreed to participate freely in exchange for money, personal satisfaction or career progression. Of course, MacKinnon can deny that it is pornography, yet that is counter-intuitive and, worse, (morally but not legally) banal. If the object of her critique is to bring to awareness the moral wrongness of forcing an agent to do what he or she does not want to do, then many moral thinkers have already done so and agreement would not be controversial. If she wants to say that a person cannot – in his or her right mind – profit from an ability to perform sexual practices for money, then it is puritanical. On this point, consider the concluding words of her critique: 'In a society in which equality is a fact, not merely a word, words of racial or sexual assault and humiliation will be nonsense syllables. Sex between people and things, human beings and pieces of paper, real men and unreal women, will be a turn-off' (MacKinnon, 1993: 109-110). If by this she means that, in such a society, our sexual tastes will be perfected, I am not convinced: I still eat KFC greedily, even after being married to an Italian for nigh on fifteen years. If she means, in such a society, arousal will not occur through sexual images because I am not aroused by the sex, but by the humiliation and the domination of gender, again I feel it is the sexual activity that arouses me, and arouses me more, especially if I were to consider the scenes in *Sex and Lucía* as against standard pornographic films which do use domination as a leitmotif. There is no reason that persons who are good at sex and happy with their sexuality cannot freely engage in arrangements that use such talents to their advantage. The only reason is if one is a puritan and believes there is something wrong with sex. Of course, MacKinnon believes there is something wrong with contemporary relations of sex, but her real target is contemporary society and inequality.[12] On that I agree and we shall return to it in the next chapter because we find we are no longer concerned with moral, but political, issues.

Just to expand slightly, consider Nussbaum's rather cryptic assertion that the criminalization of prostitution will do nothing, and may even harm the dignity of women, whereas her position on the use of the body in pornographic material is less clear and one-dimensional (1999: ch. 11). Nussbaum feels that MacKinnon's reasoning is sound, but that there is still no basis for prohibition as many feminists would want. She is careful to strip away puritanical objections to the idea that the sexual act and sexual imagery is something that no women would in their right mind be prepared to participate in for the purposes of making money, otherwise how could she not reject prostitution. Take, for example, her own utopian hope for the future of sexual activity, which apparently still leaves room for the representation of this activity and the consumption of such representation: 'It may therefore be not too utopian to imagine a culture in which men's sexual desire for women will not commonly be associated with projects of possession and control, and in which female sexual agency will not inspire fear and suspicion' (Nussbaum, 1999: 12). Feminism of this sort resolves itself, quite rightly, into a subspecies of Marxism. Nussbaum does not reject the idea of legalizing prostitution, but sees pornography as necessarily harmful to first and third parties. The reason why, though, has little to do with feminism and male–female hierarchy, it has to do with relations of production. With prostitution, the supply chain and the constituent participants (once one removes the pimp) confer on the prostitute control over the product if she freely engages in the activity: when it is to be supplied, how and what the limits are. She is in full control of the consumption of the product and hence meets Marx's requirements for free activity: she sees what she produces as worthwhile and valuable to herself (one feels she is talented and perfects her technique through time) and others; and she knows that it is her free choice to produce it (that is participates in the decision-making process which decides which goods are to be produced) (Marx, 1993: 610–15). But, pornography exists at the centre of competing interests, a confused web of production relations and a host of social connections from the studio, through the actors, including the director and the producer and the distributor. The actress (or actor) is alienated from the product: she has not decided what is made and very rarely sees it as worthwhile. And who is in charge of the product? A careful Marxist would show it is the system of economic relations which alienates both capitalist and worker such that worthwhile activity is actually impossible under a system of private property. A vulgar Marxist would decide that the capitalist, through an act of will, alienates a class of workers. This type of feminism seems to be vulgar Marxism, replacing the 'capitalist' with the 'male' and it is empirically true that the pornographic business is dominated by male capitalists (but not the literary market – where female authors seem to excel). Biological sex, though, is contingent; what matters is not that they are *male* capitalists, but that they are male *capitalists*. The participant in pornography is no different from the factory worker, the wrong is alienation from one's project and that is not a wrong with pornography but a wrong with labour relations in the contemporary material conditions of existence: 'The sex is not chosen for the sex. Money is the medium of force that provides the cover of consent' (MacKinnon, 1993: 28).

And we shall return to this below, but, for now, let us summarize what has been argued. The production of pornography, like the production of other artefacts may involve wrongdoing, but such such wrongdoing has to be of such a serious nature to negate completely the value of what is produced. Severe wrongdoing in the production of pornography is best understood in terms of the coercion of the participants in pornographic production, whether it be determination, exploitation or deception of the individual's will. Although empirically such wrongdoing does occur in the production of pornography (as it does in other industries), there is no necessary relationship between the presentation of sexual activity for exchange and coercion. Any attempt to prohibit, restrict or sue for damages against pornographic material on the basis of universal coercion in its production is, rationally, bound, then, to fail.

3.6 Consumption

Considering once more the Gauguin scenario at the beginning of the chapter, one can once more deny the similarity between Gauguin and pornographic production, because the wrongness is not located in the production process but in the consumption of the object. There can be no wrongdoing in consuming a painting of Gauguin, but in pornography wrongdoing is repeated every time it is consumed. Some critics of pornography would assert that the consumption of pornographic material harms the consumer in various ways such as seducing them into pursuing worthless activity and valuing the wrong sort of goals. Feminist critics would argue that the consumption of pornographic material harms women as a group every time it is consumed. Gauguin's wrongdoing stops once the painting is produced (or when he dies). The painting then exists independently of the wrongdoing. With pornography it is different as its existence perpetuates and increases the wrongdoing in a way that Gauguin's painting does not.

Wrongdoing in consumption is a more subtle consideration and the purpose of this chapter has been to highlight that any discussion of wrongness is pornography really should separate the production issues (which border on puritanism) from the consumption issues. It might just be that critics of pornography should ignore the production and concentrate on the wrongness of consumption, but many rely on the rhetoric of the former to motivate the latter. If the argument has at least moved the debate in that direction, then it has been worthwhile, but let us consider this a little more deeply. After all, ontological pluralism still applies: wrongdoing must be put against aesthetic value. Imagine that looking at Goya's *Saturn Devouring his Son* inspired certain individuals to be aggressive towards others. Would we then put it away in the gallery's basement or in a *Gabinetto Segreto*? Wrongness in consumption must be of the requisite severity and we must consider who the victim of such wrongness is: the consumer him or herself, individual women, women as a group or culture.

Beginning with the harm to individuals, it seems that such a claim raises a problem with liberty: should I be free to consume X if I know that X has undesirable consequences? Children are excluded from the consumption of pornographic objects, whether aural, verbal or visual because it harms them in some way. In fact, in most countries, pornographic images, if legal, will legally exclude a certain age group (usually those below eighteen). Consuming pornography, like smoking, is – one might argue – self-harm. Behind this are some rather odd empirical presumptions, from the downright false belief that masturbation is harmful to more subtle claims about harm to the ability to form healthy social relations. The one who performs masturbation, we were once told, suffers because 'His intellect becomes sluggish and enfeebled, and if his evil habits are persisted in, he may end in becoming a drivelling idiot or a peevish valetudinarian' (Acton, W. (1857) *The Function and Disorders of the Reproductive Organs,* cited in Tang (1999: 30–31)).

Empirical claims, and such assertions are empirical in nature, are going to be inconclusive and necessarily so because of what Rawls (1993) refers to as the burdens of reason. In matters of ethical discussion, social science and axiology, evidence may be complex and hard to assess and, even if we agree about what counts as evidence, we may disagree about its degree of relevance and so reach different judgements. Furthermore, concepts are vague and rely on interpretation which is, of course, affected by personal experience. Normative values can appear to conflict and be incommensurable and it is not possible to respect all values given the constraints of social space, so priority decisions will also have to be taken.[13] To agree on the harm of pornography requires agreement on what pornography is and what constitutes harm, how to gauge the degree of harm and how to value that harm against other benefits (such as liberty). However, it is intuitively not ridiculous to say that children are not allowed to view sexual activity because they do not engage in such practices and hence cannot understand what the aim of such practice is. By viewing it with no understanding, they will learn a distorted form of behaviour. Once this is recognized, we can accept that the consumption of certain materials will have an effect on enthusiasts and perhaps distort their view of relationships. Moreover, modern liberal democracies are multicultural. Just as children cannot understand the representations of sexual activity, there are groups within a plural culture with very different bases of understanding. Judgements ought to be along the lines of films are suitable for X, Y and Z and unsuitable for A, B and C. Like children and ages. Yet such an approach is problematic; first because there are too many groups and differences in groups; and second because the age '18' is a bright line which is easy to draw whereas the identification of specific groups is not. More pertinently, it is problematic to start picking out groups in this way (and who is to say feminists are not a group who need protection from offensive-to-them material). It is too complex and discriminatory. Simple common sense ought to preside: if I as an individual identity (given my upbringing, personal experience and so on) do not like blasphemous films, I should not watch them, but other people's right should not be violated. By putting '18' on a DVD and a minimum amount of information which is now the norm, the individual can make up his or her own mind.

Be that as it may be. A viewer of Damien Hirst's pickled animals may feel nausea and horror, a smoker may be harming his lungs and a mountain climber may be risking physical injury. All of these are undesirable consequences but the individual surely has to decide for him or herself whether aesthetic value outweighs physical discomfort, whether pleasure is worth more than possible disease, and whether thrill is worth possible injury; and that what is what differentiates children from adults. With the consumption of pornographic materials, seemingly only the subject can decide if his or her own harm is a consequence, whether or not it is worth the pay-off. If viewing such material made it uncontroversially the case that consumers in all probability suffer (as is the case with certain chemical substances), then there would be a *prima facie* case for restriction of the materials.

The feminist would change the tack of the argument and deny that self-harm is the issue anyway, rather the consumption of pornography involves harming others (Russell, 1988; Mackinnon, 1993). It is more akin to smoking in a public place, where it is not your harm that is the priority but harm to others, who did not choose to smoke but find themselves passively inhaling your second hand smoke. And like legislation against smoking, those that suffer have to be protected because they have no choice in receiving or not receiving the ill effects of personal consumption. The feminist critique of pornography is based on the claim that women are specifically and exclusively wronged in the production and consumption of pornography. Some align this with exploitation, but that is not gender specific and has been discussed above. So, why women exclusively? There are two more aspects to this critique: pornography harms individual women; and pornography necessarily degrades women as a group.

First, pornography harms individual women because it encourages their maltreatment at the hands of males, most prominently in a causal relationship with instances of rape (Russell, 1988; Russell, 1993: part 3; cf. AGCP, 1986). The claim that the consumption of pornography causes rape is contentious and, to be intelligible, must be akin to the assertion that 'smoking causes cancer'. Such assertions have two aspects: the conceptual or theoretical; and the empirical. The theory explains the relationship between one event and the other in terms of a causal chain. With smoking, the tar in cigarettes contains sixty chemicals which are known carcinogens and the inhalation of the smoke brings such chemicals into the body. Empirically, a correlation has to be established between smokers and persons who develop cancer, and must show that the instances of those who develop cancer is higher than in a control group. The causal relationship is then probabilistic and would take the form of 'smokers are more likely to develop cancer than non-smokers', but such an assertion can tell us nothing about any specific individual smoker or non-smoker.

With pornography, empirical studies would need to establish a probabilistic relationship between consumers of pornography and instances of rape, which is already problematic because one might want to say that agents with a predilection for rape are more likely than other individuals to seek out violent pornography for arousal. Note here that there is no analogy to this in smoking; one cannot claim that individuals with a greater genetic risk of cancer are more likely to find pleasure in smoking. The interest such agents have in (violent) pornography correlates with an interest they have in non-consensual sexual encounters, and the former is not a cause of the latter but both are symptomatic of some other attribute of the agent. Such considerations highlight the fact that any empirical study of pornographic consumption and rape will remain contentious and never fully resolved as it falls foul once more of Rawls's burdens of reason. Yet, these are only secondary problems. What is first of all required is some theoretical connection between the consumption of pornographic (and not necessarily violent) material and instances of maltreatment of women in a more general sense. The causal relationship must be conceived in these terms: a consumer is caused to form certain ideas about the probable wants, desires and pleasures of women by confusing the represented woman for actual women. The man may see a women first and foremost as a sexual object, as inferior to him, as wanting him and therefore amenable to his approaches, even if (or even because they are) forceful. As such, his perception of that women has been distorted. The supposed relationship of equality between the two agents has been distorted (A. Dworkin, 1981;

Eaton, 2007; cf. Vadas, 1987). Yet, if that is the case, then the man sees women in general in this way and not just an individual or particular: '... pornography shapes the attitudes and conduct of its audience in ways that are injurious to women' (Eaton, 2007: 677).

On the one hand, art itself is not responsible for how it is received. Films are certified by age restrictions: we protect children from certain scenes because they are not able to control themselves nor respond to the scenes in an appropriate way. That viewing images has a causal effect on certain individuals tells us more about those individuals than about what is being viewed. As such, it is a matter of responsibility. Unless pornographic films are designed to provoke harm to others, like films that provoke racism, then our normal legal understanding is that the individual who reacts is responsible and not the film maker, because how we interpret works of art, and how they change our understanding of the world about us, is a matter of rational, theoretical activity. The majority of pornographic material is intended to arouse and not to incite violence.[14] To prohibit certain genres or representations is to treat human beings like children and not allow them to order, prioritize and assign value to those features of their social and moral existence which would actually constitute who they were. So, it is still a matter of liberty and autonomy.

On the other hand, just as the causal relationship with reference to rape seems bi-directional, so too can a deeper point be made here. Contemporary pornography is more likely to be symptom of contemporary gender relations rather than a cause of them. After all, the patriarchal society existed prior to pornography. There is nothing specific to pornography about the representation of women and many rap and hip-hop music videos are far more demeaning in their objectification of women: 50 Cent's 'P.I.M.P.' being a prime example, but it is by no means alone in the genre. Other genres (one thinks most notably of romantic comedies) can often be as involved, if not more so, in the reproduction of these cultural conventions. In an Adam Sandler film, Jennifer Aniston, whose character is witty and intelligent, only becomes the object of desire when she strips down to her bikini to reveal that she is attractive as well (Dugan, 2011). Language too seems to reinforce this point. In sexual activity, there is no real difference between what the man is doing and what the women is doing, but language assigns activity and passivity. He is penetrating, she is being penetrated. (Why is she not enclosing or embracing?) He puts his cock in her mouth, she takes it in her mouth and so on. Now such statements can be rewritten, but it is very natural to assign the active forms to the male actions and the passive forms for female action and that reflects the disparity.

None of these considerations absolve pornography, though. They accuse other discourses and they too could be the subject of moral judgement akin to the moral judgement of pornographic objects. Moreover, pornography may be doubly guilty: pornography reinforces and sustains the unjustified inequality of contemporary society. It represents women in a hierarchical relationship with men. But, then, the victim of pornography is not women as such, but the idea of equality. Contemporary pornography is such that all enthusiasts are determined to objectify social relationships in a distorted way. Its wrongness, then, lies in its representing relationships between males and females, which distort equitable relationships and maintain and support institutions of inequality. Persons can only attain fulfilment through equitable relationships (and I here only assume this because otherwise feminists would argue for a *reversal* of roles and they do not). A rational, axiomatic principle of our society is equality and the vast majority of pornography is incoherent with this principle. This deviates from the feminist critique in saying that not just a specific group of society but all society and all human relationships will be harmed by the unrestricted production, exchange and consumption of pornography (Dyzenhaus, 1992; cf. Skipper, 1993). The accusation is again no different from other aesthetic objects: film, television, music, literature, and so on which form the basis of individuals' self-understanding by supplying the basic concepts and forms of social relationships (Gastil, 1976). Any hierarchical social power relationship which is unjustified and rests solely on power, as Hegel would tell us and as we shall consider below, is injurious to both parties (though not to the same degree): the dominator cannot understand his own freedom fully when he is uncertain whether his understanding of a relationship is reciprocated. The representations of social relationships at the heart of pornography do not allow men or women (or other sexualities, races and so on) to appreciate or partake in practices and relationships that would be beneficial to their own development and self-understanding.

Pornography, then, should be restricted because its consumption has an effect on the agent's understanding of himself or herself and others. Children, for example, are not allowed to consume violent material in the media because such images need to be clearly categorized as either fiction or fact. Mass media represent, almost universally, violence as desirable, as a resolution and rarely represents the real consequences of actual violence. A child who is unable, due to a lack of experience and knowledge, to distinguish between the representation of violence and the reality of violence will engage in practices that are undesirable. If children were allowed undiluted access to these images they might well procure certain undesirable moral attitudes: that might is right; that power is desirable; that violence is a solution, and so on. Only the subtlety of 'adult' drama, film and literature can do justice to the complexity of violence and its relationship to our society. Similarly, adults who lack the requisite social and emotional intelligence may view pornography and form attitudes concerning social relationships that are undesirable: the lack of consequences of emotional entanglement, the superficiality of emotional exchanges, the over-determination of sex as a constituent part of a healthy relationship, the necessity of sexual dimension in all relationships and so on. And these attitudes do not just relate to male–female relationships, but also to black–white, hetro-gay and gay–gay relationships (Collins, 1993; Soltenberg, 1993). Unfortunately, for as many Shakespeares, Tolstoys and Dostoevskys as there are for our Seagals, Willises and Schwarzeneggers, there is very little adult pornography for the childish, immature sort.. It is even possible that pornography could be a way to address and abolish the unjustified, cultural inequality between the sexes. One can make a pornographic film which empowers women. The film *Baise-moi* seems to attempt this, whether one agrees that it is successful or not (Baron, 1990). So, if such critics hold that pornography is always the reproduction and maintenance of institutional inequality, they make a descriptive error and they should be more concerned with the activities that promote inequality of which some, but only some, belong to the set of pornographic objects. MacKinnon probably does. Again, the separate ethical issue of 'pornography' seems a distraction from the real problem.

The issue is now more political than moral. It concerns the right to freedom to express ideas which are counter to cultural norms, hence a liberal right, and also the idea of equality and its value.

Interlude 3 The Marquis de Sade

The artistic and philosophical output of the Marquis de Sade is problematic to say the least. Much of the latter is delivered through the mouths of characters and necessarily exists at a distance from the man himself, and much of the former is interspersed with intellectual commentary in order to raise it above a simple judgement of obscenity. Obscene, though it is.

And violent.

And depraved.

And one might want to hold it up as a prime example of what ought to be prohibited because the aesthetic merit is, at times, quite minimal, from the scientistic reporting of needless details and numbers to the point of deliberate uneroticism in *120 Days of Sodom,* to the ridiculous narrative and character of poor Justine in the eponymous novel. More than these considerations, though, it is the sheer unrelenting and intense sexual violence in Sade's libertine novels that truly challenges the limits of what it is acceptable to write, no matter what the aesthetic worth is.

Sade's existence and his place in the literary canon is controversial and he has been the subject of much critical attention in the twentieth century, perhaps enough to suggest that reading his work is worthwhile. It should be remembered that no one participates in the production, that no one is actually hurt in the writing of the novels. It is, after all, verbal and it would take a peculiar mind indeed to have it play a causal role in violence just because such a mind would require Job's perseverance to cut through the meticulously theatrical nature of much of the imagery in order to find it motivating in the slightest. At times, it is philosophical, spinning a heady mix of materialism and atheism (inspired by d'Holbach) into a particular anti-Rousseauian philosophy of nature. At times it is political: *120 Days of Sodom* is an overt attack on the hypocrisy of the four pillars of political power: custom (aristocracy); religion; law; and capital. But, then, Sade is too cynical to be truly philosophical and too committed to the isolated nature of human beings to be truly political. He is always a religious iconoclast, celebrating sexual pleasure for its own sake and never for procreation. Sometimes, he is didactic, offering us moral tales inverted in line with his own axiology, offering the chance of enlightenment, development and intellectual and moral freedom through sexual and violent transgression. And transgression is used in a very aesthetic and moral way: we are shocked and, in that shock, what we take for granted, what we believe to be natural and right, is revealed to us as only one possible code of right amongst many codes of right, and a Nietzschean commitment to the strongest as the rightful masters of their species emerges as somehow inevitable and awe-inspiring.

Sade is contradictory and problematic.

If it is a matter of the aesthetic worth or cultural value of an artefact, first and foremost, which is of interest to those who would ban it, then the Marquis de Sade poses an interesting dilemma. The content of his representations, and his evident disregard for human nature and the claims of the weak, surely undermine most, if not all, of the artistic value of his work. Perhaps, then, the politics of the man, the expressions of brute freedom and the refusal of customary oppression demand attention. One thing that remains in his defence is a sort of nobility, a misplaced nobility which avoids social convention and speaks the truth about the human condition. For Hobbes, every facet of human behaviour could be reduced to the concept of power; for Sade, it was reducible to lust. He had a nascent prescience (much like Hobbes) of Nietzsche's full metaphysical picture of power as a universal, tidal force and agents as no more than the foam at the crest of its waves. Agents who mistakenly believe they are deliberately surfing the waves themselves. Sade was as radical and out of time as both Hobbes and Nietzsche, but ultimately, one needs to ask whether the drive to state what one holds to be true is justification enough for works that, given contemporary critiques of violence in pornography, exist definitely on the periphery of the most extreme portrayals of depravity.

4

Otherwise, We'll Have Words: The Politics of Pornography

4.1 A heady mix

Sexually explicit material has been political since its inception. It was often, and perhaps still is, revolutionary and bitingly satirical (Tang, 1999: ch. 3). In pre-revolutionary France, salacious and scandalous tales of the aristocracy and the rulers helped to undermine their putative moral authority and hence their right to rule. Stories and images of the aristocracy attacked the ideology of the *Ancien Régime* by casting doubt on hereditary lines: if the Queen was a promiscuous pervert, how could we be sure that the royal blood line, and the divine prerogative to rule, had been properly transferred? Such a scurrilous insinuation neatly mirrors the contemporary theoretical challenges one finds to the divine right of kings in Locke and Rousseau. One need only open Chaucer or Boccaccio to find less directed use of sexual representation in order to lampoon the putative moral authority of clergymen and aristocrats. In the sixties, the director and writer Lasse Braun, privileged by diplomatic immunity, smuggled pornography across European borders and produced hardcore films in Franco's Spain as part of a pagan, Nietzschean political agenda. Ronald Dworkin himself makes a less than casual association between the prohibition of pornographers due to the demands of moral protection and the justification of the McCarthy witch hunts by national security considerations (1991: 102).

One defence that contemporary pornographers might be able to offer for the existence of their productions could be based on the right to freely express ideas of sexuality. These producers may well argue that any prohibition of their creations will be due to reasons and moral opinions that are historically contingent, reflect the privileged interests of a specific class or merely the tyranny of a moral majority that wishes to censure what is at base a matter of personal taste and individual liberty. The right to produce pornography may well be protected for political reasons: pornographers must have a right to express their own ideas, opinions and beliefs just like anyone else and to censure this is an unjustified limitation of individuals' liberty. The prohibition of pornography, like the prohibition of dissenting political voices, might actually reinforce and secure the inegalitarian *status quo*. Words express: they express ideas, opinions and viewpoints. In a constitutional democracy, the individual's right to conscience is supported and maintained by the protection of the expression of these ideas. Any medium (recorded words, images, sounds) that expresses ideas is similarly protected. Freedom of the press and rights to conscience and free speech maintain and support the autonomy and liberty of the individual against interference from an authoritarian government or the tyranny of the moral majority. *Prima facie*, it seems, we must deal with the claim that protecting pornography is demanded by the right of free speech. Not to do so would be to undermine the above acts of political resistance. Of course, *prima facie* motivations do not often stand up to scrutiny.

4.2 Liberalism: Ronald Dworkin's free speech defence of pornography

Ronald Dworkin does not much care whether or not pornography is produced, consumed or exchanged. So long as no obvious, uncontroversial and direct harm is involved in its production or is the consequence of its distribution, then it is to be protected like all other expressions of beliefs, opinions and ideas by the right of free speech. Of course, such a right is not the theoretical basis of his claim, rather the grounding concept is a commitment to equal respect and concern for individuals' interests. His framework for the discussion of the free speech defence of the production and consumption of pornography has been adopted as the point of departure in the political debate. It is, therefore, worthwhile to summarize how a liberal argument that owes much to Dworkin's theoretical framework would be structured. At the base of such an argument are three liberal truisms: one, governments abuse their power to curb free speech for authoritarian reasons; two, moral, metaphysical and religious commitments are not valid reasons to curb the activities of other individuals unless shared by all; and, three, ethical innovation, experimentation and ultimately social progress require a free market of ideas which is damaged by state intervention. However, it is perhaps worth alerting the reader that Dworkin is concerned with liberty of the individual above all and his major worry is that the drive to prohibit, censor and limit ideas is a conservative agenda that seeks to maintain and secure the *status quo* simply because it is the *status quo*, whether dressed up as feminism, postmodern thought or simple moralism.

The theoretical basis for Dworkin's work can be best grasped by the consideration of a simple question: if barring access to pornography diminishes harm in the community significantly, then why should we not do so? As such, he sidesteps the fraught empirical questions of whether or not pornography does in fact cause harm. After all, free access to education and a health service are good social policies because they, in straight forward utilitarian terms, increase the common good. Much government work is carried out due to such principles (and utilitarianism is in its element at the social and not the individual level). Contrastingly, prohibition of certain drugs could be justified by an appeal to the effect their consumption would have on the efficiency of society as a whole. For Dworkin and most liberals this would have to be coupled with harm to the individual and also, most importantly, the fact that such substances would be addictive and hence have an effect on practical reasoning in the individual. Let us say for argument's sake that the existence of pornography has a detrimental effect on society as whole. The government, then, has a reason to implement a policy that controls the distribution and consumption of pornography. Such an argument is grounded on a policy: a goal-based argument whereby a state of affairs is to be achieved through which the community as a whole is better off. It need not be simply utilitarian. One could replace the good of welfare with other goods: aesthetic perfection, creativity, substantial equality and so on.

Now, unlike our Victorian forbears, such harm is not understood to be to health; we no longer believe we are harming our eyesight, encouraging hair growth on our palms or becoming 'a drivelling idiot or a peevish valetudinarian' by consuming pornography. The harm from consuming pornography is to be understood as a moral harm, the majority would disapprove of one's consuming pornography because there are more worthwhile things to be doing. One could be reading Dostoyevsky, or learning to play the harp, or trying to penetrate the musical genius of Stockhausen. But, here's a funny thing: I may want to watch the football match, or listen to Iron Maiden – such pursuits a good (cultured!) majority may equally disapprove of as being worthless. And, as a matter of empirical fact, let us say such pursuits do in fact have an adverse effect of general social utility: for the common good, I should be reading Russian literature about the human condition whenever possible rather than wasting my time watching Aston Villa lose again. Here we have an equally good case for government intervention. But, hopefully, we are a little more uneasy about this. To do otherwise, to tell people what they should or should not do in their own spare time, is an attack on individual liberty and personal autonomy. Pornography is easy to attack because its desired prohibition coincides with a long tradition of ideological puritanism, but we need to ensure that it is reason and not just tradition which motivates our intuitions. We need to ask ourselves what is the exact difference between the worth of Iron Maiden and pornography such that it is easier, not just to disapprove of the latter, but also to compel others not to waste their time on it.

For Dworkin and most liberals, governments must treat those that it governs with equal concern and respect. No objective, rational judgements can be made about the comparative value of personal interests or preferences since, in a liberal democracy, no agreement on comprehensive moral values is possible. Consensus on moral matters cannot be formed because, under free institutions, dissenting voices will always contest the majority opinion and moral values are either conceptually or empirically contestable. The government cannot interfere just because a majority of people disagree with the importance I assign to watching football matches. As an individual I have the right to have my interests treated as sympathetically as everyone else's interests. Moreover, if I believe that my aesthetic education is to be perfected through head banging to Iron Maiden rather than rubbing my chin to Stockhausen then others are able to express their disapproval, but they are not allowed to forcibly obstruct me in this, whether it be for my own good or not. In order to resist such prohibition of certain activities, we might want to agree that to diminish harm is a good, but there are other goods which the banning of pornography will destroy. Broadly understood this is the pluralist position I wish to propose in the coming chapters and have already hinted at in the last. It is of course, not Dworkin's response (although he does acknowledge it as a possibility). Dworkin's tack is different: a proper understanding of harm (utilitarianism) will show that it is significant or trivial against a background theory that also justifies commitment to the 'rights as trumps' theory in general and the right of moral independence in particular. Basically, persons are to be treated with equal concern for their interests and with equal respect for their conception of the good life.

Of course, ways of life or interests (say the aesthetic serial killer who sees his work as artistic expression) that harm others directly contradict this very principle in that the victims of such behaviour have not been treated with equal concern. My listening to Iron Maiden is neither here nor there to you, but my engaging in serial killing is. What makes the former trivial and the latter significant is a background theory of deontological rights. Whereas the former are mere preferences, the latter are 'external preferences': a preference that counts twice. For example, I belong to a religious minority who worship on what has traditionally been a work day in the calendar of our country (say, Friday). All things being equal, under social policy considerations where individuals count as equals, our preferences should count as one each and can be accommodated: there should be an allowance that I can indeed worship on a Friday and I have priority in claiming that day of the week off. However, in our society, Sunday has traditionally been put aside for the day of worship and my preference for worshipping on Friday means that others will have to cover my work. Let us make it the case that in our example certain crucial cooperative work must, by necessity, be carried out on Fridays and Fridays are the busiest day of the week. My preference is then not just my preference but it also counts against you (working on Friday is an imposition and ought to be distributed fairly). So you suffer doubly if all preferences are to count as one. What is wrong is that my lifestyle (the Friday worshipping sect), due to its belief commitments, has double the value of your own (the non-Friday worshipping sect) and that is unfair. (Of course, the external preference can here be reversed if a Muslim is overlooked for a promotion or a job because, in a secular society, he refuses to commit to working on Fridays when asked.) The obvious actual parallel of such double weighting is in racist social policy: certain roles and positions in a society are only open to a specific race (W) at the exclusion of another race (B) and this does, as a matter of empirical fact, benefit society as a whole (there are a minority of Bs, GDP for some reason increases, and so on). One member of B wants to become a university lecturer but cannot because this is one of the roles that is denied to him or her. Such preferences are justified by a policy argument (segregation leads to better well-being for the community as a whole) that harms a portion of society or specific individuals doubly: my preference for segregation acts in my favour (less competition for prestigious roles) and to your disadvantage (your opportunities are obstructed) at the same time, much like my worshipping on a Friday both benefits me and harms you at the same time. One notices that the policy itself is objectionable on the grounds of principle because the policy (segregation) conflicts with the principle of equal concern and respect.

Privileged over arguments of policy, then, are what Dworkin calls arguments from principle: 'Rights ... are best understood as trumps over some background justification for political decisions that states a goal for the community as a whole. If someone has a right to moral independence, this means that it is for some reason wrong for officials to act in violation of that right, even if they (correctly) believe that the community as a whole would be better off if they did' (1981: 200). External preferences are to be discounted from social policy decisions because they are unfair: they are preferences that count both for the agent and against another agent. Although the language is contemporary, we find the Lockean liberal defence against abuses of power: the individual's axiomatic rights (life, liberty, physical integrity, property) act as a bastion against interference in that the only way they can be violated is by that specific individual's own consent. Rights theory limits utilitarian social policy as a matter of principle.[1]

So, let us return to the original question: if barring access to pornography diminishes harm in the community significantly, then why should we not do so? Assuming it to be empirically the case that society would be better off without pornography, a utilitarian or goal-based policy could be proposed for its prohibition. There is a good utilitarian argument for a social policy of prohibition, but certain specific individuals will suffer because of this policy: the moral majority who disapprove of pornography have external preferences, they have a positive preference to free themselves of the material and a negative preference against pornographers who, on the other hand, have a mere positive preference to pursue their own interests. These latter individuals must have rights that trump the policy. Equality demands that the external preferences of those who wish for prohibition be ignored because the rights of those who wish to consume pornography are vulnerable to them: '... if pornography makes the community worse off, even in the very long run, it is nevertheless wrong to censor or restrict it because this violates the individual moral or political rights of citizens who resent the censorship' (Dworkin, 1981: 178). Dworkin bases his defence of pornography on the right to moral independence and not the right to free expression: 'People have the right not to suffer disadvantage in the distribution of social goods and opportunities, including disadvantage in the liberties permitted to them by the criminal law, just on the ground that their officials or fellow-citizens think that their opinions about the right way for them to lead their own lives are ignoble or wrong' (1981: 194). Pornography is just an expression of personal tastes and preferences which have the right to be respected because they are representative of autonomous individuals.

Here is how the argument for freedom of speech proceeds in its barest and simplest form: free speech is to be protected otherwise governments can become totalitarian. We can allow pernicious and false ideas because – following Mill (2011) – the truth will affirm itself in an open and fair debate. Freedom of speech allows for this open and fair debate and maintains and reproduces the autonomy of the individual through the institution of a right to freedom of conscience and speech. Such an understanding frames the debate in terms of an authoritarian government versus individuals who want to express their 'genius' or 'dissent' against the tyranny of the moral majority. It reinforces Dworkin's suspicion that feminists are, as the football chant more or less goes, conservatives in disguise. Put like this, those who support the prohibition of pornography are cast as allies of the authoritarian government:

> But now the political maps have radically changed and some forms of negative liberty have acquired new opponents. Both in America and Britain, though in different ways, racial and gender conflicts have transformed old alliances and divisions. Speech that expresses racial hatred, or a degrading attitude toward women, or that threatens environmental destruction has come to seem intolerable to many people whose convictions are otherwise traditionally liberal. It is hardly surprising that they should try to reduce the conflict between their old liberal ideals and their new acceptance of censorship by some redefinition of what liberty, properly understood, really is. (Dworkin, 1991: 103)

Yet, there is an obvious sleight of hand here. We are all liberals now and to deny that liberty is a good is to exclude oneself from moral and political discourse. To say that it is the only good is, however, less uncontroversial. There are two possible ways to respond to Dworkin's framework in a rational enough manner to remain in the conversation: one, agree that liberty alone matters, but that it has an equivocal meaning from which Dworkin profits; or, two, agree that liberty matters but insist that equality, too, matters and is not reducible to the former. Dworkin claims that feminists do the former, dismissing the anti-liberal nature of their 'positive' interpretation of freedom, whereas one may rightly hold that feminists actually do the latter.

For Dworkin, the right to free speech is not a natural right, but an empowering right: the institution of free and open discussion is a way to maintain and secure equal consideration of one's moral independence. And such equality is required, otherwise the liberty of the individual, understood as the autonomous personal capacity to determine oneself and one's life according to personal values and chosen projects is vulnerable to the caprice of others. Equality is a good and it is reducible to liberty. But before we join Dworkin on that last monist step, the feminist critique of pornography is for the most part premised on the claim that the existence of pornography is detrimental to the equality of individuals (specifically gender equality). If one were to be monist, then, it would undermine personal liberty. If one is pluralist, then equality matters intrinsically. The feminist argument, then, seems like an argument of principle against the existence of pornography and not an argument of policy, so the question of free speech may well just be a side issue. What is truly at stake is equality, whether it be as a value in itself or as valuable for liberty.

4.3 Metaphysical errors: doing, saying, being

The right to consume pornography is based on the metaphysical assertion that pornography is a form of expression. It expresses ideas, opinions, beliefs. Such expression is protected in a liberal society by freedom of expression, which is required to respect the equality and liberty of individuals.[2] The obvious question that needs to be asked is whether or not pornography is really speech. Does it express ideas at all? One could plausibly argue that it is mere emotional arousal or the stimulating means to an erection, to 'be horny', as a coke advertisement makes one salivate and 'be thirsty'. However, the capacity to arouse may well be a necessary feature of pornographic material, but it does not exhaust its properties. In many ways, pornography is a saying. It says: 'This is pleasure, this is love and happiness lies in this'. For MacKinnon, though, the free speech defence is mistaken because viewing pornography as an expression of ideas is a metaphysical error akin to believing the statement 'the Sun sets in the west' to be a truth (1993). The consequences of believing that it is true that the Sun sets in the west is to assume that the Earth is fixed and the Sun orbits around us. Such a belief would have an undesirable effect on our capacity for space flight. The consequences of believing that pornography is 'only words' is that it is protected under the right to free speech and it continues to commit wrongdoing. MacKinnon wants us to see pornography for what it is: the action of subordination. The *saying* of pornography is more properly understood as a *doing*.

That saying is also a doing is, on one level, rather obvious: it involves a desire to express something on the part of a unified organism as a cause that instigates the movement of body parts (the movement of the mouth, the expulsion of air by the lungs) such that effects are substantiated in the world (to put it in the most naturalist of ways!) That this occurs through the instrument of sayings, or writings, or pictorial representations, or through narrative, and so on, is by the by. Expressions are actions because they belong to the subset of events brought about by agents aimed at specific ends: we say, write, film, photograph, all to achieve aims. The distinction between actions and expressions, whereby the former are subject to moral or legal judgement and the latter are to be protected if we value liberty and autonomy, comes about for specific historical reasons, much like the concept of responsibility moves from the group to the individual level to respond to particular judicial problems (those of the socially destabilizing effect of vendetta). Morally and politically, we need to protect the freedom of conscience and speech due to our social investment in the value of autonomy and the background of normative individualism. But, that is not the point when we say some words are actions.

Liberals do, of course, admit certain expressions are actions and such actions are not protected by either rights or their underlying rational structure. Such words are of two types: one, those that cause direct and immediate harm. So saying, 'Kill!' to an attack dog or, 'Fire' in a crowded cinema are not protected. Such words are *legally* best understood as simple actions rather than expressions. There is no content to the expressions that has worth independently of their perlocutionary aspect: there is no real difference between saying 'Kill!' to an attack dog and pulling a trigger on a gun; nor is there any great difference between shouting 'Fire' in a crowded cinema and deliberately rolling a stone down a scree-laden mountain side with people climbing up. Neither of the latter actions would be protected by a liberty claim because, quite simply, they involve the foreseeable harm of others. Such expressions are then, for legal reasons, best viewed as simple actions. So, the doing with words that needs to be legally sanctioned is immediate actions of a criminal nature that also happen to be communicative (shouting, 'Fire!', sending race-hate literature into a racially tense neighbourhood). Such speaking is to be prohibited under the legislation of rights-violation according to some form of harm principle. Pornography, it is sometimes claimed, has a direct causal relationship with rape and, if this were true, then it would be a simple action akin to these (much like the agent who holds the women down and encourages the rapist in a gang rape) (Russell, 1988). It would be akin to barking the order, 'Rape!' at the audience. We have already discussed this claim in the previous chapter and I shall repeat that it is difficult to identify non-controversial, immediate harmful effects of pornographic consumption. If they can be found, then they would necessitate prohibition of such materials.

Other accepted limits to free speech include defamation, libel and slander. Libel, defamation and slander harm an individual (or group) through falsehood. Imagine the jilted lover taking revenge on an ex-girlfriend by falsely accusing her of the most mendacious of behaviour in a letter addressed to a person with whom he knows she is about to sit a job interview. The jilted lover's words are directly responsible for creating an impression of her in the mind of others that inhibits her opportunities and possibilities. He falsely represents reality to the detriment of an other and surely it is plausible to think he should not have the liberty to do so and his actions now demand to be sanctioned. In short, he has harmed her interests. There seems little difference between his sending the letter and physically keeping her locked in a room so she cannot attend the interview. Had he published the letter in a national newspaper, the same considerations would apply. Of course, the media can defend what they have printed by stating that it is an opinion, an editorial piece and so on. The legal purpose of such cases is to determine whether freedom of speech is to be upheld because the material is an expression of ideas or, in fact, a direct act of harm.

MacKinnon's claim is that most defences of pornography invoke the First Amendment (freedom of speech) because when pornography harms, it is perceived to do so in the same way that hate-speech harms a group. One can tolerate sexist or racist attitudes and expressions – and given we live in a constitutional, plural democracy, we are obliged to tolerate them – so long as such words do not translate into direct action or violence. So, one can express racist attitudes in a philosophy seminar on fascism, but not shout them in front of a crowd of civil right protesters. Or, to use another example, one can tolerate Hegel's rather Neanderthal discussion of the role of women in the modern state because it occurs within a scholarly text that is to be debated in a classroom (1991: §§161–169). Yet, one cannot tolerate the classified employment advertisement which openly states 'Females need not apply' because this discriminates against a group. Such statements or propositions have a content but also a performative aspect. 'Shut the door' can either be a command or a request depending on the tone used. And the performance of the same content establishes social relationships and hierarchies: a request is usually given to an equal, a command to an inferior. So, the performance of the same statement can assign different roles and the response to the performance determines the consent to or rejection of these roles. The performance aspect of the proposition is what determines whether it is an expression of an idea or an action of violence, and consequently determines what is to be tolerated and what is to be silenced. Hegel's words are a performance of philosophy and he is asserting. It is then a matter of truth and a matter of discussion. No actions which are harmful are to follow. The advertisement is different. The words are not just a simple case of direct harming but the words constitute and embody social practices which distribute burdens and values to individuals that have an impact on their liberties and opportunities.

Just as words can be action, so actions can be words: posting faeces through the letter box is very clearly a violent request to move house.

Waiting for the female executive in the boardroom to pour the tea is a way of communicating putative superiority and so on. Such behaviours deserve to be legally sanctioned and so, according to MacKinnon, 'Protecting pornography means protecting sexual abuse *as* speech, at the same time that both pornography and its protection have deprived women *of* speech, especially speech against sexual abuse' (1993: 9). Therefore, the defence of pornography rests on identifying it as 'speech', as opinion or a viewpoint that has a 'right' to be expressed. Her claim is that pornography is akin to racial discrimination. It is wrong because it discriminates on the basis of sex. Such acts, even though they are only words, cannot be defended by free speech arguments. Defamation occurs when the communicative content of a statement is harmful to the status of an individual or a group rather than being a direct harm. Defamation is discrimination when a sign in a hostel has the word, 'Vacancy' conditional to 'Blacks need not apply.' What happens is that 'social inequality is substantially created and enforced – that is, *done* – through words and images' (MacKinnon, 1993: 13). MacKinnon's argument against the free exchange of pornographic materials rests on two premises: one, pornography performs the action of abuse in its production and consumption and subordinates women by its very existence; and, two, pornography differs from ideas (protected under the right to free speech) because it is an action, a performance and that performance is abuse. If her argument is valid, then the legal protection of pornography as free speech is simply misplaced because pornography is a form of discrimination.

4.4 Catherine MacKinnon: pornography as discrimination

Let us look more closely at the basis of MacKinnon's argument, beginning by again quoting her definition. Pornography *is* subordination:

> 'the graphic sexually explicit subordination of women through pictures and/or words that also includes one or more of the following: (a) women are presented dehumanized as sexual objects, things, or commodities; or (b) women are presented as sexual objects who enjoy humiliation or pain; or (c) women are presented as sexual objects experiencing sexual pleasure in rape, incest, or other sexual assault; or (d) women are presented as sexual objects tied up or cut up or mutilated or bruised or physically hurt; or (e) women are presented as in postures or positions of sexual submission; (f) women's body parts – including but not limited to vaginas, breasts, or buttocks – are exhibited such that women are reduced to those parts; or (g) women are presented being penetrated by

objects or animals; or (h) women are presented in scenarios of degradation, humiliation, injury, torture, shown as filthy or inferior, bleeding, bruised, or hurt in a context that makes these conditions sexual.' In this definition, the use of 'men, children, or transsexuals in the place of women' is also pornography. (1993: 121–2)

Several things need to be said about this definition. One, it is normative: pornography is conceptually bad. Her whole argument is included in the definition and hence it is either begging the question (see Chapter 2 above) or she has a narrow definition in mind and 'pornography' can be replaced with another definition, such as violence or abuse (MacKinnon, 1993: 66). She identifies a subset of what I earlier defined as pornography, so we can encircle the set of erotica (my pornography) of which a subset (MacKinnon's pornography) is bad. Her aim, though, is normative through and through. The definition is the basis for suing someone for discrimination caused by the production, exchange or consumption of pornography. If I drive a car with faulty brakes due to a mechanical error never rectified even if known to the producer, then the car company is liable to be sued when the failure of those brakes leads to harm to myself or to third parties. If my particular car has faulty brakes and yet I still decide to drive my friends' children to football practice, then, if anything happens, I am liable. Similarly, the producers and consumers of pornography are susceptible to being sued for the damages that its existence causes; if a particular woman is passed over for promotion at work and there is a connection between this evaluation and the boss's consumption of pornography, then the producers and consumers of that pornography can be sued for damages.[3]

Two, the definition seemingly includes objects that are not intuitively understood as pornography, such as sexually charged music videos, for example, as they meet the disjunction (a) and the scene from *Flash Gordon* under conditions (b–f). Most interestingly, Winterbottom's *9 Songs* falls foul of clauses (b) and (d), yet is one of the most progressively authentic representations of a sexual relationship that does not seem to either silence or subordinate women. It seems that the definition used could be too prohibitive. However, the ordinance is not aimed at the prohibition or censorship of the content of pornography (as Ronald Dworkin seems to assert), as it would under freedom of speech and the claim of offence or harm in the expression of ideas and beliefs. Rather, it seeks to allow victims the opportunity to sue the producers and distributors of pornography for damages. It is civil and not criminal law. So, *Flash Gordon*, if used to discriminate against an individual, could be the basis of a civil claim against the distributor who used it in a certain way (publicly displaying it in the workplace, for example). The film itself remains untouched.

Three, MacKinnon uses the word 'presentation' rather than 'representation' deliberately. She does not feel that any of the actions can be simulated because of an essential realism in pornography. When a woman is penetrated, she is actually penetrated. When a gang rape is simulated on film, she is actually gang raped. More pertinently, her definition identifies pornography with abuse because she believes it is a presentation rather than a simulation. If pornography is abuse, then of course it should be banned. And if one cannot simulate gang rape but only perform it, then films containing a scene of gang rape are abuse. And if one cannot film sex without it being non-consensual, then all sex films are abuse. *9 Songs* again raises a problem in that we have two actors engaged in an example of cinema verité with artistic aspirations in which they attempt to *represent* an authentic sexual relationship (as kissing would be used to *represent* two persons falling in love in another film). Again, though, MacKinnon's central claim is about the existence of pornography. We need to distinguish the claims that 'wrong is done in the production of pornography' and 'wrong is caused by the consumption of pornography' from 'the existence of pornography constitutes or causes a wrong'. And that wrong is abuse. So, a man who watches *9 Songs* and believes women all enjoy light choking has opened the film to a suit for damages incurred by the women he chokes. Of course, in such cases, the court is to rule whether responsibility lies with the individual or the film (which oddly means pornography is ultimately defined by legal judgement).

The definition constitutes the first two premises of her argument, that is pornography performs the action of abuse in its production and consumption, and subordination in its existence. Pornographic material is abuse in its production, existence and consumption. A later quotation helps us to make her argument clear:

> What pornography does, it does in the real world, not only in the mind. As an initial matter, it should be observed that it is the pornography industry, not the ideas in the materials, that forces, threatens, blackmails, pressures, tricks, and cajoles women into sex for pictures. In pornography, women are gang raped so they can be filmed. They are not gang raped by the idea of a gang rape. It is for pornography, and by the ideas in it, that women are hurt and penetrated, tied and gagged, undressed and genitally spread and sprayed with lacquer and water so sex pictures can be made. Only for pornography are women killed to make a sex movie, and it is not the idea of a sex killing that

> kills them. It is unnecessary to do any of these things to express, as ideas, the ideas that pornography expresses. It *is* essential to do them to make pornography. Similarly, on the consumption end, it is not the ideas in pornography that assault women: men do, men who are made, changed, and impelled by it. Pornography does not leap off the shelf and assault women. Women could, in theory, walk safely past whole warehouses full of it, quietly resting in its jackets. It is what it takes to make it and what happens through its use that are the problem. (MacKinnon, 1993: 15)

Here we see why Hegel's opinions of women as stated in his philosophical work are tolerated whereas a classified advertisement that states, 'Only males need apply' is not. Hegel engages in conversation and offers ideas that one can assent to or reject. They are first and foremost ideas, opinions and beliefs. Thus, they are the sort of thing to be protected under the right to free speech. Pornography is more akin to the advertisement because it is direct violence to the rights and status of women, whether in actual violence (in production) or in the maintenance of unequal relationships of power (in its existence) or in the violation of a woman's right to equal treatment (from the effects of its consumption). So, pornography differs from ideas (protected under the right to free speech) because it is an action (or an action other than 'assertion') and that performance is abuse. By allowing pornography to be defended by a right to free speech, MacKinnon asserts that a metaphysical error has occurred such that what is first and foremost an action (abuse) is treated as an expression of ideas and opinions (speech). Abuse is a criminal act and answerable to law. So, too, should pornography be.

4.5 Langton's spade work

MacKinnon's work, for all its merit, contains several levels of confusion: between the wrongs done in production and consumption and the wrongs done by the simple existence of pornography posted on a garage wall. There is the further conflation of moral, political and legal wrong with scant attempt to separate them. She often mixes up the causal claims about the effects of pornography with the role pornography plays in constituting behavioural patterns and attitudes. Her primary audience is not, though, philosophers. It is constitutional lawyers and judges. And especially North American ones (of which I may say more in a while). Luckily, the spade work in clarifying her position has already been expertly carried out, even if the substance of the argument remains the same. MacKinnon is perhaps what Nussbaum (1999: ch. 9) describes as 'prophetic' (although her example is the even more polemical Andrea Dworkin), so it is fortunate that there exists an invaluable, 'philosophical' clarification of MacKinnon's (and one also supposes Andrea Dworkin's) theses in the work of Rae Langton. Prophetesses are not necessarily erroneous, they are just hasty in their expression because of the urgency to say what needs to be said and the required actions that their words elicit.

Let us then begin again from the premise of the free speech argument: pornography is an expression of ideas and opinions and, as such, is a possible object of protection from the intervention of those whose moral or aesthetic conceptions seek to silence it. If pornography is speech, though, what does it say? MacKinnon famously claims that the free speech argument rests on a metaphysical mistake. Pornography is not an expression of ideas, it is an action and thus subject to different evaluations because actions bring about changes in the world. If pornography is an action, what does it do? Langton adopts MacKinnon's answer: the content of pornography is the subordination of women and what it does is subordinate and silence women. It is akin to the slave master putting chains on his serfs to sell them at the market and gags around their mouths so they cannot cry out in pain and protest.

Langton is rightly put out by Ronald Dworkin's rhetorical alignment of feminism with conservatism. His claim is based on the coincidence between conservative and feminist claims that they, as social critics or intellectuals, are able to gauge the worth of an idea or production. 'Bad art harms the development of free individuals and societies', would be one such claim (even a possible assertion of a Mill in a possible world arguing with his godfather prime!) and Dworkin sees the spectre of judgements about what individuals should want made by a person who is not that individual. He then attempts to show that feminists pretend to be liberals by hiding the fact that they are interested in positive and not negative liberty. Langton (2009: ch. 2) believes this to be a red herring and she is right to a certain extent. There is something forced about Dworkin using the language and one feels it was perhaps a homage to Isaiah Berlin. However, it is not a simple red herring and it does play a role in what is to be said below. Liberals should be in favour of permitting pornography by virtue of being liberals and they should tolerate bad taste, aesthetically poor judgement and moral divergence from their own concepts of the good. To interfere in such judgement, to employ censorship for such ends, is to use the instruments of the state against the individual: '... if pornography makes the community worse off, even in the very long run, it is nevertheless wrong to censor or restrict it because this violates the individual moral or political rights of citizens who resent the censorship' (Dworkin, 1981: 178).[4]

Langton's challenge is rather straightforward: Dworkin's argument does not address radical feminism at all. Moreover, her argument seems to show that a radically feminist perspective is demanded by Dworkin's approach (Langton, 2009: 108). Her liberalism is confirmed by a commitment to the value of free speech, but she argues women's freedom to speak is impaired because pornography silences them. They are not allowed to speak freely.

> If you are powerful, you sometimes have the ability to silence the speech of the powerless. One way might be to stop the powerless from speaking at all. Gag them, threaten them, condemn them to solitary confinement. But there is another, less dramatic but equally effective, way. Let them speak. Let them say whatever they like to whomever they like, but stop that speech from counting as an *action*. More precisely, stop it from counting as the action it was intended to be. (Langton, 2009: 31)

And this silencing is a consequence of the subordination of women prevalent in the social structures of contemporary culture and of the existence of pornography which determines women's inferior civil status. The existence of pornography has an effect on the equality of women, so there is a conflict between the liberty to say what you want and the equality of persons.

The tree clearing of analytic philosophy carried out by Langton begins with the familiar speech-act theory of Austin (1962). An assertion such as, 'The door is open' communicates a particular meaning in that a grammatical subject (the door) is ascribed a property (open). The meaning of a proposition is its *locutionary* aspect. Saying that, 'The door is open' in the presence of my children may make them close it, thus the proposition when uttered acts as a cause of an effect (closing the door). The consequence of a proposition is its *perlocutionary* aspect. Austin sought to address the fact that there is another aspect of uttered propositions that had, at that time, received insufficient attention in the philosophy of language, that is the *illocutionary* aspect. I can assert (and philosophy truly loves this particular performance) that 'the door is open' as a truth claim to be assented or rejected ('No, it's closed.'), I can hypothesize ('No, it is closed, the draught must be coming from the open window'), I can suggest (and my children may close it) or I can order (and my children *will* close it). The illocutionary aspect differs from the perlocutionary in that it concerns the formal nature of an uttered proposition: it is the action constituted by the utterance itself (a claim, a hypothesis, a suggestion or an order). Such performances are different from their consequences given the fact that they can misfire, either through resistance or misinterpretation, so my children can refuse to obey my order (all the worse for them) or simply answer in the affirmative (misreading what I wanted from my statement). For Langton, there is an empirical truth-claim that pornography depicts subordination and a secondary empirical claim that the perlocutionary effects of pornographic propositions may be harm or subordination, but there is also a conceptual claim that what pornography does in its depictions is the illocutionary act of subordinating and silencing women.

One can compare pornography to a racist statement that could be prevalent in a possible society (not unlike fifties Britain). Imagine the existence of a sign in the window of hostel: 'Vacancies. Blacks need not apply'. The sign communicates the fact that the hostel has rooms available for specific (non-black) individuals. However, the specific culture determines who belongs to which group (which rarely coincides with the simple, empirical fact of skin colour). Such speech, one might intuitively think, should not be protected by free speech because it attacks the liberty of a specific group to do what they want, and will have the effect of perpetuating a putative value hierarchy (that non-black clients are preferable – have more value – than blacks) determining an inequality in the treatment of individuals in other instances. Such speech therefore harms both the liberty and opportunities of individuals and should not be protected by free speech legislation. These constitute the perlocutionary aspect of the sign, but its illocutionary aspect is to immediately exclude and subordinate. A particular ethnic group is singled out and excluded from enjoying specific liberties and they are determined to stay elsewhere in (no doubt) worse housing and more dangerous neighbourhoods, with addresses and postal codes which will be discounted by possible employers when written on job application forms. It is worth noting immediately that such performances rest on institutional and structural support from the cultural environment: putting the sign 'Vacancies. People whose surname begins with "R" need not apply' would obviously misfire as a performance if one intended to subordinate that specific group. People would find it silly or they would ignore it. The socio-ethical stratum determines (as will become clear) why certain performances are successful and others not.

Of course, what this depends upon is the authority of the hostel-owner to decide who can and who cannot stay in his or her residence. The formal acting inherent in the statement only works if the utterer can actually do what he or she intends. I can order my children to close the door, but they can choose to disobey or ignore me. My managers at the University can advise me to publish in certain journals, but I can choose to ignore them. The state can order me to pay my taxes, but I can ignore it at the risk of sanction. There are two connected aspects of this: there is the *de facto* power (force) to do what one wants and the *de jure* power (authority or legitimate power) to do what one wants. The state has both the right and power to enforce payment of taxes, as does the parent over his children. If a hostel owner has an unconditional right to grant or withhold access to his or her hostel, then he or she will be protected by law in excluding an ethnic group. And such exclusion will subordinate a specific ethnic group. He has the authority to do so (and can count on the force of the state to execute his or her want). If the right to permit entry is limited by Race Relations Law (the hostel-owner can refuse entry to who he likes, but not based on ethnicity) as a species of equal moral treatment, then the hostel-owner can be sanctioned by the state and the sign can be ignored or challenged by the non-white who wishes to stay in the hostel (and his power to do what he wants will be backed by the state). It is worth noting in passing that the unconditional right corresponds with an unconditional right to free speech under US Law and the limited right corresponds to the UK approach in race relation legislation which limits what can be said: '... should they be free to incite racial hatred, for example? British and American law now give different answers to that specific question. The United Kingdom Race Relations law makes it a crime to advocate racial prejudice, but the First Amendment to the United States Constitution forbids Congress or any of the states from adopting any such law' (Dworkin, 1981: 177).

Pornographic materials and their content depicts subordination; necessarily so given MacKinnon's own definition, but actually so in the majority of cases right down to mainstream and putatively 'feminine' *Fifty Shades Darker* examples (James, 2012). It may be the case that they have the effect of sexual discrimination and they may cause harm to individual women (but this is to be proven beyond doubt and has been considered above). However, in what sense does the utterance of pornography constitute an action of subordination? Just as the sign in the window subordinates a group (by limiting their opportunities) and the non-interference of the state confers authority on the hostel-owner to do so, so 'Pornography makes the world a pornographic place through its making and use, establishing what women are said to exist as, are seen as, are treated as, constructing the social reality of what a women is and can be in terms of what can be done to her, and what a man is in terms of doing it' (MacKinnon, 1993: 25). It would be a category mistake to say that pornography itself subordinates just because it depicts subordination (Parent, 1990). Pornography creates or supports the conditions that make possible or facilitate subordination of a certain group. It is an element in the system of subordination in the same way the hostel sign itself does nothing but is still an element in the system of subordination. The action of pornographic propositions is the 'making' and 'establishing' of women's identities and the social reality that supports those identities. And if this is the case, then pornography (like the sign) discriminates as MacKinnon claims.

Like the sign though, for pornography to subordinate, it must come from an established authority (the sign might be a printed political edict) or it must be supported by the non-interference of the state (as is the case with the sign in that the freedom to select access to one's hostel is unconditional). With pornography, there is seemingly no state-funded or produced pornography (current employment laws and maternity rights might seem to be subordination in this sense), but Langton is asserting that if pornography is protected under freedom of speech, then the state is allowing for the subordination of women through the non-interference in practices that subordinate. Note here that, articulated in this way, the claim that pornography subordinates is not a category mistake because pornography does not subordinate, but creates the conditions that make subordination possible. Ronald Dworkin's claim that feminist arguments are a form of conservatism is here exposed because the feminists do not seek the prohibition of pornography on aesthetic or moral grounds, but on the purely political grounds of discrimination and equal treatment. No doubt concerns close to Dworkin's own heart.

There are two main objections to Langton's claim that pornography constitutes a social reality of gender subordination. The first concerns the agent and the second whether – as MacKinnon claims – pornography *creates* subordination. One, with the sign, we can identify who is responsible for the discrimination (the hostel-owner) because he wrote the sign. Yet this is in itself overly simplistic. His writing of the sign is merely a repetition of an attitude prevalent in his culture:

> Such a reduction of the agency of power to the actions of the subject may well seek to compensate for the difficulties and anxieties produced in the course of living in a contemporary cultural predicament in which neither the law nor hate speech are uttered exclusively by a singular subject. The racial slur is always cited from elsewhere, and in the speaking of it, one chimes in with a chorus of racists, producing at that moment the linguistic occasion for an imagined relation to

> an historically transmitted community of racists. In this sense, racist speech does not originate with the subject, even if it requires the subject for its efficacy, as it surely does. (Butler, 1997: 80)

By citing the hostel-owner as responsible for the discrimination and as the subject to be punished, one ignores the very real history of those attitudes in his own identity formation. We ignore the role of the state in its permitting of the freedom of access or of prohibiting arbitrary discrimination. We ignore how the sign, as an act of power, creates an identity that did not exist prior to its being written (the excluded immigrant class). With pornographic films, we have a director, a producer, a distributor, actors, technicians, writers (I suppose, although it is often hard to tell!) and so on. The idea of individual responsibility requires that we identify one, some or all of these as the agent who is subordinating.

MacKinnon's claim, though, is different. She is stating that it is 'pornography' which subordinates, not the individual producers. She is, after all, offering a civil case against individuals who discriminate because they have consumed pornography and, so, she is talking about pornography as one talks about the Post Office as in 'the Post Office delivers letters': that is as an institution. And this complicates matters more because the anthropomorphism involved in these practices is very much the target of Butler's critique: a subject is constructed by language in order to fit our moral demands. If my letters are lost in the post, I demand compensation not from the postman or sorter, but from the institution. The institution is constructed as an agent to blame, but has very little metaphysical reality. What Butler may have correct is that feminists in the MacKinnon mould are seeking the Male (the ur-Father?) who has subordinated them when, in fact, there exists a prior non-chosen origin of the male/female relationship constituted by the system (language) which has made this subordination possible. It is for this reason that the sign which uses the word 'blacks' was successful in fifties Britain whereas the one which (hypothetically) used surnames beginning with R would not be. The system ought to be the true target of critique rather than some imagined father who originally, historically, subordinated women (a claim we return to below in succeeding chapters). When Butler states that 'The power to "race" and, indeed, the power to gender, precedes the "one" who speaks such power, and yet the one who speaks nevertheless appears to have that power', we see that the responsibility for the *creation* of subordination does not lie at the door of pornography, even if subordination's perpetuation does (1997: 49). The *how* of pornography's subordination coupled with Butler's intuitions about the slippery intentional nature of pornography problematize the citation of a single agent's will as responsible for causing the injury with words.[5] With the sign, a Marxist would look at the sign as an ideology, as belonging to the superstructure and hence to be understood in historically material terms in relation to the base. Responsibility, to use a word seemingly more and more inappropriate, lies with the economic system.

Butler criticizes Langton's two ideas that pornography subordinates and silences. The first because it rests on an assumption of some sort of divine command, identifying an imagined, ideal agent who can subordinate easily and simply through the invocation of simple words. However, no amount of saying what a woman is can make the woman that without the woman's complicit submission. In believing in such a relationship, feminists are disrespectful of women's own individual power. The second because a text allows for a reinterpretation and a deconstruction of its original meaning through irony, which makes it into a fantasy. The latter is a claim about the possibility of objectification that we shall consider in the next chapter, but the former is pertinent here. Butler asks this: if pornography acts by undermining the intention of the woman to say, 'No', and to say what she wants to say, then why is the intention of pornography stable and that of the women not. The answer (even to the non-radical feminist) ought to be obvious: authority. Pornography functions within the realm of state power in terms of deriving its legitimacy from the capitalist-constructed relationships between persons. Silencing of women is permitted because pornography has an unconditional right to say what it wants and, given cultural conditions, its voice is louder than those who would oppose it (like the non-white who asks for a room at the hostel). The point is that the intention seems divine because the claim 'subordinate' is made by the system. Langton assumes it to be made by the will of men as a collective or Man as the fount of political power. This is problematic.

Butler's critique may well be an exaggerated claim about the idea of intention but she is right to show that in an act of social formation through political power there is an excess which escapes, the difference as it were, from what is enframed in the saying. However, her attack on the sovereignty of the subject in the speech-act is neither here nor there in one sense: the sense that relocates the whole problem to the concept of power. There exists a prior question to be asked: what are the conditions of possibility of contemporary pornography? And the answer is the present subordination of women (and race and class) already by the social system of coding that makes meaning possible. Pornography as subordination is a symptom of the already present subordination of women and not the cause of subordination. However, we still treat symptoms in the health context as the selling of Lemsip testifies. Much discussion of pornography occurs in the context of legal theory and specifically US legal theory with its fetishism for free speech protection (much more than Mill ever demanded). Personally, I am not interested whether a judge deems that the burning of a cross in someone's garden is protected speech under the Constitution or not. The act is morally wrong, it should not have been done. Whether a state can find grounds to sanction or exonerate the perpetrator tells us more about that state than the action. I want to hold the person who burns the cross responsible as an individual but, simultaneously, I also want to know whether I participate in practices that reproduce hidden conventions making and encouraging such behaviour. And if so, I want to change the coding of my meaning or those conventions to match my moral interests. I engage critically with the system of meaning. Equally so with pornography. Just as morality and moral judgement conjure up a subject who can be blamed, so language and its performance conjures up one who can perform. Just because such subjects are 'fictions' in Butler's Nietzschean sense, there is not yet a compelling reason to undermine the morality just because it rests on a supposed metaphysical error.

That such discourse fixes a continuous chain of events (or a doing/a becoming) into a singular deed can still serve a purpose. Such an agent may well be an historical constitution but this does not necessarily undermine its worth. Many ideas are historically constituted and some are more rational than others. Just because something is a metaphysical illusion, does not mean we cannot divide it into necessary fictions, unnecessary fictions and injurious fictions if we are either pragmatists or idealists. That such a discussion occurs at all demonstrates how law fails morality and is often used to cover the immorality not of individuals but of the social fabric itself. Here one can return to US versus UK legal approaches to hate speech. The latter privileges equality because equality of unprotected speech without equality of moral standing and power distribution makes free speech an empty right. Take the example of my tutorial groups: everyone can question my opinion and my assertions and all can equally assert, but I would be foolish to ignore who the members of the group are likely to listen to when he or she asserts by virtue of the relationship teacher/student. Such a relationship is rational because either the students want to pass an examination or truth is best tracked by following the words of the expert who is suitably accountable. The social system determines the discourse, but what MacKinnon (and Langton) are seeking to show is that pornography plays a role in this subordination by reinforcing and perpetuating subordination and it does so through a performative or illocutionary act.

Let us weaken the claim slightly and hold that pornography cannot create subordination, only maintain it. Especially as MacKinnon defines it. It has to be the depiction, or reproduction, of an already existing state of inequality. This is very different from causing it, which is perlocutionary. If pornography subordinates as an illocution, then it makes sense to identify an intention and an agent. Even if, at the moment of utterance, that agent and the object of that utterance are created because, then, one's critique is aimed at resolving how it is possible to identify one as an agent and one as an object within a specific milieu.

Langton is well aware of this when she identifies the agent who utters pornography as: '... pornography's voice is the voice of the ruling power' (Langton, 2009: 44). Pornography's voice has to be the ruling power for it to have the *de facto* power of subordination and the *de jure* power for this subordination not to be challenged. The state rarely rises to the defence of the subordination of women, especially not in liberal democracies. According to Langton, liberalism's putative defence of the sanctity of the principle of free speech confers the authority on pornography. What this means is that subordination of women is reinforced by the fact that subordination is protected from being challenged. The voices of those who would oppose subordination carry no weight and are, in effect, silenced. Protestors or critics can be physically silenced, they can be placed where no one will hear them, or they can be denied the language that will allow them equal participation in political discourse. Just as a knowledge of Latin was once required to have political power, a language that excluded large parts of the populace from participation, so subordination is perpetuated by the absence of a challenge in the correct language and pornography is one of those elements of modern culture that ensures that a certain group (women) cannot learn or use the language proper to such discussions. Thus, their utterances are seen as hysterical, exaggerated, emotional, irrational and so on. So, for the radical feminist, it makes sense to talk about the subject of pornography performing the act of silencing and this silencing as an illocution leaves subordination unchallenged. It is an utterance akin to the 'Don't be silly,' to the child which is an act of imposing silence and inactivity.

Mill was well aware of this exclusion of women from public discourse and also well aware of how women will their own domination through cultural influence: 'Exactly the same thing may be said of the women in the harem of an Oriental: they do not complain of not being allowed the freedom of European women. They think our women insufferably bold and unfeminine'. This could just as easily be used to describe the undesirable and unfeminine popular characterization of radical feminists (Mill, 1869: loc. 1370-72). The silencing then has a priority over the subordination: 'But if pornography not only subordinates but *silences* women, it is not easy to see how there can be any such fight. At this point the second feminist claim demands our attention. Whether women can fight speech with more speech depends on whether, and to what extent, women can speak ... If speech is action, then silence is failure to act. If pornography silences women, then it prevents women from doing things with their words' (Langton, 2009: 47).

The second objection to the claim that pornography causes subordination is more significant: if the effect of pornography is the subordination of women, then all we need for equality is the removal of the cause (pornography). Such a counter-factual is plainly false. One may claim it is one cause amongst others, but it is hard to see how the equality of women would be improved by prohibition. Pornography belongs to a set of social practices that perpetuates (rather than determines or causes) subordination. On the one hand, pornography as both Langton and MacKinnon conceive of it, would not be possible unless there were not an already existing hierarchy of power relations. Such a relation obviously existed historically before the emergence of pornography and probably had a causal role in its appearance. On the other, the claim that pornography silences would not have any sense unless the women in question who wish to raise their voices in disapproval were not already in a state of subordination. The perlocutionary or causal effect of pornography is the perpetuation of relations of power and domination that exist as part of a social fabric not the creation of it. That does not make it any better, but it is important to understand in what sense pornography is said to *cause* subordination. In fact to say that pornography subordinates is to say that the victims of subordination or the oppressed cannot resist and especially not resist with words because their words lack power. This is the silencing argument.

MacKinnon expresses the silencing argument as ever with rhetorical zeal:

> When any one of them tries to tell what happened, she is told it did not happen, she imagined it, she wanted it. Her no meant yes. The pictures prove it. See, she smiles. Besides, why fixate on the pictures, on the little artifact, at most a symptom? Even if something was *done* to you, how metaphysically obtuse can you be? The pictures *themselves* do nothing. They are an expression of ideas, a discussion, a debate, a discourse. How repressed and repressive can you be? They are constitutionally protected speech. (1993: 5–6)

One can be silenced by being gagged. The gag physically stops the air exhalation forming the words which express ideas and opinions and from satisfying the desire to speak. The gag is an attack on your negative liberty to speak and the utterance on this account can have no content; the content of one's ideas is quashed. You know what you want to say but you cannot physically say it. The state or an authority can threaten sanctions if you speak. This is silencing through abuse or threat of intimidation. MacKinnon's quotation suggests that, for the most part, women can form words. Pornography does not act as a gag, it offers no physical impediment to the protest of women as the existence of radically feminist critiques testifies.

One can be silenced by having the content of one's utterances ignored. One is allowed to say what one wants, but one's words are without any discernible effect, they are merely sounds for the other person who does not change their behaviour with respect to their content. One can say, 'But these words have no effect because you have no power or authority'. Here, the perlocutionary effect is negated. The woman may know what she wants to say but cannot say it because her words fall on deaf ears: MacKinnon's critique is that of the hysterical woman, the one whose content is suspect. That her claims are taken to be hysterical is due to the existence of pornography which shows us what women really want, what they desire. Such silencing can also occur at the illocutionary level. The actor, to borrow an example from Davidson, acting the warning, 'Fire', may see an actual fire, but his audience believes he is still acting. His intended action (to warn) misfires. Pornography creates a constant state of misfiring statements for women, they say 'No', but they mean 'Yes', because, say the consumers, we have all seen it in the films.

One can be silenced by being excluded from the table of possible participants, or from being included at the cost of losing the possibility to determine rules governing rational sentences (the syntax), and the permissible content of such sentences (the semantics). One speaks but fails to perform the action one intended (to dissent, to reject) because one has no power to create the rules that govern the interactions between persons. The most noticeable example would be the use of Latin in church. One must learn the language, but in learning the language one acknowledges the right of certain individuals to have power and of certain laws to form what one says. The interest of not paying the tithe because you do not believe in Heaven is not an interest you can have if you learn to speak the language properly. In order to be able to express interests at all requires being educated by that very institution with its axiomatic beliefs that subordinate. MacKinnon's quotation seems to capture such silencing in action: pornography determines the discourse of desire, its objects and its expression. If you want to participate – and you do because you are a sexual being seeking companionship – this is what you must say and how you must behave and by choosing to participate you agree to a certain set of desirable objects and practices.

The first of these 'silencings' is constituted by women's inability to express the content of their ideas, the second that their words have no consequence and the third that their speaking lacks the formal structure of doing. When a woman says, 'No', the existence of porn subordinates because her 'No' is a mere sound, or goes unheard, or it is taken as complicit agreement. It is one thing to talk about the philosophy of language but most political philosophers would have noticed a much more apt analogy between these three forms of silencing and the three dimensions of power proposed by Lukes (2005). One can have power over another when one's presence alters the way in which that person would have behaved. The presence of pornography gags women, were it not present they would speak openly because they know they do not want its subordination. One has power over another when that person knows what he or she wants but his or her interests are not treated as equal on the political agenda. The environmentalist may want to reduce the number of cars per family, but no political party exists to further these interests, so such interests are ignored and the individual's desires frustrated. The existence of pornography keeps the interests of women in a subjected position, as though they are not serious interests at all, merely the whims of the hysterical. The first two dimensions of power share a significant feature: they identify a fixed subject with known desires who has these desires frustrated. If the mugger had no knife, I would not want to give my money to him. I can sincerely say that if he had not been present, I would not have wanted to give away my wallet. Similarly, I know that I want cleaner air and that this can be achieved by reducing the cars on the road, but as no one can represent my interests, my wants go unfulfilled. I know what I want in both cases, but the presence of obstacles or absence of means through the will of others frustrates me. The fixed, female subject of these aspects of power is the target of Butler's critique. Where the third dimension differs is in the fact that the subject, by participating in activities or discourse, has his or her desires determined by what it is permissible to say or to do. If one wants to be liked by one's young friends, I must agree to be in their gang and obey the rules of what to wear and how to shake hands. As I do so, I am complicit in my own subordination; I will my own domination. What it means to be a 'sexual woman' (determined in no small part by pornography) may be the very acceptance of interests and wants that were the system not to exist, she would not want.

What is significant about changing the perspective from concerns with language to the concept of power is that silencing is revealed as the instrument of subordination. Pornography silences women from either expressing wants and interests they are aware of, or it silences them in such a way that the interests they would have, if pornography were inexistent, are consigned to the unconscious because they cannot find expression in the rational part of an agent's identity. And when Langton dismisses Ronald Dworkin's discussion of negative and positive liberty as a red herring, the possibility of considering the use of power in discourse disappears because she cannot talk about sincere and forced intentions, about a higher and an empirical self. Why she does so is perhaps because Langton fears falling into the Foucauldian or postmodern trap of seeing power as some sort of metaphysical given in discourse: a force that determines the barrier between the conscious and the unconscious and the formation of agents and intentions. Since her critique of liberalism is based on the misfiring of illocutions, this would undermine her whole approach. There is no reason to understand power as an exclusively productive force, though. Power is also a relation between agents or institutions and agents. And those agents have intentions prior to these relationships. Whether such intentions are due to other relations of power, or are fixed, or are transient, makes little difference. I am frustrated when I cannot satisfy my desires (to not have sex with you) or when I am unable to think or articulate what I would want for myself because someone has the power to determine my wants prior to my participation in their formation. The subject of pre-power creation is akin to the Sartrean for-itself that, if it denies the necessity of empirical engagement with others and the world, is guilty of one of his forms of bad faith (a point we shall return to in the next chapter) (Sartre, 1991). If pornography plays a role in such relationships, then perhaps there is a problem: the silencing perpetrated by pornography reinforces the subordination of a specific group (women).

With the concept of power now put into play, there are two ways to understand a limit on free speech: one, free speech is to say what you want without obstruction (negative free speech). What stops the agent from saying what they want are others who impede them either legitimately (with the State's approval) or illegitimately. Such exercises of power either impede or ignore the interests of individuals. The putative assumption is, given that we live in a liberal democracy, free speech is everywhere and one can say what one wants when one wants with very soft limitations. So, women are able to say 'No' if they want to (it's just that they don't), or they are able to lobby for prohibitions on materials they find offensive, but such lobbying is only a preference equal in weight to those who wish to consume or make pornography. Such free speech is threatened when the state wants to silence ideas that threaten its authority. Dworkin sees the defence of free speech as the defence of liberalism. Two, free speech is difficult because what you want to say is silenced before you speak. The limit to what one can say comes from culture, discourse and language itself which silences one through censorship. Censorship is everywhere and such censorship is legitimated by state techniques of deciding which utterances have value and which do not. Those that do not hardly count as speech; it is the speech of children, of lunatics and of women. Pornography maintains such censorship through the determination of the formal and substantial content of sex discourse: what one should like, how and when (and perhaps most importantly, with whom). Hence arguments against pornography are irrational, like political challenges to the *status quo*, or taken to be complicit endorsement. Putatively, the former position holds that women are just as free as others to speak and their preference just happens to contradict those of pornographers and hence the state (in a liberal democracy) must remain neutral and let both speak. The latter position, on the other hand, holds that speaking is already unfreedom, but all speaking is unfreedom so, thinkers of Butler's ilk will hold, the pornographer who subordinates can no more be blamed than the women who speaks can be lauded.

However, both positions are unacceptable exaggerations of real social existence. Langton uses the perfect example of Linda Boreman's (the actress Linda Lovelace) description of her own abuse at the hands of pornographers, which is received not as an expose, but as yet more pornography to titillate (Lovelace, 2006). What she wants to say can find no expression because it is taken to be material for arousal, though she is saying she hated it, she cannot be serious at all. When she says 'No', we all *know* it is a game of coquetry. Langton, though, is complicit in the structuring of the problem as a choice between polar opposites. By debating the problem in terms of simple speech-act theory, we are seemingly left with the choice between these two extreme opposites. By introducing the concept of power into the discussion, though, we can see how pornography may well be power as a relational concept (the first two dimensions), but also at the same time, as a productive force (the third dimension) without conceding the normative project: if it is an act of power in the first two dimensions, then there is a subject who is accountable; if it is an act of power in the third dimension, then there is a social and moral fabric which requires evaluation because a pre-power subject (as empty as such an entity may be) must either comply with or reject social meanings.

Ronald Dworkin understands the feminist claim that pornography silences women as a claim that pornography deprives women of the negative liberty to speak. He compares the feminist argument to the demand that everyone has a right to be heard sympathetically and in a liberal state everyone has the right to say what they wish. So, for example, people who believe the Earth is flat have a right to speak, and we respect them as persons who can articulate beliefs, but there is no corresponding right for the beliefs themselves. I can still hold that the belief that the world is flat is absurd, but that does not mean I can prohibit them from having the right to believe such absurdity and express it to others. To do so, to change their views and beliefs through political power, affects their positive liberty to speak and that is an attack on my valuing them as an equal. Pornography, holds the radical feminist, expresses beliefs that need to be silenced. A feminist inclusion of free speech, then, has to be a positive liberty claim. Women cannot determine themselves because they don't have the language – they are silenced. For Dworkin, you can't be silenced by the government in this way, because it is not liberal.

Langton's response is that the negative versus positive liberty debate is a red herring, but it is not so obvious that she is right. If the problem is one of power rather than purely speech-acts (which it has to be), then the silencing operated by pornography is about women determining themselves. Dworkin, for her, has a narrow conception of free speech: speech as freedom of locutionary act (asserting content) and he misinterprets the feminist claim as one about perlocutionary acts (the effects of asserting). This may well be correct and, if so, he ignores or does not engage with the real critique, that is the illocutionary claim. The woman who says 'No' but is taken to mean 'Yes' is not analogous to the flat-earthers because the silencing stops her from the illocutionary act of doing something, that is resisting the will of an other. Yet, it seems that both Langton and Dworkin make a mistake. He, because the feminist claim is not about locution or perlocution and hence saying what one wants when one wants, but about the illocutionay act of being able to do what she wants when she wants (we may respect the wills of those that assert the Earth is flat, but laugh at their ideas – with a woman, the right to say what she wants is not respected). The woman who wants to decide what to do with her body cannot; she is not respected as an equal because the existence of pornography limits the contents of her will and wants.

Consider how Langton develops the idea that pornography silences the illocutions of women through the creation of the limits of what can be said and when. She claims that fiction rest on a background of fact, hence we can learn from it but, given the nature of fictional works, the factual web that supports a work of fiction can generate mistakes in readers. First, a reader may mistake background for mere fiction (and does not learn what he should learn). For example, a novel about Africa may talk about the Nile flowing through Egypt, but the reader assumes it is a work about a parallel Earth with different geography and fails to 'learn' the location of the Nile. Second, a reader may mistake mere fiction for background (and learn what he should not); for example, that time travel is possible through worm holes. The latter would seem to be the case with pornography: the pornographic film asserts that 'Women mean "Yes" when they say "No".' Or, pornography may represent women as compliant yet coquettish and such a characterization is necessary for the narrative to function (hence is background) in the same way time travel is a necessary background for certain science fiction films, yet is fiction. As such, if the background structure is taken to be true, then pornographic films affect the possibility to enunciate (illocute) and the effectiveness (perlocute) of an act of dissent: 'Pornographers, we have suggested, are liars, or background liars, or background blurrers' (Langton, 2009: 194). Of course, Langton goes further (obvious from this quotation) in holding that the blurring is intentionally brought about by the agency of someone who has something to gain from such and such a mistake. Furthermore, it can be worse: some statements when delivered by the relevant authority make it thus and so. 'Guilty' delivered by a court may a wrong judgement, but what it does is make the accused guilty *de jure* and hence the *de facto* counts for nothing.[6] Pornography's silencing of women rests on a claim about the construction of social reality and that moves the critique to one about equality and objectification, not about free speech or speech-acts at all.

4.6 The silencing-subordination claim and its relation to objectification

It is perhaps pertinent to revise what we have learnt. The MacKinnon-Langton critique basically challenges Dworkin on the following point: it matters little what pornography 'says'. What matters is that it makes impossible equal concern and respect for individual members of a specific group (women). It does so against a social background of inequality and therefore perpetuates the subordination of this group. The silencing of women can only work against a background of subordination and is an act of power in that women are not allowed to articulate what they want not because they are obstructed from doing so, but because their wants are not considered worthy of equal respect, or because language and the discourse of sex make it possible for them to express their wants only at the cost of their own rationality. Pornography depicts a world which rests on a particular view of what a sexual women is in order to satisfy the interests of the non-woman. To say, though, that a decision has been taken by a will other than the woman's, that is, by the Male's wish to subordinate women in such a way, and to conceive of such an act as a momentary, ahistorical and precise act of will is to rely on a rather mythical, metaphysically problematic conception of the Male. It is not that the negative versus positive liberty debate is a red herring, it seems the whole free speech debate is a red herring. What matters is equality and not what is being said at all.

MacKinnon's argument is a legal one and not a moral one as such (1993: 71). It identifies what may be a metaphysical error (pornography is legally understood as speech when it is in fact an action) and traces out the legal consequences of this error: the conflict between free speech and a deeper commitment to equality. What is left unsaid is the Hegelian point of why we have free speech at all: in order to ensure equality and liberty for all individuals in the modern state. The concern for equality and liberty should almost always trump free speech and such a point of view is common to both Ronald Dworkin and his supposed opponents, the feminists. What is more, it is a peculiarly North American problem, where a true left agenda and defence of equality has never actually happened (MacKinnon, 1993: 87, 90).[7] Free speech is a problem because of the distribution of power. When MacKinnon discusses the proposed fascist march in Skokie, Illinois, free speech is used to defend the march, but equality and equality of groups' needs and races is not used to condemn it (1993: 82-5). There is a contrast between US formal equality (we are equal and thus possess equal rights under the law to protect individual space from violation) versus the United Kingdom or Canadian substantial model of equality, which is that power in society for historical and economical reasons is distributed unfairly and any laws and institutions of equality should seek to acknowledge and change this.

Yet even in MacKinnon's discussion, the figure of the original Male and His act of will is to be found. To attack the first amendment is to cut off one's nose to spite one's face, though. Dworkin's point is valid: if we agree on equality as a fundamental value, then once we start ascribing what can and cannot be said, then the best defence against inequality is seemingly lost. Dworkin sees the rise of radical feminism as an attack on liberalism as he conceives it (a monism where the be-all and end-all of moral and political discussion is value of liberty). He frames the debate as a repetition of the long-standing face off between conservatism and liberalism in which feminism is cast as the new form of conservatism. He is, in many respects, right to do so, but not in all respects. To cast it in such a way is too easy, we are all liberals now and to characterize feminists as illiberal is to swing the pendulum of rational weight too far in his own direction before the discussion has began. In some respects, though, feminists are conservative but in ways that they could recast themselves as the liberals to Dworkin's libertarianism. After all, liberals like the value of equality as well as liberty and do not, to a man, see it as reductive to the prior value of liberty *à la* Dworkin. Labels are doing some of the arguing for us and we should always be wary of that.

One way to comprehend the feminist worry about the existence of pornography is to compare it to Irish jokes. Since the Irish are always represented as foolish in English jokes, it has an influence on the agent's understanding of an individual who happens to belong to that group. One is more likely, due to unconscious associations brought about in early character development by these jokes, to prefer an English lawyer to an Irish one, contrary to equal opportunity. And such an association (as is clearly the case here) may well be ideology which requires reflection and refusal since it is due to historically conditional circumstances (such as the social exclusion of Catholics in British society). It could plausibly be argued that the representation of women in pornography reinforces and reproduces institutional inequality in that, when seeking advice, one is more likely to prefer a male lawyer to a female one. The existence of pornography obstructs the possibilities and opportunities of *all* women. This is Langton's ideal policy argument and puts it in line with the UK Race Relations Act in that pornography can subordinate and silence women because it is involved in the formation of rules governing the discourse of sexual relations and gender perception. It constructs a social reality in which the equal concern and respect for women's status is diminished.

Yet, the MacKinnon-Langton critique of the liberal tolerance of pornography is based on the claim that the existence of pornographic material reinforces the subordination of women through silencing. The techniques of the silencing are intimately bound up with the representations of women in pornographic films. Just as the person who refuses to participate in Irish jokes is cast as a killjoy because the jokes are 'harmless' and the person has 'no sense of humour' or they are even an example of 'political correctness gone mad', so the woman who denies that the representations in pornographic films are desirable is a prude, or frigid, or lying to protect her virtue. Women's expressions cannot be trusted, in short, unless they agree with the males and so, women are complicit in their own subordination. Such persons as refuse to play by the rules are excluded at the beginning of the game by what Langton calls, in her chapter on 'scorekeeping', the rules of accommodation (2009: ch. 8). Nussbaum demands that 'Feminists ... should ask whether women can really make progress in areas such as rape law and the prosecution of domestic abuse, when a jury of their peers has been raised on images that depict such abuses as exactly what women are about' (1999: 250). There is nothing specific to pornography about the representation of women and many hip-hop music videos are as demeaning in their objectification of women and their celebration of hierarchical relationships; 50 Cent's 'P.I.M.P.' being a prime example. Yet, these too could be the subject of moral judgement akin to the moral judgement of pornographic objects. So much the worse for hip-hop videos. The feminist, though, makes a stronger claim. She holds that there is a conceptual link between pornography and inequality, whereas it is only an accidental link in the case of music videos. Music videos can or cannot reinforce these relationships, whereas pornography cannot but reinforce these relationships.

Mill was well aware of the need for the constituent elements of culture to be rationally evaluated, notwithstanding his liberal credentials and his investment in methodological individualism as an explanatory theory in the social sciences. He argued 'that the principle which regulates the existing social relations between the two sexes – the legal subordination of one sex to the other – is wrong in itself, and now one of the chief hindrances to human improvement; and that it ought to be replaced by a principle of perfect equality, admitting no power or privilege on the one side, nor disability on the other' (Mill, 1869: loc. 7–10). It is not just in the interests of the subordinated sex, but in the interests of 'human improvement' that inequality is to be overcome. It needs to be overcome because a fraction of the population is subordinated and that subordination is perpetuated through a silencing carried out, in part, by the existence of pornography. An unequal culture is undesirable, one might quite sensibly hold, and inequality is perpetuated by the existence of pornographic material because of the identity of women is constructed as not trustworthy when she expresses her desires. As such, we are now concerned not with subordination (which pornography has not caused), nor directly with silencing (which is only subordination's means of execution), but the social reality of inequality and the identity of women in this social reality. It is to this discussion that we now turn.

Interlude 4 Baise-moi

Baise-moi is an artistic failure and it is undermined by a single one second frame around 52 minutes into the film. When T. S. Eliot (1997) described *Hamlet* as an artistic failure, he did so in the certainty that it would be controversial, that it would generate debate. I doubt the description of *Baise-moi* in a similar fashion even registers on the seismographs of literary criticism. Its failure, though, is for much the same reason as *Hamlet*'s failure (according to Eliot): cohesion. Hamlet's relationship with his mother is forced in the play, because we find no explanation of it, nor reason for it, neither in terms of an explanation nor in terms of a catalyst for the plot. It is a brute fact about the characters that has its origins extraneous to play and thus ruins the harmony of the whole. Or so Eliot would tell us, who seemingly forgets that people do have extraneous baggage and life itself is not cohesive. Who is to say that characters should not mimic reality?

As I have said, there is an element in *Baise-moi* in the 52nd minute which undermines the message of the film as a whole.

The film recounts the story of two objectified and brutalized women who are unable to recognize themselves in the categories of understanding imposed on them by society: poor; immigrant; woman; subservient; a sexual object; obliged to satisfy of man's desires and wills, owned by men, and so on. (The title has been translated into *Rape Me* in English rather than the more obvious *Fuck Me*, perhaps, oddly, to avoid censure and offence. The directors have objected to the former translation.) The characters' existence is bleak, meaningless and violent. The opening of the film illustrates how women, especially economically disadvantaged women are treated by men. They are waiting to be possessed, wanting it and ready for it when it is needed. Their sexuality can be bought (one of the characters is a prostitute) or represented (the other character has appeared in pornography films) and basically the world is one by which women as objects are constructed by the mentality of the consumer of contemporary pornography; hence what the women say is silenced (in graphically and brutally violent ways) and they are kept in subordinate positions (the initial rape scene is cleverly juxtaposed with a prostitution scene, making the viewer all too aware of the connection between physical threat and economic need). And the men remain uninterested in the women as women. When the boyfriend of Manu, the rape victim, learns what has happened to her, he blames her for wanting it and then becomes angry and seeks revenge, not for what they did to her but what they have done to him, since she was his.

It is this scene which is the catalyst for the plot. Manu kills her boyfriend and, simultaneously, the other central character, Nadine, kills her room-mate. Whereas the former is explicable in terms of the situation, the latter is purely arbitrary, but both express the wish that things be different. Killing is a liberation and empowerment for them and, after a chance meeting, they take on the roles of Bonnie and Clyde or Thelma and Louise. The violence and poverty of their prior existence makes the existential morality, the arbitrariness of social conventions of behaviour, which are binding only because we choose them to be so, materially real in a way that shames its playfulness in the white, bourgeois, male thinkers who scribbled the philosophy itself down. Once social conventions no longer bind them, they revel in the arbitrariness of their actions, the doing of things for the sake of doing them and the attempt at the creation of their own values (especially in the attempts to be witty killers and characters other than themselves).

Men are made to be subordinate, as are other women. Sex becomes theirs; they determine it, they decide it. The two characters are all that matter and we see the full deconstruction of male objectification in the scene where they copulate with two anonymous males in the same hotel room. The scene is voyeuristic and explicit, the activity pornographic, but what is of interest is that the camera turns to one of the anonymous males who states that it would be nice if the two women had sex with each other. In a pornographic film, such lesbianism for the sake of men, rather than for the participants themselves, is standard fare. The viewer expects it, it is part of the genre. Here, though, the male is sent from the room and excluded. He is dismissed. This is not about his pleasure, it is about theirs. The male who remains, who does what they want, is rewarded. At that moment, the male viewer is thrown reflectively on himself because that is what he had expected and wanted to see. But he is now, like the other anonymous male, excluded and cast away. (Similarly in another scene, when asked to perform oral sex, Manu vomits on the recipient, revealing the exact consequence of deep-throating to males.) The viewer feels shame and one perceives that the women for the first time take control of their own sexual desires and journey. The viewer is left to respond to them rather than, as a normal pornographic experience dictates, them responding to what we, the male, want.

The scene almost redeems the film, but not quite because in the next anonymous pleasure sex that Manu seeks, she makes herself into an object for a man. She is taken from behind, but the true failure is the use of the 'money shot', the ejaculation of the man on her buttocks outside of the vagina. A very familiar trope from pornographic films but it undoes the deconstruction hitherto employed in the film. Manu has become the object for the male and a particular male once more. The scene is unharmonious and has no justification in the film as a whole. It fails.

Baise-moi is an attempt at the cinematic deconstruction of expectations of unequal hierarchies employed in the representation of women in general and sexual activity in particular. It seeks to show that the structures which hold women in their social positions are both economic and sexual, but also fundamentally chosen by both the oppressors who benefit and the oppressed who, in displays of existentialist bad faith, seek to be what they are viewed as, and avoid the risk of being nothing. Inauthenticity is a choice and so being authentic must also be a choice. There is a way to resist what people expect, even if in the film that road is extreme violence. Ultimately, though, one brief one second frame undermines its whole objective.

5
Rae Langton's Photo: Domination, Subordination, Equality

5.1 Choosing photos

This chapter will begin rhetorically and a little bit ironically. Please do not fall into the trap of the indignant fool. There is a point to be made.

On the back of Langton's comprehensive and illuminating book on the subject of pornography is a small monochrome photograph of the author. The fact that it is black and white recalls Steve Pyke's portraits of philosophers, but there the resemblance stops. The image is a close up and out of focus. Having seen her in real life, the image is somewhat disingenuous: she is more handsome than she chooses to appear. Her mouth is moving. Langton is animated, in motion and, one surmizes, in conversation. She is the philosopher in action, doing what philosophers do, engaging in ideas. She is also a woman, but she obviously does not want femininity to distract from her 'philosophity'. No doubt she was happy with the choice of the photograph, perhaps sending it herself to the publisher.

What does this photograph tell us of her? That she is serious, unconcerned about her being captured unaware on film and, hence, apparently, indifferent to the aesthetics of her appearance. She is more interested in the ethics of her appearance – how she lives, in conversation – because this is more who she is than what she looks like, which is just what she seems. Langton is telling us who she is: a serious person of letters who happens to be a woman. Her photograph projects an image of her for us to interpret, but on her terms; by grasping the photograph we are brought to an understanding of who she is. She has subjectivized herself through an image, but the first step was the objectification of herself into the image and then the appropriation of it by us.

On my website is an image of me when I still had long, curly hair. I no longer do.

5.2 Agreeing with feminists, but disagreeing with their conclusions

There is a very famous article on the issue of abortion that utilizes an approach worth copying (Thomson, 1971). As with most debates in applied ethics, the choice of one's grounding normative theory is often determined by our pre-rational commitments to the conclusion we wish to support (although philosophers are loath to admit such a phenomenon). So, with the subject of abortion, if one is pro-choice, it is easiest to argue in terms of consequences and possible future welfare, whereas if one is (forgiving the rhetorical auto-designation) pro-life, then it is easiest to talk in terms of the person and their rights. What Thomson does is to allow the controversial statement that a foetus is a person to stand and still argue that this is insignificant if we consider the rights of the pregnant woman. She turns the debate on its head by agreeing with seemingly pro-life premises (about the personhood of the foetus), only to advocate a pro-choice position on the basis of individual rights. On the issue of pornography, feminists seemingly do the same thing: they agree with all the theoretical commitments that seem to justify a pro-pornography stance, only to come down against pornography. Whereas Thomson is critically subversive though, most feminists are flatly contradictory and rely on obscure metaphysical concepts to justify their arguments. In this chapter, I agree that pornography is objectifying, but at the same time I shall deny that any normative requirements follow from this.

Here is a very uncontroversial series of statements: all human beings have a right to liberty and also to physical integrity. The latter right can be understood as an ownership of their bodies. Consequent to these rights, is the right of human beings to use their body as they see fit and to deny access or use of their bodies as they see fit. Women are human beings. These are the basic tenets of any feminism, but one does not need to be a feminist (at least in any robustly theoretical sense) to concur with them. And, of course, to say that they are uncontroversial is a hostage to fortune for most philosophers out there who are, perhaps at this very moment, chomping at the bit to interject. But, it is very useful to remember that ethical discussion begins in the tutorial or seminar, and its most pertinent intricacies are interrogated there. Ethical statements, unlike those of epistemology or metaphysics, have to meet the standards of common sense in public discourse because they are not the prerogative of specialists or experts alone. To draw a rather fanciful analogy, pure mathematics has to concur with the mathematics that actually puts rockets on the moon, otherwise it is mere speculation and so ethical ruminations must at least offer themselves to the court of public judgement.

And it is in the court of public judgement that such basic feminism is uncontroversial. No one would want to contradict these statements and would do so only at the cost of his or her rationality and risk exclusion from rational debate. Of course, that 'one' who uncontroversially agrees must belong to a culture much like our own. It is a necessary fact that women are human beings. As human beings, it would be uncontroversial to assert that women can decide what to do with their bodies, how to use them and what labour to engage in for reward. And these statements are uncontroversial in a secondary way: they are actually supported by a constellation of religious and metaphysical doctrines. Kantian ethics and other, broader liberalisms would immediately support such statements. So, given these statements and their wide acceptance, it would seem feminists would see pornography as morally permissible without yet touching on its desirability or value. Pornography could be conceived of as valuable and worthwhile by feminists in the sense that it allows women to pursue well paid careers and to exhibit talents for fair reward or to develop personal projects.

Of course, some feminists do not think pornography, especially most examples of the genre, is permissible. And that, given all that was said above, seems initially odd. But the last chapter has shown us why. Women are equal to men in terms of worth and deserve equal moral concern but, in contemporary society, for traditional, historical and non-rational reasons, there is a residue of hierarchical inequality. Women are not paid equally, they have to prove themselves not just the equal but better than their male colleagues to succeed, their words carry less weight then their male peers and so on. The justifications of such inequality occur at the hidden level of the cultural subconscious, mixed up with religious echoes, poor medical understanding and supported by techniques of social coding and meaning. Part of the population is subordinated by the wishes and interests of the other: as a man, I benefit from higher pay, have an easier ride at work and have more putative authority in my words. This is unfair but to my interest.

Let us return to the example I touched upon in the last chapter concerning Irish jokes. Since the Irish are always represented as foolish in English jokes, then it has an influence on the agent's understanding of an individual who happens to belong to that group. One is more likely, due to unconscious associations brought about by these jokes in early character development, to prefer an English lawyer to an Irish one, contrary to equal opportunity. And such an association (as is clearly the case here) may well be ideology which requires reflection and refusal since it is due to historically contingent circumstances (such as the social exclusion of Catholics in British society). It could plausibly be argued that the representation of women in pornography reinforces and reproduces institutional inequality in that, when seeking advice, one is more likely to prefer a male lawyer to a female one. The existence of pornography obstructs the possibilities and opportunities of *all* women. So, the liberty of one woman to do what she wishes may well not be in her interest because it harms the conditions which are required for the realization of equality between the sexes. The techniques of subordination are played out through the identification of an individual with a trait that does not belong to her through the conventions which govern our understanding of others. In short, we objectify the individual according to general categories of meaning.

The inequality prevalent in society is perpetuated through techniques of subordination whereby individuals who belong to certain classes or groups are understood in a way that they have not chosen, nor do they recognize themselves in them. If they protest, their voices go unheard or are ignored. Objectification of persons then supports the silencing and subordination of these very objectified individuals:

> As pornography consumers, teachers may become epistemically incapable of seeing their women students as their potential equals and unconsciously teach about rape from the viewpoint of the accused. Doctors may molest anesthetized women, enjoy watching and inflicting pain during childbirth, and use pornography to teach sex education in medical school. Some consumers write on bathroom walls. Some undoubtedly write judicial opinions. (MacKinnon, 1993: 19)

The best argument against the existence of pornography – which is part moral and part political – is that the existence of pornography reinforces unjust inegalitarian relations between genders or reinforces subordination of women through objectification. The aim of this chapter is to agree with the claim that pornography objectifies women as a group and hence harms the individual, but to deny that the remedy for this is to prohibit or censor pornographic materials. Rather, the objectification of persons requires an aesthetic medium for the individual's overcoming of such determination. The argument that pornography needs to be prohibited or censored due to its necessary objectification of women seems to have much to offer, but ultimately rests on several problematic assumptions: one, it confuses a conceptual definition of pornography with a normative judgement; two, it does not consider that the inequality is as undesirable for males as it is for females; and, three, it rules out the possibility of any progressive or morally worthwhile pornography (even if permitting – or better, tolerating – certain forms) which could actually question and overcome the institutional inequality at the heart of contemporary pornography.

5.3 Objectification

What exactly is objectification? Colloquially, the accusation of objectification is perhaps most easily laid at the feet of the heterosexual male who prowls the nightclub in search of prey. He scans the women dancing before him, or standing by the bar, as the shopper in the supermarket 'ums' and 'ahs' before packets of detergent: this one is cheap, this one has three active ingredients, this one increases the shine; this one is a 'dead-cert', that one has nice tits, and so on. What he does is to behave towards the women in the same way we evaluate detergents, and such behaviour is unidirectional. You can objectify the women, but you cannot objectify the detergents. Objects cannot be objectified because they are objects through and through. Nor, as we shall see, are objects easily 'subjectified' – what we mean is that they cannot be sincerely anthropomorphized. There are cases of 'subjectification' and we shall see whether or not there is a problem here beyond the epistemic one: when my computer crashes, I hurl abuse at it, I take to it with my seldom used squash racquet and blame it for destroying my masterpiece (and leaving this poor copy of a text you are now reading before you). What is true, though, is that I am well aware that my behaviour is absurd, that the computer can no more be blamed than a slice of bread can be chastised for its flavour. I know that the computer is an object, my violent outburst is merely a way to diffuse my frustration and anger. I know that the computer is a thing and that I am making a category mistake when I ascribe certain properties to it, so at worse I am guilty of epistemic bad faith. However, from such bad faith, no moral normative consequences of worth follow, as they would if I were to demand that the police arrest the computer. What is significant about this attitude, though, is the parallel of the epistemic bad faith at the base of such 'subjectifying' and objectifying judgements and its origin in human interest and desire.

Let us return to our nightclub crawler. What is true about his comportment toward women is that he knows that they are subjects, but forgets (or represses, or denies, or undermines) such a status. His behaviour, if we were able to penetrate his barely articulate internal soliloquy, is reprehensible because of this fact: there is an appropriate way of understanding what is before him, a demand made by the nature of the thing to be known, that he, because it suits his interests, or just because he can, given the structures of his consciousness, revels in denying. And unlike the computer, moral consequences follow from his epistemic bad faith: the computer can be understood wrongly: this is neither here nor there for the computer but it is very significant for the women to be understood as they are. The women must feel, quite rightly, that he is treating them as objects (or even as an object!) and they could, again quite rightly, demand that he stop.

It is worth noting how quickly the colloquial understanding of objectification requires philosophical elucidation. One wonders whether it was a philosophical concept through and through which was dragged into lay discourse just because of its sheer appropriateness.[1] The radical feminist tradition of objectification attempts to cast the objectification of the female by the male in terms of simply treating a subject as a thing (MacKinnon, 1993; A. Dworkin, 1981). As such, the tradition's indebtedness to an unlikely figurehead is apparent, that is the moral position of Immanuel Kant. The second formulation of the categorical imperative, which we have previously noted as peculiarly apt to discussions of pornography, reads: '*act that you use humanity, in your own person as well as in the person of any other, always at the same time as an end, never merely as a means*' (Kant, 2012: 4:433). The behaviour of the nightclub prowler is wrong because he uses the women as a means-merely: they are to be consumed for his own sensuous arousal unbeknownst to them. He does not ask permission or seek consent. He treats them as objects on the shelf of the supermarket knowing full well they have the capacity to resist (or to concede) his determination of them as tools for his own use.

For the radical feminist, objectification is bad because it cuts women off from full self-expression (it silences them) and self-determination (it subordinates them). Just as Irish jokes internalized in early childhood may later play a subconscious role in deliberations of adults and harm the self-determination and self-development of Irish individuals, so pornography, the challenge goes, creates a social and conceptual framework and the conditions of knowing whereby the objectification of women by men becomes an easy repression, as though the epistemic bad faith is always already present in the pre-understanding of men. The history of early pornography films determines the audience and the hierarchies of domination: stag night films where women were excluded. It creates an ideality of a male subjectivity and female objectification: the point of view or gonzo approach is nascent in these early stag films and the mechanisms of voyeurism feature heavily. The gonzo trope feigns a subjective possession of an object before the viewer, it attempts to immerse the viewer in a situation so that he or she becomes the actor holding the camera. The woman remains an object before the viewer. And unlike other film genres this structure has yet to be undone or subverted. The pre-understanding of the Irish is as fools and the pre-understanding of women is as never saying what they mean or not being truly aware of what they want. Women, if asked, would have the choice of dissent (of having a voice) or acting as they wished (being able to determine themselves). With Irish jokes, the Irish would have an equality in consideration when applying for jobs. Pornography is therefore morally bad. And it is morally bad, once more, for Kantian reasons relating to the person and his or her rights.

According to Nussbaum, the designation of objectification as a practical activity of a mind is a cluster-concept involving seven, possibly related, aspects (1999: ch. 8). Under some of these aspects it can be good or bad depending on the context and, perhaps, under some of them it is *always* bad. She does, however, depart from traditional feminism by admitting something more than problematic for it: being an object for others can be a wonderful sexual experience, so it cannot always be bad. Her question is simple: is treating a subject in these ways a priori bad or is it relative to the circumstances and context of the objectification? A visit to the doctor for an infection will reduce 'me' to a body part (the infected one, I hope) and to a natural organism. The doctor sees me as nothing more than connected tubes and mechanisms with fancy Latin names. Yet, such objectification is permissible given the context. If objectification is of this nature, then Nussbaum wonders whether we are looking at the wrong concept. Langton (2009: ch. 10) adds three more aspects and it is perhaps pertinent to list all ten before discussing them. In the following list, one to seven are from Nussbaum and eight to ten from Langton: *I treat a subject as an object when I see him or her as ...*:

1. a tool to further my own interests (instrumentality);
2. lacking autonomy and self-determination (denial of autonomy);
3. lacking agency and/or activity (inertness);
4. interchangeable with other objects of the same or other types (fungibility);
5. something that it is permissible to break up, smash or break into, lacking in boundary integrity (violability);
6. as something that can be owned, exchanged (ownership);
7. whose feelings and experience need not be considered (denial of subjectivity);
8. reduced to his or her body or parts of the body;

9. reduced to his or her appearance;
10. being silenced by the conditions of my perception.[2]

The paradigm example of objectification is perhaps the institution of slavery where a subject is reduced to the mere tool of his or her master. It also works as an example to link objectification to subordination: by reducing your subjectivity to an objectivity, I make you an object of my will and hence deny your freedom to decide and act for yourself. Reading Aristotle's *Politics* which divides the natures of humans into masters and slaves and describes how slaves benefit from the superior decision making of the masters, we could see an epistemic mistake with normative consequences (1912: 1252–1255). The basic fact is that for someone who belongs to a economically privileged class and has an interest or a want in the use of the free or cheap labour of others, then non-critically following Aristotle's argument reinforces what we want to believe, it allows us to satisfy our interests more simply by employing a form of epistemic bad faith. The psychological repression required for our interests to be satisfied is that much easier. Pornography serves a similar function to Aristotle's ideology. It depicts subordination and perpetuates such subordination in the same way that ideologies such as the Great Chain of Being, Laissez Faire-ism, Electivism and so on depict and perpetuate classism, racism and other political hierarchies.

However, let us begin with a less controversial example and concentrate on my brief nightclub narrative. Let us assume our nightclub crawler is an avid consumer of pornography and because this depicts women as objects and as meaning what they do not say, he finds it easier to believe this about women because it helps to satisfy his own sexual preferences. Looking first at Langton's eight and nine, we can see that this is in fact a correct description of what the prowler is up to: he is reducing the women to their bodies or to their appearance. In fact, there is no difference between these: when we say he is reducing the women to their bodies, we do not refer to him as a anatomist who sees persons as bodies, bones, arteries and organs, nor to the photographer who uses bodies and limbs (without consent) in picture compositions, nor as the painter who sees the model as limbs and torso. It is the way in which he reduces women to their bodies: either as parts or as their appearance as an embodied whole (and this is what truly separates the anatomist from the prowler, because the latter makes a normative judgement and that is what is meant surely by 'appearance').

The reduction to appearance is not in itself something undesirable. One does so day in and day out and much labour depends on being reduced to an appearance (the model, the maitre d', the shop assistant and so on). We care about ensuring our children do not go to school with the stains of *ragù* on their white tee-shirts from lunch the day before. What is wrong is that our prowler reduces the women to *mere* (there's that word again!) appearance and thus denies their autonomy, denies they are something more or something beyond his apprehension of them (and this is Langton's empowering sense of objectification). He fully represses the epistemic mistake of seeing them as objects because he knows that if he were to ask (in most cases) the women would object to his ogling. Or, at least, he is not prepared to risk the satisfaction of his interests by seeking consent. So, putting to one side number ten for now, it is not clear what Langton's other two aspects add beyond elucidation (which in itself is not to be ignored). What they seem to entail is a denial of autonomy in that the person before me is not, for me, a person but a mere appearance because if they were a person I would have to ask if they minded being evaluated on their mere appearance.

The nightclub prowler, though, is also guilty of denying the personhood of the women by perceiving them as fungible or interchangeable. Like the detergents, he makes comparisons based on their appearance and features which can be compared: their breasts, their legs, their faces, their clothes and so on. He is using a type of instrumental practical reason (not a million miles wide of a bizarre egoistic hedonist calculation) that denies the very central value of personhood. We object to such treatment because we like to believe that we have value because we are individual persons with our own desires, projects and tastes. I cannot be reduced to just a number as Patrick McGoohan was wont to inform us. There is a principle at stake here and our moral perturbation stems from this: an individual is an individual and ought to be treated as such.

However, there are many instances which are seemingly morally legitimate in which the individual is not treated as an individual. There are legitimate ways of object-making such as the social scientist who sees individuals as atoms that obey certain laws. Much utilitarian social policy is of this sort: education policies, distribution programmes and so on. Before political libertarians see this as grist to their mill (no pun intended), there is a much more obvious case in point: advertising. I am categorized by a label which relates to my age, my gender, my geographical location, my income, my sexuality and my familial situation (plus many other factors). For the advertising company, I am interchangeable with any other member of my set. Is there any difference between the objectification of the nightclub prowler and the advertising company? One may want to bite the bullet and say no and demand an end to such categorization wholesale, but there is an interesting point to be made here: one could plausibly argue that there exists a mutual, accepted agreement between me and the advertising company because by categorizing me they can better inform me of products which may be of interest to me rather than those that are not. In short, they respect what I probably want and desire even if they do not ask me (or ask me directly). The nightclub prowler differs because he does not assume any sort of proxy agreement on the part of his 'categorizations'. He engages in an objectifying attitude, that is viewing persons as a mere tool or as a body part. The aim of his categorization is purely egoistic; either immediately through the pleasure of perceptual consumption or mediately in terms of what he would use the women for. His objectification, then, consists not solely in the interchangeable nature of the women for him, but also in the denial of their inwardness (desires, preferences), their autonomy and their reduction to a use for him as an instrument to his own pleasure.

So far, then, we have seen how objectification involves a cluster of overlapping epistemic attitudes (for want of a better word) that allow us to repress an error at the base of our practical attachment to the world. I understand a hammer before I pick it up (I have to in order to pick it up by the handle and not the head!) and this allows me to use it in an appropriate way. I might not know what a hammer is and use it the wrong way round, with some success, but it impairs my capacity to act in the world. By consuming pornography, one may view women as to be used, as objects, but such treatment of the female results in normative consequences: one denies them an essential part of autonomy, the capacity to agree or not to participate in one's plans. And as such, one subordinates them through a denial of their autonomy (Number 2) because they are solely material (Numbers 1,3,8 and 9), have no inner life worthy of consideration (Number 7) or are interchangeable with others and thus have no intrinsic worth as an individual (Number 4). Only when such attitudes are in place – much like only when we have accepted Aristotle's argument about differences in kind between human beings – can we see such things as to be owned and once owned, exchanged, destroyed, broken and so on. In short, Numbers 5 and 6 are, it would seem, consequences of objectifying attitudes and not actual objectifying attitudes. The final attitude of silencing is also a consequence of the objectifying attitude: only when I deny your own self-determination can I truly and sincerely believe that I know better than you what you meant when you uttered words; only when I see you as an object can I hold that your remonstrations and denials are actually playful affirmations every time you deny that they are. And as we have seen silencing is just a form of subordination: it is the negation of the practical will of the agent in order to satisfy the will of he or she who has power.

There is no way that the nightclub prowler when asked to respond with sincerity would ever express such views, but it is clear that in the nightclub he does repress what he knows in order to satisfy his interests. And we have all done something similar. What pornography does, according to radical feminists, is make possible the repression of the knowledge that women too are agents with their own desires, preferences and will and also the capacity to communicate such wants. Pornography makes it easy for the male to reduce women to the status of child, lunatic or animal. These are things that seemingly express what they want but they are simplistic – we (the males) know really what they want (Williams, 1981: 58). For Nussbaum, the crucial understanding of objectification is instrumentality and we see the seeds of this in Aristotle as well as Kant: I know what is best for you and it is best that you serve my interests otherwise you, as an individual, will suffer. Langton disagrees and, for her, autonomy denial is the empowering concept.[3] Pornography subordinates and silences women through objectification in that the male represses his knowledge that the woman is an autonomous agent with her own desires, projects and wishes. It allows him more easily to operate the epistemic bad faith necessary for autonomy denial. Langton firmly belongs to the Kantian and not the Aristotelian model: for Kant, there is something about sexual activity which makes it override our seeing others as ends and can only be regulated by institutional marriage. Practical activity becomes confused and unreliable because desire is central to sexual activity and desire is individual and not rational (Kant, 1963: 163-4).[4] According to a simplistic reading of Kant, our nightclub prowler would be able to treat the women as their own masters only if he were not sexually interested in them. His desire for them to be objects then rests on the plausibility of willing to believe the fact that they are not subjects. If a system of knowledge can be erected that can, first, determine what the women should want and thus what it is to be a woman (think of magazines that prescribe how to be sexy, how to catch your man); second, map this on to a want of women (to be part of society, to be like everyone else) and, finally, supply this want, then women have become complicit in their own domination. In order to be normal, to be desirable (and this is what they want), they must becomes what the system of knowledge demands them to be. The true subject, the Woman, can exist outside this system of rationalization, but her wants are inarticulate (she is weird, she is not normal). She is silenced so she can be subordinated: by wanting to be ogled, she agrees to her own inequality before men, her own objectification. A true f*ait accompli*.

5.4 Projection and social reality

Langton, therefore, notices that it is not objectification itself, or solely, which grounds the feminist critique. For her, the role of projection is of equal importance whereby a reality of known objects is constructed by the mind in order to perpetuate an epistemic system which serves not truth but human interests. Of course, in our social reality, such interests are not universally human, but specifically male: 'Women's oppression stems from the operation of large-scale psychological or linguistic forces, shaped by unconscious and irrational desires, or shaped by the structure of language itself, a "language of the fathers"' (2009: 242). Projection of this sort is a conglomeration of various techniques which all generate beliefs on the basis of desire (rationally the wrong direction) and beliefs begin to fit desire rather than the other way round. She is keen to trace such social, epistemic construction to the Scottish Enlightenment thinkers, culminating in Hume (2009: chs. 11 and 14). However, such constructions of social reality and knowledge systems through the power of human interests and desires is central to at least two other traditions: one, the pluralist Italian tradition and especially its apex in Vico, as well as, two, the more widely recognized post-Kantian idealism of the German tradition, most notably in the thought of Hegel and, more controversially, to a lesser extent, in Marx.[5]

Intuitively objectification would seem to be a problem because it falsely represents reality: the content of the propositions claim that women are not agents or are not subjects. Objectification is a result of desires and interests forming beliefs. However, there are other, less morally controversial, propositions which are normative in nature and *cause* reality to be what it is. In the mid seventeenth century in Europe, for example, a claim that had its origins in Christianity began to surface: all humans are equal. It was clear that as a statement of fact, this was (and perhaps still is) false but, rather, it was the declaration of a moral and political project which would play out over the next four hundred or so years. What the people who held this claim wanted was a world in which this was true and through political activity, rebellion and revolution, they made such a statement more or less true in the construction of institutions which would guarantee the equality of agents. They made the world become what they wanted it to be. The desire then became a truth. The internal sentiment that all humans are equal confers a value on an object (members of a lower class, women, slaves) which strives to be taken seriously as an objective feature of the object. Or, the desire for something to be thus and so generates the belief that something is thus and so (so the desire for equality actually makes us believe people are equal). However, projected desires can also be negative. One, the desire of men for women creates the relationship between perpetrator and victim in that the woman is cast in the role of 'wanting' or 'asking' for it, a stereotype all too prevalent in much unreflective pornographic material. Two, the commodification of women's sexuality through pornography is a way of creating the coding of desirable women, so that the desires of men are reproduced and complicity accepted by women who wish to be desired (in order to further their own interests). If the women want to have their own interests satisfied in our society, then they must conform to what society expects them to be.

Let us concentrate, though, on two other cases first. One, the statement that 'all humans are equal', cannot be linked to an objective fact in any simple sense which correlates, or does not, with the statement. Moral reality is constructed through and through. In reality, people are not equal and so I therefore labour on the world to make this the case: I demand institutions which ensure the fair treatment of individuals as individuals and not as members of specific economic classes, races or genders. Desires cannot seemingly make other things true in the same way. Two, I really want to believe in Santa Claus and become fixated on the idea that the impersonator at Fenwick's grotto in December is, in fact, Santa Claus. My desire for there to be a Santa Claus generates the belief that he is Santa Claus and my willingness to dote on him confers on him the very values of Santa Claus: generosity, patience and kindness. Yet such a belief is untenable because he will take off his costume and he won't come to my house on Christmas Eve. Reality has a tendency to crush inappropriate beliefs. Not least because he may well deny he is actually Santa Claus, claiming instead that he is Bob who works nights in the ice-cream factory. Yet, I ignore that. I take his words to be those of play, denying what he actually is in order to keep his secret. I silence him by not letting his words mean what they mean. I can act in the world to make this true only at the expense of his freedom of will: by forcing him to be Santa Claus, to live eleven months of the year in Lapland and to descend down every chimney on Christmas Eve.

Sexual objectification falls between these two extremes. Our nightclub prowler illustrates this point perfectly. He has a belief that women are agents with wills of their own and the consequence of such a belief frustrates his desire to take non-consensual delight in their mere appearance or in treating them as objects of consumption. To further his interests, it would be better that they were mere objects subject to his will and choice, without desires and an inner life of their own. To view them in this way requires epistemic bad faith: he must repress the knowledge that they are subjects and hope that this repression is not revealed to him at an inopportune moment. Feminists would claim that his consumption of pornography (amongst other social institutions and conventions) allows him to perform his master-stroke of epistemic bad faith, to create the neurosis akin to that of the Santa Claus believer. What separates them is that the Santa Claus believer is vulnerable to the revelation that his belief is false because the world will not conform to his desires, whereas the male fabricated world of social reality, according to the feminist, maintains and supports the epistemic bad faith of the nightclub prowler. His belief is not vulnerable in the same way because it is shared and being shared with his peers:

> Pornography's knowledge *is* harm, because the creation of knowledge, through pornography, and the objectification of women by pornography are two sides of the very same phenomenon. On MacKinnon's way of thinking, pornography is a certain kind of self-fulfilling projection. That is what makes it a source of knowledge, and that is what makes it a kind of objectification. Part of the harm is in the *shape* that is projected: the vision of what women are like – servile, inferior, less-then-human. And part of the harm is also in the *shaping*, the fact that the projection becomes, in the contexts of oppression, a self-fulfilling one. (Langton, 2009: 307)

Langton embellishes her feminist critique of pornography by bringing to the fore pornography's role in projection with a rather rhetorical thought experiment (2009: 261-266). She imagines a conspiracy designed and implemented by, one assumes, an evil, male genius whereby the origins of the need to see women as objects is separated from that need and given the convincing veneer of naturalistic science. Moreover, the limits and rules of what constitutes science is set by the same male genius who also dictates what is to count as evidence that confirms or falsifies a belief. Over a period of time, the cultural and social institutions of the world created by this genius will begin to actually confirm these propositions as truth: if a certain race is kept in slavery for a period of generations and excluded from education, then such a race will *in fact* exhibit the properties of servility and dependence. What we are presented with is the creation of knowledge by a desire-driven being who is best characterized as the ur-Father of feminist critique. The world has been made male through and through, for the desires and interests of the male, and the woman, if she is to speak at all, is to speak in the language of the male.

Like the projection of desires on the world, though, such a process, if one strips the rhetoric from Langton's example, is neither negative nor positive intrinsically. It is the construction of the social conditions of knowledge consistent with accounts found in thinkers such as Vico, Nietzsche, Freud and the German idealists. Unsurprisingly, we turn to the most prominent of the latter group, that is Hegel, to offer a neutral description of knowledge construction, cultural institutions and progress in order to show that human interests and desires can form the historical basis of moral values. The aim of the following excursus into idealism and moral projection is to understand Langton's thought experiment couched in a supporting philosophical theory and to reveal that the requirement of male interests in an original event of domination is not the main moral problem.

5.5 Hegel's moral idealism and progress through projection

Hegel's absolute idealism and historical dialectical progression is a neutral account of how ideas and human interests shape political institutions, moral systems and the world. Truth in this case follows belief and the direction of fit is from the human mind to the world itself and not, as is most commonly believed, from reality to what we believe. His absolute idealism originates in the appropriation and reformulation of Kantian transcendental idealism which, itself, was an attempt to overcome the epistemological limitations of realism (most commonly understood as either empiricism or rationalism). Let us begin with the intuitively most plausible account of belief formation in order to draw out what is at stake here, that is empiricism.[6]

According to the simplest form of empiricism, beliefs are a response to the causal effect of reality in the knowing world. In short, I believe there is a red table before me because light has reflected off a surface and has entered my retina setting off a chain of causal relationships that form the belief in my mind. The representation in my brain of the 'red chair' stands in for something in reality that is causally efficacious and constitutes knowledge (under the right conditions). The truth theory rests on an assumption that the perceptual faculties adequately and appropriately represent the world, but why do we assume that our perceptual faculties adequately represent the world? One can justify the faculties of knowing only by making an appeal to some other story: God's providence, evolution, *et cetera*, yet none of these can be justified in the terms of empiricism itself. They are not verified by simple sense-data nor propositions that correspond to real objects empirically understood. So, the epistemological investment in the adequacy of perceptual faculties is either an assumption or justified by metaphysical theories, but in either case the ground is beyond the simple verification processes of empiricism. Empiricism, in short, cannot articulate a convincing account of the subject–object relation without assuming that perceptions are just adequate and appropriate to the task.

Kant overcomes this problem by more or less ignoring the problem of reality and making the human mind active rather than passive in the construction of propositional content. Intuitions are 'given' to the mind, but the mind actively engages in the world at the same time in a form of behavioural filtering. The mind applies categories to the intuitions such that they can be propositional knowledge: the object before me *to be an object* must have form, substance, quantity (be one), quality (for example, a colour) and so on. Unless we understand objects in these ways, then there cannot be objects at all and hence no knowledge. These categories or ways of understanding the world originate in the rational mind itself and not from reality.

However, one might object, that the same problem arises: how does one know that these categories are adequate to represent the world? The answer was extremely radical: truth is no longer correspondence with an external reality – these categories do not need to be adequate to represent the world. Since these categories are hard-wired into a rational mind (according to Kant his transcendental arguments have shown that knowledge is only possible on the basis of the possession of these twelve categories), truth is no longer about correspondence with an external reality, but consensus with other rational agents. If knowledge is now understood as *how* a rational being would perceive the object (how it would appear for rational beings in general), then we can still assign the value of truth: things are empirically real if it is how a rational subject would construct the object; if rational beings would judge it to be thus and so. And since for Kant reason is universal – the same for all minds, at all times, in all places – we will all form the same judgements if we are not partisan, irrational or in error since the categories are hard-wired in the mind. Error arises from using the wrong categories, applying metaphysical errors by using categories that do not exist and from false reasoning. (And reasoning is susceptible to the problem of desire, and for this reason Kant does not like sex: it makes us reason badly and on a particular rather than a universal level, sex is a virus which corrupts thinking and relations between rational agents.)

Hegel, like thinkers before and after him, does not exclude human interests and desires from the construction of knowledge: it is because we *want* the world to be rational that our desires make the world thus and so for us.[7] Neither does he see the twelve categories, those of the rational being rather than the particular, historical individual, as being adequate to the task Kant assigns them: for propositions to have content, many more historically relative concepts and meanings are to play a role in the agent's reasoning. Unconstrained by the universality of reason, though, truth once more becomes problematic. If propositions are not constrained by the imperative to correspond to reality nor the imperative to cohere with propositions which *all* rational beings can assert, then they can be different for different cultures and societies. The position raises the problem then of how one might claim that modern physics is better or truer than mediaeval physics; or whether there can be an external standard by which one can judge the adequacy of these meanings and categories. Ignoring the epistemological question and concentrating on the ethical problem, one can offer a response to his problem. Hegel holds that moral categories and concepts, axiomatic prescriptions such as equality and freedom, are necessary in order for the subject to have moral experience. However, as abstract concepts they are too formal to dictate substantial obligations and these can only arise from the content of a specific way of life with its implicit description of what is good (interests, welfare, respect). Hence his reworking of Kant's transcendental idealism. So, one can formally state equality for all, but substantially one must say what equality entails (opportunity, respect, or resources) and to whom it is to be extended (members of my nation, human beings, rational agents). Hegel's point is that this will be supplied by or be a product of my social context or moral fabric and not the workings of practical or pure reason (Hegel, 1971: §§507–516). And this seems to open his position to the charge of relativism.

Different cultures have different approaches to building houses. In Japan, for example, there are next to no arches. Now, there is no correct way to build a house, rather a constellations of approaches that serve the interests of those for whom the edifice is constructed (be it shelter, entertainment, celebration, and so on). These techniques are passed down from generation to generation and they change with innovation, the emergence of new technology, and contamination from other cultures. Such progress makes one revise and reject building approaches of the past. One could build 'blind' as it were, that is build a house with no glance at the tradition of building but guided only by an understanding of the laws of applied mathematics. Such a builder might get lucky, but he really ought to look at how buildings have been built in the past and recruit a very experienced builder if he wants to be successful. What is rational has form (the conceptual cognition of philosophy) and content (reason as substantial essence). This content is justified through its historical development and existence, and it is passed down from generation to generation (Hegel, 1991: Preface). Ethics is more akin to building than science: ways of life supply one's moral obligations, but such obligations may become obsolete or inconsistent when new moral problems cannot be adequately articulated or comprehended by the existing moral structures of experience. Inconsistencies between the moral categories and the substantial content of a way of life can arise internally (problems of abortion, for example, that puts a strain on the religious origin of most moral precepts) or externally (the idea of intellectual property rights and non-capitalist, indigenous people when a pharmaceutical company chooses to use the people's knowledge for profit), and *progress* occurs due to these conflicts. Moral concepts, value and meanings are rationally redefined by the process of historical development. The task of philosophy is to become aware of this change and not to instigate it. The relationship between mind and the world itself fires the change.

To make sense of the idea of progress, one needs to reference the enigmatic aphorism which somehow embodies the difference between normal idealism and absolute idealism: 'What is rational is actual;/ and what is actual is rational' (Hegel, 1991: 20). Kant's idealism holds that intuitions are the content of experience but that experience is structured by the subject. This corresponds to the second part of the aphorism, the actual has to be rational in order to be experienced. Hegelian absolute idealism differs in that not only does the content of experience have to have a rational structure, but the rational structure of the mind must correspond to the real structures of reality: what is rational has to be actual. (Put flippantly, an agent can freely impose another theory of gravity on the world and this will allow him to have consistent experience, but it might hinder him when he wants to walk off a cliff or build an aeroplane.) The difference between normal idealism and absolute idealism hinges upon the relationship between intuitions and knowing: with the former, intuitions are passive and knowing active; with the latter, intuitions and knowing are in a reciprocally active relationship. And the litmus paper for a set of beliefs about the world is human interest and practical activity: if I believe the world to be thus and so, will my interests be satisfied? A moral principle is not a simple assertion, but a prescription – it determines the way in which the knowing subject structures experience. For Hegel, this is a reciprocal process: our categories of understanding must be adequate for us to labour in the world, and reciprocally the world has to live up to our categories – especially the moral ones. His idealism is described as absolute because one day the subject's categories of knowing will adequately fit the world and the world will have been made rational, by labour, in order to correspond to such categories and this is guaranteed by his philosophy of history, which embodies the concept of progress.

Hegel's historicist philosophy opens a space for an immanent critique of current social structures. The existing state of affairs, that is the contemporary and real structures of society, its practices, institutions, conventions and laws can still fail to be actual. They may exist but not be fully rational. Social reality can fail to be actual in that it is a mere appearance and contradicts what is essential to the state. Take, rather pertinently, the issue of sexual equality. Women may have been given the right to vote in 1918, but law itself could not express the will to freedom until such time that the structures of the family changed and institutions and policies were introduced to give them economic freedom. Without these social transformations, the majority of women voted as their economic masters (the male, the father, the husband) told them to do (De Beauvoir, 1969: 689). Progress is made possible by the demand that a law be comprehended. What is the rationality of the law in giving women the vote? It is to express the principle of liberty conceived of as autonomy. Yet, without social structures changing, this is a hollow law since it does not achieve what it should. And this is not to be underestimated as a form of social critique: the divine right of kings remained in place and lingered on as an ideology long after the waves of change instigated by Italian humanism and the Reformation began to shape the world with the implicit demand for equality. Even in the eighteenth century, political writers were still concerned with dismissing the idea of divine prerogative as a viable account of political obligation. For Hegel, this would be an example of the need to make actual what is rational.

So, let us return to Langton's accusation of a male conspiracy behind the construction of knowledge. If one takes seriously the sort of moral idealism consistent with Hegel's account above, then we can see how desire and human interest lie at the origin of moral prescriptions and concepts. Human needs dictate what is right or wrong in the first instance. Metaphysical and religions systems are then built to rationalize these prescriptions separate from the human need which gave birth to them. Imagine, to live in a group, one must pass part of one's produce to the group itself. Together, through cooperation, we can live more comfortably. But certain individuals are lazy, some work too hard and so on. Conflict will arise, so religious prescripts are put in place to explain why we must give away some of our produce to the group and why it is important to rest at times. Such explanations make no reference to the human need for cooperation and are evidenced through religious data: the coming of the seasons on a regular basis, the vision of the Shaman and so on. As new problems appear or new encounters are made, these beliefs develop. This seems to be a valid account of moral reality and it is ultimately about whether the human needs and desires at its origin are satisfied. That such systems are not wholly rational, that certain individuals are privileged, that others are excluded, is something that history must confront. If Langton's critique requires that, at the origin of moral development, the Father and his male friends grouped together in a deliberate manner to exclude women from the sovereignty of reason, then the idea of an original *intention* to exclude women made by an individual or individuals and reproduced each generation by all males would mean we could identify our wrongdoer. Moral values, though, are the products of an historical narrative which is far from coherent. These values are rationalized by engagement, which is what philosophy seeks to do. What Langton's critique reveals is that inequality is a by-product of historical development and that it should now be confronted. Moral accountability moves from the original intention to exclude certain individuals to satisfy specific interests (which remains conjecture) to the claim that the behaviour of individuals reinforces and maintains a system of inequality. The existence of pornography, then, is one of the tools which allows the perpetuation of these interests of a specific group at the expense of others.

5.6 The feminist claims about objectification

The feminist claim that pornography objectifies may well be true, but only in so far as any aesthetic media objectifies. Pornography cannot but objectify given the nature of what it is. The question is whether or not it objectifies in a way that results in negative normative consequences for individuals or groups. Take, for example, Bram Stoker's presentation of the West African servant, Oolanga, in *Lair of the White Worm*. It is without doubt offensive, the character's face being: 'unreformed, unsoftened savage, and inherent in it were all the hideous possibilities of a lost, devil-ridden child of the forest and the swamp – the lowest of all created things that could be regarded as in some form ostensibly human' (Stoker, 1911: loc. 256). Stoker's presentation is racist because he uses putative generalities of race to determine the particular aspects of an individual character to confirm contemporary widespread ideas about a specific race. We are not presented with an individual, but with a type, and particular claims about an individual character are referred to general claims about his race. Such a presentation constitutes 'background lying' and makes it easier for subjects to form beliefs about other races that are in their interest rather than true.

Both Stoker, in particular, and pornography, in general, utilize 'background lying' in order to make the reader mistake mere fiction for background and hence learn what he or she should not (Langton, 2009: 194). In both cases, what he or she learns supports attitudes towards race and gender respectively by creating the conditions for the epistemic bad faith of denying that a particular individual is an individual. If we read Stoker unreflectively, we may form attitudes towards West Africans determined by perceiving them as savage and violent. If we listen to Irish jokes as a child, we may believe that the Irish are characterized by a higher than average foolishness and treat the individual Irishman in front of me as a fool without realizing it. With pornography we may form the belief that women enjoy rape, that when they say no they actually mean yes or, less rhetorically, we may learn that the roles in the power relationships between the genders are 'naturally fixed' in a male–female hierarchy rather than the result of artificial, cultural transformations.

Does pornography *necessarily* do the same thing with gender that Stoker does with race? What is truly at stake in the feminist critique of objectification are two claims:

1. the existence of pornography creates, maintains and informs social and cultural conditions of understanding such that it easier for knowing subjects (both male and female) to perform the epistemic bad faith required to objectify persons belonging to a specific set;
2. such objectification has negative normative consequences in that it undermines the moral value of a subset of persons by reinforcing inequality (subordinating) and denying the autonomous and rational status of this subset (silencing).

Hence, we see how objectification plays a role in the moral problematic of pornography. We now have an unholy triangle of objectify-subordinate-silence in much the same way that religious ideologies have, in the past, obfuscated debates about the moral status of the stranger, the foreigner, the other, the child, the animal and the woman. The existence of pornography, like the wearing of specific items of clothing or the telling of racist jokes, determines identities and attitudes towards identities. The problem is that, for the most part, it is enough for the feminist to say that pornography objectifies woman for it to be condemned. But objectification is only bad, it could be argued, if it has negative normative consequences (Claim 2). If the feminist wants to say that objectification is bad, then romantic comedies can be as harmful, if not more so, than pornographic films. Take, for example, the recent comedy, *Just Go with It* (2011). A simple plot in which a man cannot see what he has before his own eyes: he is forced to change the object of his desire from the young, nubile image of beauty to the woman who is older, has as sense of humour and is 'beautiful inside', as the cliché would have it. So far, so Hollywood! We are invited to learn the trite moral that beauty on the inside my count more than external beauty. However, at what moment does our male hero undergo this revelation that he might in fact love the older, intelligent woman? Only when she strips off to show that her older body in a bikini can at least hold a candle to that of the younger woman. That is, only when she proves she is attractive externally – that she has a hot enough body even at her age – to carry off a bikini. Then, it is permissible for the hero to desire her. The objectification and its relationship to subordination and silence is obvious: I will only listen to your jokes and your opinions and I will only love you if you conform to the idea of beauty and femininity first and foremost. If you are different, if you do not do and say what I expect, then your voice will go unheard, and you want to be heard, so conform to what I want.

Of course, the feminist will rightly hold that such films are objectionable, trite and offensive. Surely such representations of women are as harmful and, more importantly, harmful in the same way, as the charges laid at the feet of pornographic material. Rather than bite the bullet and demand wholesale censorship of Hollywood, the feminist might instead say something like: romantic comedies are problematic and some do objectify women, but some do not. On the other hand, pornography necessarily objectifies women and cannot but make them into objects of desire whereby their subjectivity or equality to men is challenged. However, that 'necessarily', required for the argument to work, opens the feminist up once more to the charge of normative silliness: there is a presumption of an irresolvable inequality in sexual activity. Once the sexual activity is represented, then the representation has to objectify women as subordinate. That is absurd, surely there can be equal sexual relations and, like romantic comedies, some representations reinforce inegalitarian tropes whereas some deconstruct them. The 'necessity' of pornographic objectification is plausible only if sexual relationships are always already unequal, and that is a modern form of puritanism.

Such puritanism seems to be reflected in Langton's thoughts on solipsism and the feminist interpretation of it. One form of solipsism is the belief that I alone exist, that is I am the only subjectivity in existence. Such an epistemic attitude will damage the agent's interactions with others because, if others do exist and yet he believes they do not, he will treat persons in the same way as he treats other things or objects. Langton then reduces this to a 'local' solipsism: the subject treats some persons, specifically women, as things. The consequence of such a local solipsism is, according to Langton, the transformation from having sex *with* (reciprocally) someone and having sex *with* (that is using, like I cut the wood *with* a saw). Pornography, according to the feminist, represents sex as having sex with women as in the sense of having sex using women, doing something to them (as one moves the saw back and forth), using them as objects to achieve an end independent of them and their desires.

Langton sees objectification as a form of solipsism, but this is mistaken. Solipsism is the theory that there exists only one subjectivity amongst objects, some of which feign to be subjects. You cannot, however, objectify an object, as we have seen. If one were a sincere solipsist, objectification would be impossible. Objectification requires the recognition of the other as a subject in order for this subjectivity to be negated in an act of objectification. Sartre, as we shall touch on below, knew this better than most, but he – too – found it impossible to overcome since he began from a Kantian–Cartesian understanding of intersubjectivity, which is premised first on the I and then the extension of the I to others (Sartre, 1991). Most feminists seem to suggest that there is something about sexual activity which makes reciprocity impossible, otherwise pornography could possibly represent sexual activity which was not normatively problematic. The claim that A. Dworkin and MacKinnon make in their work, that sexual activity is seen as a form of subordination harks back to an almost pagan understanding of sexuality:

> The threat of passivity was the threat that you lost self-control, that you became the object of somebody else's desire. In the ancient world, desire is something very rarely reciprocal. You don't want to be loved back by someone you love. That's a modern invention. For the Roman citizen, you should desire somebody and not be the object of desire. You had to be the master of your body and its desires. The worst thing that could happen is that you become the object of somebody else's mastery or desires. That is to say, a slave, or indeed a woman. Hence being penetrated or even, at an extreme, being desired makes you not the subject, not the master of your own being. (Simon Goldhill, in an interview for Channel 4, cited in Tang (1999: 37))

The Roman morality that to penetrate is good, to be penetrated is weak is already hierarchical, linking weakness to facts about anatomy in a way that exemplifies the naturalistic fallacy. What, though, is wrong about making yourself an object for others at times? The wrongness seems to come from a commitment to the context of reciprocity, that is the 'modern invention'. To make a direct connection with the pornography problem, actors in films objectify themselves all the time, as do workers on the factory floor. Both actors and workers do the bidding of another's will, reduce themselves to an atom that is fungible (they can be replaced by other actors and workers) and become a tool for someone else's plans. The Dworkin/MacKinnon/Langton argument rests on the claim that sexual activity itself is hierarchical because one is necessarily an object for the other's desire and ends. And this is always the case in heterosexual sexual relations for them. Only given this form of puritanism can the representation of sexual activity be 'necessarily' damaging to the moral value of a subset of persons.

This is not true of all feminists. Remember that Nussbaum admits that being an object for others can be a wonderful sexual experience (1999: ch. 8). There is no necessity that objectification has necessarily negative consequences unless embellished in deeper cultural understandings. Similarly, the second premise is supported by a specific theory of objectification that views any treatment of human beings (including oneself) as an object as being morally suspicious. This is Kant's theory of moral rightness. In sexual activity, one is the body and desire and that is not to be trusted because when desire is ruling the practical will, one cannot be rational. One can only be an instrument for another, for Kant, when one freely consents to participate in their plans and that requires that both parties are recognized as rational and governed by rational principles. For Kant, when we have desire in the picture and (more generally) the body, reason becomes unreliable, so consent cannot be granted (unless grounded in the legal contract of marriage). Kant's theory rests on a dualism between body and mind, whereby the mind is reduced to body for the purposes of subordination (hence a person is treated as a thing). The radical feminists seem to repeat this Kantian presupposition about the use of others as objects, but there are perhaps different – equally plausible – ways to understand objectification.[8] Sartre and Hegel both offer the theoretical underpinnings of an understanding of objectification. Rather than merely accept that objectification is the reduction of an agent to non-agent, or a subject to its body and assume that this is always wrong, it would be pertinent to comprehend how and why subjects actually objectify others. Sartre's thought reveals the structure of the objectifying act of cognition and Hegel's thought forms the basis for a normative distinction between kinds of objectification.

5.7 Alternate theory of objectification 1: Sartre

Radical feminism may depend on the wrong theory of objectification or, at least, on an under-articulated understanding of the objectifying action. What is needed is a theory of objectification that can articulate a difference between bad objectification and good objectification. On the basis of such a distinction, one could then distinguish between good and bad romantic comedies and good and bad pornography films. Nussbaum and Langton's theorization of objectivity is not seemingly able to articulate this distinction (even if the former thinker does hint at it). For them, all objectification is a form of Kantian wrongdoing. Neither can Kant himself, especially not when desires and bodies are involved (and, of course, between persons, desires and bodies are *always* involved). Sartre and Hegel reject such a distinction between body and mind: the mind is embodied, it is one's body. To be master of one's body is to be free. I am my acts and I am my body. If I make my body do what I want, if I infuse it with my subjectivity then it is mine. There is no mind, independent and separate in a theoretical realm as the Kantian idiom leads us to believe.

Sartre's theory of subjectivity and objectification, if one can do it justice in a couple of paragraphs, is based on the instrumentalization of the world by the free for-itself or consciousness. The human being is a negation of its present and its past through a projection to the future, it exists for-itself in the presence to its being as not being what it is. So, the human being is not what it is (I am not what you describe me as or categorize me as being, I always escape that because as soon as you describe me I can choose to accept or reject your categorization); but, I am present to that categorization as its negation (this is what constitutes the fact of my existence or my *facticity*). To deny such facts is a form of bad faith, as we shall see below, and I am not what I am in the sense that what I truly am is my choice to be something in the future, a projection of what I can be but am not yet. The world, or the subject's being-in-the world, is characterized as a matrix of tools through which I am either able to achieve or am frustrated in achieving my aim. How the world is for me reveals what my original choice is. An agent's encounter with a mountain and how it 'appears' to that agent reveals more about the agent than the mountain itself. If it is 'too steep' or 'daunting', then the agent has already made a choice not to climb it, to resist climbing it. If it appears 'challenging' or 'exciting', then the agent encounters it having made the choice to scale it. (And in this example, we see the shadow of the self that chooses before the me articulates and how the 'me' and the world are constructed on the basis of this original choice; the self of the pre-power construction.)

Original choice structures a world-for-me as well as simultaneously being an act of self-objectification: in order to be what I am not, I have to make myself and the world through practical actions on the world and these acts amalgamate into an empirical 'me' (an object, at this stage, in my world) which has the relation to the for-itself as being that which the choice must overcome, hence the temporal and not fixed nature of human existence. At the heart of Sartre's account of freedom and human nature is the notion of self-objectification brought about by the desire to be subjectified or what Sartre calls the general project of being for-itself-in-itself, that is being what one is freely. Since the for-itself is freedom, it can only be what it is through the negation of what it is, so the ultimate project of human existence is futile. The project to be for-itself-in-itself is the desire for subjectification and objectification at the same time: the for-itself wants its freedom to be its essence, so it pretends that 'freedom' is a determinate characteristic of its being and then attempts to structure a subjectivity on top (a limited freedom, the freedom of being an empirical 'me'). The process assumes the self is an object (a human being) which is then subjectified or given a fixed agency (a personality that is 'me' which determines my actions in specific situations). For this to be possible, the for-itself must first objectify itself as a personality, that is commit the bad faith of denying itself as freedom (I am shy, introspective, have desires for specific objects and likes for others and so on).

Objectification is implicit in Sartre's account of subjectivity. Perhaps more oddly, so too is the subjectification of a subject by itself. The subject can only be itself by being free, and freedom, the choice to structure the world according to the original upsurge or projection, is possible only through making the other into an object for the self.[9] Subjectification of oneself, that is, of making oneself an agent is only possible through the objectification of the other. Being-for-others is an immediate way in which the subject structures the world, otherwise there would be no limitations on the way in which free choice could structure the world and hence no possible identity of a 'me' in the world, nor 'my' world at all. The immediacy of the other as a general possibility is felt through 'shame' or the possibility of one's being-in-the-world being evaluated as an objectified possibility by the other. Shame and the other, then, are pre-requisites for what Sartre understands by responsibility. In short, were there no other, then my choices and my actions would not matter and there would be no 'me' as the reference to which these actions are to be applied.

The original presence of the other, that is the subject's pre-reflective awareness of being evaluated as a unity or a 'person', is the general structure of what Sartre refers to as the look: as a self-consciousness that I am either looking at or being looked at by others. Without the existence of an other as a real possibility, there would be only a non-coherent field of intuitions with no structure nor narrative. The fact that there is a 'world' and a 'for me' is a form of transcendental proof of the immediate knowledge of the other. Looking is subjectification in that I reduce the other to an object with fixed desires, projects and plans which may or may not involve me or may conflict with my presence, but I do so only with the epistemic bad faith of repressing his or her subjectivity (or looking at me). I am aware that the other before me exists as what I see only in so far as not being it, as the negation of what I make him or her out to be. I subjectify myself as the master of him. Being looked at is objectification in that I find myself an object in another's matrix of means to a future and subordinated to his will. I am 'me' only in so far as I am complicit in his ends, otherwise I am not what the other sees me as in the sense that I am what he or she sees in the manner of not being it (I am responsible for it and am present to it as the negation of it). The 'me' is in a meta-stable state. I remain as a negative presence to myself and am either subordinating or being subordinated, both attitudes which are freely chosen.

Bad faith is, after all, an existentialist term of art. And in Sartre there are three types of bad faith. Bad faith is a possible way in which the for-itself can *exist*. It is an attempt to deny the contingency of actions due to some source of meaning prior to choice. The for-itself denies responsibility for who it is and what it has made of itself in order to rationalize itself. Sartre compares freedom to vertigo in that vertigo is not the fear of heights but the awareness that, when the subject finds itself on a precipice, nothing stops the subject from throwing itself to its death. The only thing that stops it is the choice not to throw itself off. Yet, it strives to rationalize this, to offer reasons: what about my children? The pain I will cause? I have so much to live for? (Sartre, 1991: 30) But these reasons are only reasons if the choice has already been made. Ultimate responsibility rests with the subject and hence the encounter with the world is always authentically characterized by anxiety. To free oneself from this anxiety the subject seeks to make the rationalizations natural or determinant, to make them facts that cannot be denied. This is the structure of bad faith. In *Being and Nothingness*, bad faith takes three forms. First, the belief that I am determined by my facticity: the agent assumes that essential, fixed properties limit his possibilities and explain his actions. Second, the belief that I exist most authentically as transcendence, that no matter what you describe as 'me', I can negate it. I can negate all my facticity, because I am free. This form of bad faith implicitly denies my being-for-others which is an essential structure of freedom; that is, existing in the world. Finally, the 'spirit of seriousness' or binding oneself to a purpose: I am a communist, I am a Christian and my role dictates certain obligations which derive from something external to me. This is described as another way to try and fulfil my project without the anguish of choosing for myself because, as a part of a general movement, my choices are limited by the dictates of that movement. (The reader should remember an earlier remark: the true woman (subject) can exist outside the system of rationalizations, but only in transcendent negation (silence) or by being wanted (by being objectified).)

And perhaps now we can see how bad faith has lent its name to my understanding of the epistemic mode required by objectification. The first is a form of self-objectification. I overcome my responsibility by making myself into a 'me' determined by natural limitations and a past. The objectification of pornography is a way to understand myself as 'male' or 'female' and hence constrained by certain meanings and values. I am dominant, I am subservient, I take pleasure in being a victim, I take pleasure by causing pain and so on and so forth. If I am male, this is what I should be and the natural order of meanings found in my society and culture describe what is actually the case. I am as others understand me to be and nothing more. The second maps neatly on to Langton's ideas of solipsism: there are no others only things. There are no limitations, I am not male, nor female, I am what I choose to be. In so many ways this is the problem with Butler and postmodern celebrations of 'play', as though if the system is arbitrary, we are free from it. Sartre reminds us that facticity is me in the mode of me not being it. I must deny it and negate it and that is always an engagement with it. I cannot be indifferent to it. If I feel that pornography does not capture what it is for me to be 'male' or 'female', I cannot just ignore it because it is there before me, interpreting who I choose to be. Finally, the third form is the reinforcement of the first through the choice to internalize the order of meanings one finds in culture, to commit to conventional meanings. As women start to make pornography, as they start to enjoy pornography, they are consenting to their own domination. They recognize things they want and they can only want them by committing to modes of understanding which limit who they are.

However, there is no stability in these forms of bad faith. There are holes in this instrumentalization and inauthenticity where the world slips away from me: the free choices of others. I know that others are different from objects because they pull my world away from me and make my objectification and subjectification a farce. It is the shame that I feel before the look of others, either because they see me as what I am not and judge me as that or they see me as what I am not yet and judge me on my failure. For them I exist as an object, as a thing which frustrates or aids the achievement of their own future projects. For myself, I am the construction of meanings, but I exist as a meaning for them at the same time. I am both subject and object. The failure maps on to the forms of bad faith. In the first, self-objectification is impossible because there is always the excess, the presence to oneself that knows it is not what others see. The self remains the attempt to master those others and become a subject. In the second form, others will continually judge one's indifference and see it as a game, as false and insincere. And finally, the subject will once again see its objectification as not itself and try to escape it through the mastering of others and their understandings. The relationship between the self and the other is, then, inherently unstable. There exists no Hegelian possibility of mutual reciprocity because one cannot exist as a subject for the other unless that other makes themselves an object (which they are not), and one cannot exist as an object for the other unless one denies one's subjectivity, but this very denial is that subjectivity. The presence of the other is not under my control, nor am I under his or her control, like the matrix of objects which constitutes our being-in-the-world, so the relationship is inherently unstable (Sartre, 1991: 408).

Being looked at cannot collapse into a for-itself and in-itself relationship, the other remains always an embodied other, a repressed looking, otherwise the social dimension of existence, the self existing with others, would not be possible. The social world is possible through either epistemic bad faith (I conceive of others as objects) or self-objectification (I exist as a 'me' for others). Both are desirable for the subject because they are modes of avoiding free responsibility. Reciprocity is impossible for Sartre and the only possible attitudes towards the other are sadism (objectifying) or masochism (self-objectifying).

What is interesting about Sartre's account, though, is that one possibility for stabilizing the relationship between the self and the other is brought about by the existence of the third consciousness which looks at 'us' in our conflicting, indifferent or cooperating struggle. The third sees 'us' as an object for him or her and we become aware of being looked at not as two individuals but as a constituted 'us'. The third look, as such, makes possible the third form of bad faith: I can reinforce my subjectification or objectivity only through established social projects, a commitment to ways of understanding, and that requires the pre-existence of these modes of understanding. The gaze of this third consciousness fixes not 'me' and an 'other', but an immediate 'me and the other' as a group or a singular entity and hence further limits our possibilities. Sartre's consistent claim throughout his work is that a plurality of subjects can exist as the objectified 'us', through the mediation of a third consciousness, but never truly as a 'we' or the reciprocal Hegelian cooperating rational beings (Flynn, 1984: 19). An 'us' can be looked at, but it cannot – for Sartre – look. The 'us', then, can be objectified but only an I can look, the 'we' cannot look. Equality is impossible because community (the subjectivity of a 'we') and individuality (a plurality of 'I's) are, for him, mutually exclusive.

The reason why a 'we' subject is impossible harks back to Sartre's existentialism: the self or the 'I' is immediate and the 'we' is derivative, that is it can only be understood if we first understand what it is to be an 'I'. I understand a 'we' as an amalgamation of 'I's like myself hence not a real subjectivity at all. It could equally be argued that we only know what it is to be a person, though, when we have an understanding of what it is to be an 'us'. So, the human being growing up will understand itself as a son, a male, white, English and so on. Of course, for Sartre, the subject only exists as these in the sense of negation: I am a son, male, English and so on, but these do not exhaust what I am, *I am* in the sense of *not* being them. As soon as I identify myself with the 'us' of conventional understandings, I undermine my own particularity and my own subjectivity. I perform an act of bad faith in that I objectify myself for the other according to meanings I have not chosen.

Sartre, tellingly, identifies the looking as the oppressive class and the looked at as the oppressed class (Sartre, 1991: 420–1). In terms of the feminist critique and pornography, one can understand the looking as the gaze of the male and the looked at as the objectified female. Whereas the I-other relationship is unstable for Sartre, what we can see is that the existence of pornography confirms an already existing hierarchical relationship such that the objectification of a specific class of persons by another is stabilized. The subjectivity that is female is always already understood in a certain way of being and cannot negate the looking of the other. The reason is that the I-other relationship is constituted by a third self-consciousness who fixes the two subjects into the hierarchical relationship of already established power relationships: the male is the looking and the female is the looked at. Who, though, is this third look? For the radical feminist, it is the original Male or the Father: the original choice for men to be subjects and women to be objects and not the particular male who watches pornography or prowls nightclubs. Sartre, though, makes it clear that the males themselves are as much a victim of the conspiracy as the objectified females because they are caught in a characterization of an 'us' that they were not responsible for choosing and which only exists as a negative presence to the categorization. Here we can see how Butler's critique of the intentional model of feminism and the idea that there was a decision made by a subject to oppress a certain group is untenable: 'The power to "race" and, indeed, the power to gender, precedes the "one" who speaks such power, and yet the one who speaks nevertheless appears to have that power' (Butler, 1997: 49). The idea that there exists a subject who oppresses and an oppressed unaware of such oppression is the philosophical equivalent of a conspiracy theory. Yet, as we have said, the target of Langton's speculative narrative is not to identify the original perpetrators of an inegalitarian system, but to reveal the fact that accountability rests on those who maintain the system of inequality. The fact that one continues to 'speak' the language and to endorse the values of one's existence, through his consumption of pornography in one instance, even if one is aware of the inequality it engenders, is where accountability lies.

Subjectification is impossible – it is always Sartrean if one begins from the Kantian model – and solipsism is implicit to its worldview and impossible to escape. There is an unbridgeable chasm between subjects that can at best be approximated in modes of identity and conventional behaviour. Sartre, an heir to Kant in so many ways, asks whether one can in fact 'subjectify' others. His answer is only at the expense of one's own subjectivity, by admitting one is an object for them and their subjectivity. For there to be a common subject, that is a relationship between two subjects, the relationship needs to be mediated by social conventions and meanings. Neither subjectivity has chosen such meanings, though; they are quite simply thrown into them in the first instance. And this is why for Sartre to embrace such meanings is always objectifying and an act of bad faith because one does not make the codes of mediation oneself through free choice.[10]

Sartre fails because his view of objectification is always an unfreedom, a concession to the will of others whereas, for Hegel, the concession to others is what separates freedom for-itself from freedom in and for itself. Sartre's (1992) posthumously published notebooks show how he tried in vain to use Hegel's theory of recognition to overcome the impasse in his own theory of social interaction. It was futile because the other, for him, was always either an objectifying or an objectified entity, never as a subject for a subject. One feels that, as with much of Sartre's philosophy, he could not emerge form the shadow of Kant. His failure initiated his movement in the direction of Marx. The question remains to be asked whether the failure was necessary or was merely due to Sartre. Is it possible for subjects to exist reciprocally as a 'we' and not as an 'us'? The 'we' needs to be mediated by social facts, institutions and meanings and this is the third self-consciousness. It is not a subject but the will of subjects codified into structures of meaning. Such a third can make subjects into:

1. an 'us' (both objectified);
2. an 'I' and a 'she';
3. a 'he' and an 'I';
4. a 'we' (both subjectified).

For Sartre, only (1) is possible; for the radical feminist (2) is actually the case; but Hegel shows us how (4) is possible. Hegel, as we shall see, offers us a way out of the 'I/me' impasse. For him, the subject or agent is first a universal, in that he or she is constituted by the objectification of the 'us' and cultural meanings: I am a type and if I was not I could not be an agent at all (I would be nothing but a bundle of incoherent deeds and not in any sense a unity). However, Hegel too agrees with Sartre in that the particular 'I' is the negation of these determinations. The abstract 'I' can rise above these determinations to assert itself as an individual in the group (hence the 'I' is derivative from the 'us'). Finally, though, the 'I' can exist as a 'we' when the self gives itself positive and not just negative content and chooses to be or not to be what society understands it as (Hegel, 1991: §§5-7). The particular and substantial individual uses the conventions of the 'us' to objectify a chosen and not just given identity.

5.8 Alternate theory of objectification 2: Hegel

Implicit in Hegel's theory of action is a theory of objectification that, unlike Sartre, makes possible a subjectification in a 'we' of common subjectivity. That some utterances have a performative or illocutionary aspect is something well discussed. Hegel's theory is a radical reversion of this claim. Every action is linguistic in nature. What separates actions from events is not that they are intentional (or, at least, not wholly), but that their intentionality resides in the reference to the understanding of others and hence their action is an embodied meaning. Raising a hand in a class means 'I want to ask a question', standing by the roadside in a particular way means 'I want to cross', and knocking on the door means 'Please answer'. Actions are conventionally structured in that they exhibit a necessarily rational structure. Actions, like words, are done for others in a context of shared interpersonal conventions. We know an action is an action because it is meant (it is willed) and the meaning of that word is obvious. A stone falls and means nothing. A man winks at a woman and means something. We objectify ourselves every time we act or speak. The intention (subjectivity) is objectified in the action of the body. Acts express something particular about the agent by communicating his or her intention to an ideal other who, to use an apt metaphor, is able to 'read' the inner self from the outer expression.[11] Hegel summarizes his theory of moral action in one typically lucid passage which sets out the conditions of moral action:

> The expression of the will as subjective or moral is action. Action contains the following determinations: (α) it must be known by me in its externality as mine; (β) its essential relation to the concept is one of obligation; and (γ) it has an essential relation to the will of others. (1991, §113)

The first determination (α) is familiar: an event is an action if the agent's intention plays a causal role and the agent is aware of it. The right of knowledge (α) is the condition that the agent must recognize an event as being produced by him or herself for it to be an action as opposed to an event. Only those events admitted as one's own are actions, that is events to which the agent ascribes himself or herself as the author. Such self-ascription is, in the first instance, nothing but the identification of a reason conceived of as an intention in the set of causal conditions necessary for bringing about the event (Hegel, 1971: §504). Thus, the agent can distinguish between deliberately knocking a man off his ladder ('I wanted to because he had ogled my wife') and involuntarily knocking a man off his ladder ('It wasn't my fault, I tripped on the carpet.') The subject is responsible for the occurrence to which the predicate 'mine' can be attached and which is traceable to the subject's intention (Hegel, 1991: §115).

However, Hegel wants subjects to be held responsible for their actions in order to distribute praise and blame. The first determination of free action is unable to fulfil this goal on its own since it 'fails to cast the agent in his proper role' (Velleman, 2002: 123). Reasons, that is dispositions and beliefs, *cause* an intention which *causes* an action, but the agent just does not feature and it is agents we hold responsible and not their beliefs and dispositions. So, reasons must effect something (an agent) in order to become intentions and since reasons do not always produce the same intention in differing agents, something is missing in the causal explanation in order to make it plausible. Of course, one could cite the agents' differing webs of beliefs as the differentiating factor in diverse responses, but it is still possible for an agent to be moved by beliefs *despite himself*. Cases such as coercion and addiction feature an agent who is in accordance with the standard model ('I believe the robber's gun is loaded and I do not want to die'; 'I am in a state of wanting and I believe that the drug will alleviate this'), but, phenomenologically, these stories do not seem to capture the real nature of human action (Frankfurt, 1988). It makes intuitive sense to say that 'it was not me' or 'I wasn't acting on my own will' and such statements do have a legal – if not metaphysical – resonance. The phenomenology of human action involves reference to the agent and the empiricist model appears to negate this aspiration. To account for cases of coercion and false consciousness, the subject has to freely endorse his or her end for the action to be properly his or her own. Hegel puts this in terms of obligation: the intention is to be known as a good-for-me (β). In the case of coercion, the muggee has a conflict of goods: self-preservation versus fulfilling his role. The former motivation trumps the latter but the agent is not free because he is not acting from his own will. It is the presence of an external factor which obstructs his free action.

So far, so traditional. Hegel is at pains to make room in his moral and psychological theory for an element which is anathema to more naturalistic accounts of action. He wants to demonstrate that free action is identified by a subject who endorses those actions as his or her own because it emanates from an act of will which is properly his or hers. Although a purely causal account is able to explain an action, the causal model's explanations are inadequate to ground an evaluative judgement: it explains how we are able to blame the coercer and not the coerced in power relationships. One needs to move away from the person (a collection of given dispositions and beliefs) to the subject (the agent who is 'at home' with his intentions and motivations): 'Freedom is only present where there is no other for me that is not myself. The natural man, who is determined only by his drives, is not at home with himself' (Hegel, 1971: §23 A2).The criterion of 'homeliness' which Hegel proposes captures the modern, moral self as opposed to the 'I' identified by the traditional grammatical subject-sentence structure (of which the 'cup' can also be a subject as in 'The cup fell from the table'). Such a linguistic subject is a formal grammatical entity and full subjectivity requires homeliness or the presence of self to oneself in the intentions.[12]

Notice how bad faith is present when there is another who is not myself: pure facticity (self-objectification); pure transcendence (denial of subjectification); and pure conventional behaviour (objectification) in Sartre's terminology. The natural man is akin to the coerced agent or the agent in bad faith and all are 'self-willed': free if he is able to act on the content of his will and not free if he is obstructed from doing so. However, there is no full responsibility since the content of the will is given and ultimately no different from external causes, psychoses, neuroses and the will of others imposed on one. Full-blooded human action involves the proper recognition that what one did, one wanted to do and would justify if asked.

Traditionally these two determinations ($\alpha + \beta$) have been held to be necessary and sufficient conditions for free action, yet Hegel adds his third determination (γ): the intention has to be capable of reconstruction by others from the objectivity of the act itself. It is here that objectification and self-objectification reside in his theory. One way to characterize this is to say that the justification of one's good or end involves one in the activity of reason-giving and this activity is, for Hegel, inherently social. Affirming what is substantially right and good is not a matter of external, transcendental standards independent of one's peers, but rests on their recognition of the content of one's will in terms of articulated and shared categories of right. There are no constraints on a will which justifies a good or a purpose to itself: one is able to convince oneself that anything may be good (Hegel, 1991: §140 R). Reasons for action require a degree of objectivity for Hegel and this is based on reasons being a justification for all men who share my way of life rather than just for me: that is, an actual reason, rather than just wilfulness. Contrary to Kant, one's role, situation and circumstances all constitute reasons for behaviour. In offering reasons, the agent knows that, if they are good reasons, he can convince others. It follows from this that the agent's description of his intention must harmonize with the other's interpretation of the act: the agent is only fully free when he is aware how his action will be interpreted. The will of others contained in one's own will is this shared scheme of interpretation in and through which we reconstruct intentions.

The rational reformulation of the initial determinations of action occurs in a later paragraph which reduces the dialectical trinity to a new symmetry of subjective and objective aspects:

> The right of intention is that the universal quality of the action shall have being not only in itself, but shall be known by the agent and

> thus have been present all along in his subjective will; and conversely, what we may call the right of the objectivity of the action is the right of the action to assert itself as known and willed by the subject as a thinking agent. (Hegel, 1991: §120)

Here we find that self-ascription of intentions, or the right of knowledge (α), is combined with the necessary element of modern moral freedom (β) into the 'right of intention' such that the agent will only be held responsible for those actions deliberately brought about by his or her own will, thus ruling out external causality, neurotic behaviour, coercion, deception and false consciousness. An action is – independently of the protestations and affirmations of the agent him or herself – to 'stand in for' or 'represent' the will of the agent in the 'outer' world, just as the word uttered in a language is assumed to be a sincere representation of the thought and will of the speaker who is present. If the agent wishes to be understood as a free moral agent, then he or she must be aware that an action requires a commitment to the medium through which others will understand it. So, in order to affirm one's freedom, there must exist a minimum level of expectation which must be met. If the subject's acts are to be the expression of inwardness, then he must be certain that the other is going to reconstruct them faithfully. Both actor and interpreter must, therefore, share a common understanding of the way in which acts are to be rendered intelligible. Objectifying oneself according to shared conventions is a form of freedom for Hegel. Without grasping the rules and vocabulary of language, I would never be able to enter into rational discussion, so without performing specific roles set out by cultural conditions, I would never be able to enter into rational agency. Language pre-exists the utterance and, similarly, the expectations of agency pre-exist the action: the 'I' is derived from an original 'us'.[13]

Recognition, it ought to be recalled, is not just granted by the struggle to death, even if that story makes stark what is at stake: I demonstrate to you that I am free over and above my desires by risking the most fundamental drive for the sake of a principle (Hegel, 1977: ¶¶178–196; Kojève, 1969; Williams, 1997). Such recognition of one's essential rationality and humanity can alternatively be granted by marriage, whereby the agent sincerely places altruistic and universal needs over particular and egoistic ones (Hegel, 1991: §162). Without the self-certainty granted by knowledge of the intersubjective categories of the right of objectivity, the subject would be unsure whether or not he has been properly recognized or if his intention can be reconstructed faithfully from his action. In a rational social order, the agent knows the good in question because it is made immediately available to him through fulfilling his roles in the family (parent, child), civil society (worker) and the state (citizen). If I wish to be known as a good father, then my acts must accord with those judgements which accompany a good parent (love, generosity, discipline) and not those which are generally frowned upon (indifference, prodigality, severity). The significance of the right of objectivity resides in the certainty of recognition and one's social fabric is a liberation because it makes possible – and does not inhibit – free moral action. What Hegel's theory makes possible, though, is the possibility of the 'we' subject. In a household, between partners, roles and duties are distributed according to several layers of rationalization and meaning. These roles and duties create limitations and liberties for the different parties, but the household or family recognizes itself as primarily a 'we', as an interpersonal subject. Such a 'we' is only possible on the basis of a shared reciprocity. Social conventions, when rational, are the household writ large.

So, according to Hegel's theory of action, objectification occurs in every single action and we can now make sense of the four positions developed earlier and their relation to bad faith. Sartre recognizes that for objectification as an 'us' to occur, that is to move from self-objectification to a stabilized, conventional objectification, a third look is required, but this look is not necessarily a will. Rather it is the historical conditions of meaning or what Hegel identified as the will of the others as a group, the shared language of understanding. Given the objectification through this social mediation, we proposed that four outcomes were possible: (1) we are seen as an 'us' (both objectified); (2) we are seen as an 'I' and a 'she' (the feminist nightmare); (3) we are seen as a 'he' and an 'I' (the postmodern deconstruction); or (4) we are seen as a 'we' (both subjectified). Using Hegel's right of intention and right of objectivity, we can propose that (1) occurs when neither subject is able to feel at home in the structures of meaning, so the right of objectivity trumps the right of intention. (2) and (3) occur when one group or class can feel at home in the conventions of appropriate behaviour and the other cannot, and (4) occurs when both subjects find themselves at home in the conditions of meaning. (4) is our goal (some might add utopian, I choose not to because that would be to fall into Sartre's trap), but the claim is that the objectification, that is the setting of roles and descriptions of behaviour encouraged by pornography leads to position (2). As the next chapter will show, the actual critique is that pornography, if it is bad, results in position (1) and so is not exclusively a feminist concern; and this does not constitute grounds for its prohibition (actually the opposite). The consideration of Hegel's thought on action allows us to differentiate between good and bad objectification: objectification is exemplified by case (4), alienation by (1) through (3).

5.9 Objectification and alienation

Let us return to the nightclub prowler example and see whether we can make sense of these new forms of objectification. The claim is that he objectifies the women before him and, unlike the simple feminist direction of a male consciousness objectifying a female body, we have a slightly more complex story and, interestingly, one told from the point of view of *both* participants. The woman, in short, participates in the process. The prowler views the women who have chosen to visit a nightclub. They have done so for a variety of reasons: to socialize with friends, to meet new friends, to dance, to escape the mediocrity of their day lives and so on. They dress and act accordingly. The clothes they wear, their modes of behaviour objectify what they do and communicate to the prowler who they are, what they want and what they plan to do. For Sartre, such self-objectification is already a denial of one's true subjectivity, that is the presence to oneself and the capacity to not be it at any moment. We need not be so dramatically existentialist: we all wear specific clothes, have certain brands of mobile phones and participate in specific activities in order to carve out some individuality, some freely chosen 'me' from the crowd. Hegel calls such categories a liberation because they allow me to determine myself as a 'me' in the world amongst others – just as we all choose specific portrait photographs to illustrate to the world who we are.

So, the women are choosing to be who they want by being 'at home' in specific categories. They have self-objectified themselves (or subjectified themselves). The problem arises in that the prowler does not recognize their categories: for him, they are all (and who is to say a few of them are not?) offering themselves up to him as meat to be consumed, either through salacious observation or through sexual use. The women could not recognize themselves in the descriptions offered by the prowler. Similarly, one could imagine Langton's photograph in a possible orthodox religious state as being interpreted as 'slutty', as 'provocative', that is in categories of understanding in which Langton herself would never feel at home, If such a description were offered, she would vehemently deny it: 'That is not me, you have made a mistake'. At this stage we have Sartre's face off between individual consciousnesses which understand themselves at the same time as flipping between subject (looking) and object (being looked at). However, the prowler has certain cultural understandings on his side, urban myths about the type of women who go to nightclubs, what sexy clothes mean and what women want; and such myths are known to the women who can easily find themselves falling into the same objectification. Responsibility for the silencing of the women's voice arises due to historical conditions of understanding and not wilful, male actions. The women are then able to resist the objectification through transcendence (silencing themselves – bad faith form 2) or they resign themselves to his judgement and stabilize the objectification which then fails to be a self-objectification (willing their own domination – bad faith form 3).

Why is Hegel's account an improvement over the feminist model of objectification? First, it does not immediately identify the source of the problem in intentional male action which resolves itself into the original male conspiracy. Most objectifications occur at the level of the individual and are either stable or not. Stability is brought about by cultural power relations. Second, it allows a space for female autonomy in that women do not find themselves determined from before their birth by cultural conditions, but find themselves – like all subjects – thrown into systems and orders of meanings that make demands on them and offer them liberties, but which they can choose to endorse or reject. The alternative theory of objectivity developed offers a proper account of female subjectivity which feminists, as a rule, do not. Third, it allows us to distinguish between good and bad objectification or self-objectification and alienation. Self-objectification is when the subject feels at home in the objectified product of his or her action and the action or objectification of myself is recognized as mine by me and as a properly understood expression of myself. In short, I choose to be what others understand me as (the 'we' subject). Alienation, on the other hand, is when the product of my intentional behaviour (the action) is taken away from me and I no longer recognize it as mine, it is alien to me. I thus have two choices: to be what my action has been understood as (conform) or to resist and to try to determine the proper interpretation of my actions and objectifications (and risk being silenced). We can see in the second case what happens is that others deny my individuality and see me as an example of certain types. As such, 'I' am a tool in the confirmation of the other's attitudes about my type, fungible, general and one whose inner life makes no impression on the world.

In the bridge between *Being and Nothingness* and the *Critique of Dialectical Reason*, Sartre defines the spirit of seriousness in these words: 'The spirit of seriousness is voluntary alienation, that is, submission to an abstraction that justifies one: the thought that man is the inessential and the abstract the essential' (1992: 60). The alienation is *voluntary*, that is, free in the sense of self-determined, and therefore *authentic*. Where the spirit of seriousness fails is in the rejection of the particular and the individual in favour of the duties of some impersonal, abstract entity. This is the very premise which Sartre will begin the *Critique* from, that is, the need to marry existentialist subjectivism with Marxist historicism. The incomplete nature of *Being and Nothingness* resides in its consideration of an isolated individual existing in the world, but the third form of bad faith points explicitly towards the need for a sociological and political understanding of human beings. One way was through Marx's understanding of alienation, as Sartre ultimately does. Nussbaum also invokes Marx briefly in a footnote to her discussion of objectivity, but she does so only to show how her seven aspects are present in the objectifying power of labour-commodity on the worker: 'MacKinnon has written that sexuality is to feminism what work is to Marxism. In each case something that is most oneself and one's own is what is seen by the theory to have been taken away' (1999: 222). However, remember that for Marx, the capitalist is also alienated by the system of capitalism. The capitalist's own essential being is impossible to develop. His productive powers are not his own because he cares nothing about what he actually produces, only what it is monetarily worth. The analogy, then, to be faithful would have to acknowledge the unfreedom of men given the cultural conditions of sexual relations. Only with the acknowledgement of these, could the conditions be properly restructured according to equality. Nussbaum's article strives to find the 'empowering' moral notion of objectification (is it autonomy-denial, is it instrumentality?) without success because the real difference is that objectification is morally bad when there is a lack of homeliness and self-objectification, when it is taken away from me and becomes alienation. My body is my own. The question is do I or an other objectify it for you? And the seeds of such a distinction are borrowed by Marx from Hegel (where the former uses a general theory of action as a specific theory of labour and value creation): self-objectification is a liberation because through the cultural understandings and meanings in which I participate, I am able to express myself as an individual (I am a male, a heterosexual, middle-class and so on), but I am not able to be reduced to these categories, I am more than the sum of my parts.

And here I want to return to the comparison between two views of the representation of sexual activity. On the one hand, MacKinnon tells us, 'In a society in which equality is a fact, not merely a word, words of racial or sexual assault and humiliation will be nonsense syllables. Sex between people and things, human beings and pieces of paper, real men and unreal women, will be a turn-off' (MacKinnon, 1993: 109–110). On the other hand, Nussbaum asserts 'It may therefore be not too utopian to imagine a culture in which men's sexual desire for women will not commonly be associated with projects of possession and control, and in which female sexual agency will not inspire fear and suspicion' (1999: 12). Both share the grounding claim that inequality distorts sexual relationships and such a distortion is then reproduced in pornography and such distortion *acts* either to perpetuate already existent hierarchical relationships or, in some sense, to make the ideology of such inequality *true*. Yet, MacKinnon leaves no space for the representation of bodies and sexual activity as aesthetic discourse aimed at arousal. Objectification is necessarily domination, but only because it is Kantian at base with a slight suspicion of the possibility of combining rationality, freedom and sexual activity in the one person (rather than in the conflict of the bi-person, if you'll excuse the pun, between the empirical and the transcendental). Nussbaum's words do not, however, rule out the reproduction of sexual activity as long as the conditions of freedom and rationality in the participants are met. The possibility of a permissible reproduction of sexual activity requires consent. Given however, that her theory of objectivity similarly rests on the Kantian notion of using others as means and, that sexual activity is sensuous through and through, the Kantian in her doubts the actuality of such consent, in the same way that when money is involved in a transaction of labour, freedom is nearly always under suspicion.

The demand that sexual activity be reciprocal and sincere seems too high. One could imagine a couple in a long-standing, sincere and loving relationship where, after a night of watching a Hollywood film with a particularly erotic (but not pornographic) scene, they make love, with each other thinking of the scene as they do. They imagine doing what the couple in the film were doing, but neither communicates this or even reveals it to their partner (not as deception, just because they don't see why they should). That such a situation arises is more than plausible. That it is morally wrong is absurd. There is certainly a using of the other as a means to pleasure, but the question is who is actually being used here: the partner, both partners, the actors, or all three? The demand that 'we' can sincerely participate in social conditions of knowledge, though, and find ourselves at home in the cultural language which makes our sexual being possible, is not utopian at all. Self-objectification through one's actions is possible on two conditions: (i) that I see my action as a proper and freely chosen effect of my will and my chosen inner life;

and (ii) others will recognize my true intention and hence my individuality from the act itself. (ii) requires that subjects share (constitute a 'we' and not an 'us' or an 'I/she') cultural conditions of meaning in which they can feel at home. The question is, then, whether the existence of pornography makes such conditions unattainable or not.

5.10 Conclusion

Let us go back to the original claims: (1) the existence of pornography creates, maintains and informs social and cultural conditions of understanding such that it easier for knowing subjects (both male and female) to perform the epistemic bad faith required to objectify persons belonging to a specific set; and (2) such objectification has negative normative consequences in that it undermines the moral value of a subset of persons by reinforcing inequality (subordinating) and denying the autonomous and rational status of this subset (silencing). Let us look at these claims again in light of the reformulation of objectification into self-objectification and alienation elaborated above. That pornography aids in the objectification of persons is neither here nor there. In this respect, it performs the role of many other institutions, conventions and meanings in that it sets down the manner in which we can understand others and their behaviour. To describe such action as epistemic bad faith is rhetoric, because it could easily be understood as a way to subjectify myself and others: through these understandings I allow my individuality to be stated and respected.

The first claim appears particularly badly put. Of course, there is an obvious consideration which has arisen from the alternative models of interpretation, namely if the existence of pornography creates, maintains and informs social and cultural conditions of understanding such that it is easier for knowing subjects (both male and female) to perform the epistemic bad faith required to objectify persons, why is the critique of pornography explicitly feminist? There are male actors in the films as well and they, too, behave in ways that may make women form false beliefs: men are only interested in sex, men comply with the desire to make love without reservation, plumbers are horny and the average size of the male member is about twelve inches long. Such background may create a situation in which a woman (or another man) may form beliefs about the individual man in front of them because the woman wants it to be thus and so. Neither 'male' nor 'female' feel at home, let alone the bisexual, the homosexual, the asexual and so on. The latter categories are ones on which feminists only ever make passing remarks.[14]

What the feminist will say is that such beliefs are not supported by the society at large, though. They will be more akin to the belief that the man in Fenwick's is actually Santa Claus: if I were to share such beliefs, others would dismiss them, whereas the beliefs about women are more likely to be supported by others because the cultural conditions of inequality support them. Male beliefs, in short, can move from unstable objectification to cultural alienation. The second thing the feminist may say is that whereas the background lie and the epistemic bad faith of the male is in his interest, the background beliefs of the woman about men (based on pornography films) are also in his (and not her) interest. We shall return to this claim below, but it is worth noting that the average size belief is rarely in the interest of the individual male.

So, the first claim really ought to read: the existence of pornography creates, maintains and informs social and cultural conditions of understanding such that it easier for knowing subjects (both male and female) to objectify persons belonging to a specific set. As we have seen, such self-objectification and objectification are neutral: they are examples of epistemic bad faith only when the subject denies all forms of categorization (negation through transcendence or silence) or when the subject does not feel at home in the categorization but still allows it to determine the creation of their individuality (they are alienated). Pornography as a mediation of sexual identity, by supplying role models, values and instruction, is neither necessarily unhomely nor a form of interest-driven oppression by a specific group, although it might historically be so.

It is claim two which is now of interest: such objectification has negative normative consequences in that it undermines the moral value of a subset of persons by reinforcing inequality (subordinating) and denying the autonomous and rational status of this subset (silencing). This is the true feminist claim that all pornography is complicit in the construction of ways of knowing in which the female could never form a free individuality, but only an identity which is in the interest of others (males). Irish jokes do this at a subconscious level and do so in the interest of one group (the English) at the expense of another (the Irish). The Irish cannot feel at home in such an order of meanings, but are complicit in it if they wish to participate in activities which are a benefit to them (which they must to gain any form of employment in English society). The Irish are silenced and subordinated.

Of real significance in the feminist critiques (and especially in Langton and Nussbaum) is the usage of objectification as putatively negative. A Hegelian (and more broadly idealist) understanding of objectification is not necessarily always an exercise of power. Yet, the contemporary forms of pornography may be more akin to the Irish jokes. The formation of the understanding of individuals belonging to a certain group (the Irish, females) is corrupted by the existence of pornography which reflects the hidden interests of another class (the English, males). Any attempt at authentic self-objectification becomes alienation because the subject cannot feel at home in it, so they must either be silenced or subordinated. However, in order to secure other necessary goods and a life worth living, the subject must conform to the categories of understanding, thus we see how it resolves itself into the third dimension of power or the willing domination of the subject by herself or himself.

A proper critique of pornography should then be aimed at the cultural conditions of understanding and not some imagined individual who seeks to oppress a group. By assuming that one can trace the wrongdoing to a decision on the part of a fixed subjectivity, feminists undermine any true moral progress and any real understanding of sexual representation. Defining objectification as feminists have done, pornography is seen as necessarily bad just in virtue of being objectifying, but objectifying can be negative or positive. The feminist critique obscures the fact that objectification creates an 'us' in which all individuals are objectified rather than a mere set (the female). And if this is the case, we cannot go from the fact that pornography is objectifying to a conclusion that it ought to be prohibited or its existence is grounds for legal suits. There is no single or group Male to identify as the perpetrator of the wrongdoing. Under capitalism, Marx saw alienation as four-fold: I am alienated from nature; from myself (I cannot feel at home); from the product of my will (I did this despite myself); and from other individuals (atomism). Pornography is a capitalistic simulation of alienation. The sexual other is understood as an instrument for my pleasure and the individual's sexuality is seen as a commodity to be exchanged in the marketplace. The subject cannot feel at home in the modes of behaviour that constitute his or her sexuality (we do it despite ourselves) and we are in competition with others because our body can be replaced by any other object. Our sexuality is distorted by capitalism and its representations, that is pornography.

Pornography is a cultural problem and a cultural problem requires a new type of ethics which does not seek an intentional criminal and a single victim. The next chapter constitutes an initial attempt to articulate such an ethical framework.

Interlude 5 The Devil in Miss Jones

Damiano's 1973 film, *The Devil in Miss Jones,* is an existentialist classic. The 2005 remake is an example of the worst kind of capitalist drive to homogeneity.[1] But before we narrate and lament the loss of pornographic innocence and aesthetic creativity at the altar of money-making, let us celebrate the original. The film is a reworking of Sartre's *Huis Clos,* reducing the play's original 'trilogue' to a simple dialogue between two strangers.[2] The conversation between the participants resolves around the same Sartrean theme: a misunderstood and irresolvable dialogue where one discovers the futility of being something for an other and, at the same time, realizes that one cannot exist without the other. This is so above all in sexual desire, where we cannot do it by ourselves, nor even with others. The film concludes with the main protagonist, awakened to sexual desire and its rampant egoism, unable to satisfy her urges because the other has no interest in her sexually and she has no interest in him as a person: 'I can't do it by myself!' Sartre's play concludes with Garcin rejecting the sexual intimacy offered by Estelle, all three characters realizing that they cannot exist without each other.

Both narratives are a modern re-imagining of Hell, where the religious iconography of burning torture is replaced by the heated gaze of the other from who one demands to be recognized as worthy (which all the characters in life, in both film and play, were not), yet aware that the other cannot freely judge me and at the same time be determined to judge the character as they would wish. And the descent into Hell is a very Catholic imagining, bound tightly to religious and not necessarily moral conceptions of sin. The characters are condemned to Hell because of the actions for which they are wholly responsible; in the play, it is infanticide, cowardice and cruelty, and in the film it is suicide. More than this, though, the very premise of the film is grounded in the

Dostoyevskian universe where God is dead and everything is permitted. As she arrives in Hell, Miss Jones does not understand why in a life so free of sin, one single act weighs so heavily against her. In a situation in which she is damned anyway, why would cultural norms and external standards of correctness continue to determine her behaviour. She is granted a short stay in limbo where she can try what she has always denied herself in life, and had led to her suicide, one assumes, from social isolation.

The asexual man in the cell at the end is played by the director himself, aware that his creation is no longer for his own satisfaction, that he is in no way the 'director' of the film but something more, something beyond this because this reduces him to nothing but a pornography director, which unfortunately he requires the other to testify to, but his other will not.

The film is interesting because of these themes and also the main actress is not the stereotypical pornography star, a fact very much written into the screenplay: 'It is not much to look at, I know.' It is interesting because it is character (and female) led. It is Miss Jones who determines what she wants to do and when she wants to do it.[3] The male actors are directed by her words and her wants, not by the expectations of the viewers. It is the woman who is in control and enjoying what she does. She decides what is done with her, how, and to what extent. The men in the film, even the bureaucratic Cerebus and the Teacher fulfil no role but the extension of her wants and needs. The final double penetration scene is controlled by her and uniquely has the men's genitals rubbing together. She demands that they come not in or on her, but on each other. This is a scene almost impossible for a mainstream pornography that wishes to make money since it is, like the man's idealization of lesbianism being a voyeuristic pleasure for men, a reciprocal woman's idealization and eroticization of gay sex for herself. (A theme that is very much prominent in the Spanish film, *The Ages of Lulu*.)

The remake is so thoroughly modern that it is banal. The actress is very typically a pornographic actress, chosen because of her image rather than her ability to represent the character. Her 'sin' is no longer the Catholic sin of suicide, which was of interest because it was meaningless in our new moral universe: the absurdity of being condemned for something one does not understand as wrongdoing, that appears arbitrary to one. Instead, we are offered the non-existentialist account of personal responsibility: Miss Jones is now condemned to Hell because she is blamed for bringing about the suicide of another, rather than her own suicide. And that was because she ignored the sexual advances of this man. She denied him what was his right and what she wanted, even if she could not admit it. She owes him and, in the final scene, she is made to pay for this 'sin' as he denies what she wanted all along. The two in the dialogue in the final scene are no longer strangers, but are bound together by a relationship of wanting and owing.

The remake reduces it all down to male coded desire. Hell is no longer a school or college, but a workplace. The Teacher is replaced by the Devil as a woman (with the ubiquitous lesbian scene). Hell and torture are alluded to in a final orgy scene which culminates in the necessary *ménage a trois*. Although still double penetration, it is now straightforwardly heterosexual as the men remain very much apart and, rather than the woman being the centre of pleasure, she is now the source of pleasure as testified by the insertion of oral sex which confers pleasure on the men rather than her. There is no indication of the original Miss Jones's wish and the woman's viewing wish for male homosexuality.

It is obvious that, for all its failings, the original was an attempt by a production team and a group of individuals to make something of value, in which they had an interest, a product that was, in some sense, theirs. There was also an apparent attempt at aesthetic value and narrative pretence. The remake is no longer about the product, it is about the money: turning an investment into a product. To ensure maximum profit, women are cast who meet the expectations and wishes of the majority of the audience (white, blonde, banally pornographic), and make the sexual activity what the audience expect (hence we reproduce and continue to determine what their expectations are, no taking risks with male homosexuality or women's desires for the erotic). The film is put in an easy moral framework which they will understand, skewed to some odd contemporary pornographic mentality about what women really want and how they should be rewarded or punished for it. All in all, it produces what will sell and is demanded by the economic reality of our lives rather than what we might have wanted to make had we been free of the demand to see the investment in the film solely in dollar signs.

And all that philosophical pretence, existential angst and amoralist rumination is cut. Who wants to be distracted by thinking when they've got their cocks in their hands? It's a porn flick, after all.

6
'I Can't Do It by Myself!': Social Ethics and Pornography

6.1 Dworkin's secret admiration

Ronald Dworkin is very much a good example of the liberal, legal theorist who finds himself situated in late modern capitalism. Yet, he is a thinker who exists in a different world: prior to the mass proliferation of the media and the advent of the internet. He reduces the question of pornography to the eminently sensible political question of how far should people have a right to do the wrong thing. Now, we know whenever anyone poses such a question, we shall find ourselves forced to agree sooner or later to some sort of liberty or harm principle whereby the only justification for the sanction of the liberty of the individual is if that individual's actions will result in harm to others (not to himself or herself). Dworkin, of course, will position his rights theory at the border of the private–public distinction: the only way pornography can be prohibited is if it violates the rights of agents. And, of course, the prohibition of pornography violates the rights of producers and consumers of pornography, thus we are offered this strategy: '... if pornography makes the community worse off, even in the very long run, it is nevertheless wrong to censor or restrict it because this violates the individual moral or political rights of citizens who resent the censorship' (Dworkin, 1981: 178).

Feminists have attempted to show the harm and the violation of rights brought about by the production, exchange and consumption of pornography concerns specific individuals and not choices about how one should live one's life. Liberals still defend the existence of pornography on the basis of individual rights to do what one wants when one wants so long as it does not violate the rights of others. Oddly, though, Dworkin has a not so secret admiration for the 1981 Williams Report and the non-utilitarian goal-based strategy it proposes. That defence, unsurprisingly given its liberal basis, resolves into a defence of another version of the harm principle. Dworkin, however, claims that the legal proposals of the report are not justified by the theoretical approach of a goal-based strategy but merely by common sense. The authors help themselves to a public consensus on the issue to ground the apparent rationality of their arguments (but, then, it was a government report and not a work of philosophy!)[1] Only a rights-based approach can justify the intuitions, so the rights-based approach is more plausible.

The aim of Williams' goal-based strategy in the report is a society which promotes human self-development whereby individuals can make intelligent and free decisions about their lives (1981: ch. 5). A free market of ideas is required for the possibility of such ideas and hence there is a need to protect minority pursuits from the homogeneity of the moral majority (or 'collective mediocrity' as Berlin (1958) once described it). Dworkin, though, is uneasy about the vague metaphysical commitment to human development and the possibility that some agents will assume that they know what is best for the development of others. Rights theory ensures that no agent can decide for another without the consent (sometimes implicit!) of the choice-patient. Rights protect individuals and the free market of ideas whereas the goal-based strategy does not. Dworkin instead grounds his argument on the right to moral independence and *not* the right to free expression as lazy feminist critics seem to suppose: 'People have the right not to suffer disadvantage in the distribution of social goods and opportunities, including disadvantage in the liberties permitted to them by the criminal law, just on the ground that their officials or fellow-citizens think that their opinions about the right way for them to lead their own lives are ignoble or wrong' (Dworkin, 1981: 194).

Where Dworkin's position is perhaps weakened, though, is in its absolutism. He proposes an either/or dichotomy, rights or goals, and he tries to restrict goals with rights because goals on their own fail and can be pernicious. The answer is not so much either/or, but rather a fluid reciprocity. Rights matter because they support and maintain the right sort of goals and goals are of the right sort because they are maintained and supported by rights (because individuals make them self-conscious culture and not just culture). Both positions, though, rest on the experimentation of a morally reliable minority.

Things have changed. Pornography is no longer a minority issue nor does it exist in a shadowy, hidden recess of society. And, for that reason, the feminists' identification of the objectification-subversion-silence trinity goes right to the heart of both Williams' and Dworkin's positions. What is at stake is equality, whether it be understood as the need for self-conscious understanding (undermined by alienation), the need to be accepted and recognized as a morally, independent peer (undermined by silencing), or the capacity to decide for oneself (undermined by subordination). It seems that the feminist claim that for a society to be rational, it must respect the autonomous choice and equal standing of all its members, is in full agreement with Dworkin's theoretical commitments. The disagreement rests on whether his rights theory can actually deliver this goal. The direction to be followed now is to see if one can identify an ethical position that can support the Williams, Dworkin and feminist liberalisms, but in such a way that we can decide whether or not pornography needs to be prohibited, tolerated or encouraged.

As far as human development is concerned, one needs to keep in mind the intuition that whatever human development consists in, it requires the autonomy of individual agents to recognize the value of what is proposed and whether that requires protection via rights, institutions or through education, it remains fundamental to the *goal* of society. Take, for example, these words from Mill when discussing the place of women in society and reflections on their contemporary predicament:

> The moral education of mankind has hitherto emanated chiefly from the law of force, and is adapted almost solely to the relations which force creates. In the less advanced states of society, people hardly recognise any relation with their equals. To be an equal is to be an enemy. Society, from its highest place to its lowest, is one long chain, or rather ladder, where every individual is either above or below his nearest neighbour, and wherever he does not command he must obey. Existing moralities, accordingly, are mainly fitted to a relation of command and obedience. Yet command and obedience are but unfortunate necessities of human life: society in equality is its normal state. Already in modern life, and more and more as it progressively improves, command and obedience become exceptional facts in life, equal association its general rule. The morality of the first ages rested on the obligation to submit to power; that of the ages next following, on the right of the weak to the forbearance and protection of the strong. How much longer is one form of society and life to content itself with the morality made for another? We have had the morality of submission, and the morality of chivalry and generosity; the time is now come for the morality of justice. (Mill, 1869: loc. 753-62)

Mill's call for the morality of justice is for a society which guarantees equality between individuals and he seems to attack deontological theories because they rest on relations of power and ideology. His ultimate justification would no doubt be (although it is seldom mentioned in the tract in question) general happiness, but that was always for Mill happiness of the individual first and foremost. For Dworkin, a morality of justice (rights) guarantees moral independence. For the feminists, it guarantees a voice and autonomy and, for this present essay, equality is a goal which guarantees free and uncoerced identity objectification and not social and individual alienation. An ethical position is required: that does not assume that rights theory is ethically neutral (as Dworkin does); that can explain the conditions of free, human development (which Williams and his cohorts only assume); and takes into account the distinction between alienation and objectification (which feminists do not). It will then be seen whether such a position can offer a rational evaluation of the existence and role of sexually explicit representations in culture.

6.2 Sketching out a new ethical position

The preceding pages have shown that, if there is a moral or a political problem with pornography, it resides in its existence in general and its consumption in particular. Critics of pornography, if they are to be as robust and convincing as possible, must hold that the existence of pornography maintains an historically contingent state of inequality between groups, enabling the treatment of specific individuals in a way not consistent with their standing as full moral agents. In other words, pornography supports an institutional and ideological failure to confer on certain agents the respect they deserve. Thinking through the problem in discursive isolation, either as a moral problem centred on the treatment of persons or as the political problem of liberty to say what one wants, generates obstructions to an adequate discussion of the problem itself. And if one were to imagine an actual, public debate, such separation does not map moral discourse in the slightest. Political principles, moral values, social cost–benefit analysis and empirical facts all constitute various reasons for holding a specific moral belief. Of course, one would not want to unreflectively mirror the discourse of the *hoi polloi*. Philosophy is, after all, about clarifying such discourse, but perhaps moral discourse ought to be more sensitive to the social context in which we find ourselves. Perhaps there is a particular, historical problem with pornography that is in no less urgent a need of a resolution than a supposed universal problem with the representation of sexual activity. We still need a theory, though, because theories allow us to be consistent and rational and not just assertive and groundless.

The fragmentary nature of this debate may well be an instance of what Hegel saw as symptomatic about modern moral theory: the separation of politics, ethics and morality into distinct, autonomous discourses. It would be a mistake, though, to attempt to offer Hegel's ethics as a better alternative to the more traditional responses since, implicit in such an endeavour, would be the need to justify an interpretation of particular historical texts and the plausibility of this interpretation. Any attempt to defend an interpretation of Hegel's ethics is an intellectual enterprise in its own right and Hegel himself made some very silly, if excusable, mistakes in his ethical ruminations which would need to be ironed out. However, one need not subscribe to Hegel's grander metaphysical claims in order to realize that the basics of Hegel's concept of culture do offer something substantial to the debate. For economies of space, it should be noted that what follows is *Kantian* rather than *Kant, Hegelian* rather than *Hegel* and *Vichian* rather than *Vico*. It is also my first attempt to articulate the grounding ethical view in any systematic way and will surely be in need of refinement, but the position developed offers a new way of thinking in ethical theory that does not separate morality, ethics and politics into different spheres of discussion.[2]

I shall first indicate what it is for a motivation to be a value and identify those motivations which are values as reasons proper of the individual. Second, I shall assert, rather than argue for, a position of moral idealism (or irrealism) whereby what is known to be a value is derived from the social and moral fabric, or tradition, of the moral agent. Such values make moral thinking and action possible and inform the practical rationality of the agent. Contrary to Kant, though, I shall eschew any substantial universality in moral reasons as distinct from other reasons, instead rejecting monism in favour of pluralism as it better describes moral experience and does not, unlike Kant's universality, lead to moral requirements which oscillate between being too strict and too abstract. Moral idealism will, however, furnish us with universal procedural requirements of morality which, although unable to do enough moral work, will limit ethical discourse according to the treatment of people. In order to generate substantial moral requirements, the procedural approach will be augmented by an historical approach, whereby the agent is conceived of as participating in a system of values and reasons which pre-exist him or her and make possible his or her practical reasoning. Finally, in order to complete the picture, we shall see that the procedural and historical requirements also require one further condition, that of a minimal naturalism in order to rule out counter-intuitive moral requirements.

What happens when someone asks whether pornography should be prohibited? In the preceding pages, we have seen what the sort of answers offered will be, answers that are concerned with individual and group well-being, equality, the liberty and autonomy of groups and individuals and respect. Nearly all the arguments for both the prohibition of *and* the non-interference in pornography demonstrate some rational connection between its existence or non-existence and the protection, promotion or maximization of these values. These values are understood as reasons which ought to motivate agents, that is motivations worth having (Wolf, 1990). When someone does X and one says that she should have done Y, that is acted differently, or one simply says that she was wrong or should not have done that (whether for moral, prudential, epistemic or other types of reasons) what one actually means is that although she wanted to do X (and would not have done it, had she not wanted it) and though it was not necessarily wrong to want X, doing Y was more desirable or you should have wanted to want to do Y in the circumstances and situation. Take the example that my village is attacked. I have the simultaneous desires to flee and to fight. The value here is that desire which one desires to act upon when faced with these drives pulling in opposite directions and the hierarchy can be explained rationally. So, I desire to flee the invaders, but I also desire to protect my family and my staying and fighting is rationally connected to this second consideration. The second desire is privileged, that is, it is the one which I ought to act upon, because the web of meanings that constitute my society propose the values of family, honour and heroism. If I were to flee, it would make sense to say I did so despite myself, even if such a statement is metaphysically puzzling. Values are interests or preferences which trump immediate desires if they are not (which they sometimes are) immediate desires themselves.

Take a more traditional moral case of whether or not an agent ought to keep his or her promises in order to illustrate the nature of these values. Let us put some flesh on the bones of the example in order to better understand what is at stake: we bought a lottery ticket together, each putting up 50 per cent of the cost and agree to divide any eventual winnings equally, 50 per cent each. You have to, however, leave the country and I look after the ticket. I therefore agree to inform you of the result and promise to pay you 50 per cent should we actually win. We do, in fact, win a substantial amount, say twenty million pounds, but I know that you are unaware of the fact and I am pretty sure you will never learn that we have won due to the emergence of some quite strange circumstances concerning your situation and convenient memory loss. Am I morally obliged to inform you and pay you back as I have promised? As an agent, any agent, I would find myself pushed and pulled by a collection of various latent interests: greed, fraternity, prudence, guilt, altruism, egoism, and so on and so forth. Many of these are manifestations of more base emotional responses and they overlap, but nearly all can be articulated in terms of reasons: personal benefit, friendship, instrumental achievement of goals, caring about the welfare of others, caring about my own welfare, and so on and so forth. Many of these reasons are compelling, they are intelligible to most agents (who can access them simply be imaging themselves in a similar situation), and they are motivating, either being an expression of an interest or desire or being related to reasons for action or desires.

Of course, the question is about whether I should keep my promise or not and the answer would seem to be, 'Yes', notwithstanding other considerations. The interests, desire, or preference that motivates me have to be in accordance with the principle of keeping my promise if it is to be laudable. So, even if I want to keep the money in order to buy a new house, or I awake to find that I am actually a greedy and not a generous person at all, I should still inform you and share our winnings as promised. So, even if I want to keep the money, I may – and I am human – recognize in myself the wish to inform you at the same time as not wanting to inform you. Practical reason at the immediate level is too close to the id to be ruled by rational connections between desires. The difference between what is a value and what is a mere motivation is that I want to overcome my personal greed, I want to want to inform you to such an extent that my other desires are rendered insignificant in relation to it. I may know you are going to waste the money on cheap booze or that I am going to donate it to cancer research, or, I just know I am going to have a lot of fun with the money, but egoistic or prudential reasons for my keeping the money matter less than the moral reasons to keep my promise. (Given the discussion of aesthetic and moral value in Chapter 3, this is not necessarily always the case, but it is in this situation.) I want to want to keep the promise over and above all the other things I desire and want. On one level, it might just be that the desire to keep the promise is stronger than the desire for personal profit, but on another level, promise-keeping is a value. My actions when I keep the promise in spite of my very strong want to profit from the situation testify to the value and I have to make a conscious effort to do so, perhaps reminding myself it is the right thing to do. In this second case, keeping the promise (whether it be for a simple deontological reason, or deeper welfarist contractarian accounts of promise keeping, or because it is an expression of my respect for you as a reasoning thing) is the expression or the principle governed by a value, or the motivation worth acting upon.[3]

And when we introspect, we are aware of possessing a storehouse of values which inform and supply the content for our moral judgements and evaluations. These values or motivations worth having constitute a cultural a priori in two sense of Kant's meaning (although he would of course reject the idea of the *cultural* a priori at all) (Ewing, 1967: 29). First, these sorts of values are presupposed in our moral experience in that we could not form moral judgements unless we had the building atoms from which to construct such judgements. Welfare, liberty, equality, rightness and so on may be opaque but they are the sorts of terms that moral discourse requires in our culture; they enable us to understand events as moral events. Second, these values are also contributed by the thinking agent's rational structure and are not derivable from the world. Values are not supplied by God, not deontological in that absolute sense (a sense which Kant's contemporaries would have had as an echo in their collective rationality and hence making it easier for his own moral arguments to progress), nor are they non-natural facts. Values exist in the shared, moral fabric which constitutes the basis for judgement. They are interpersonal and motivate agents in virtue of that agent occupying a role in a given culture: 'In an ethical community, it is easy to say *what* someone must do and *what* the duties are which he has to fulfil in order to be virtuous. He must simply do what is prescribed, expressly stated, and known to him within his situation' (Hegel, 1991: §150R). Thus, these values are a priori (imposed by a subject on reality but not derived from that reality and required for the possibility of moral experience), but they are *cultural* through and through; we find ourselves thrown, historically and contingently, into them.

In the lottery case, an overriding principle, 'You should not break promises', asserts itself as the proper and appropriate motivation. Non-philosophically, we all know that is what we should do in the situation described above. Philosophically, we can justify the value in terms of deeper theoretical positions: indirect utilitarianism, Kantian deontology, contractarianism, and so on. Any moral theory worth its salt must conform to the immediate intuition in this case. However, in the case of pornography there is no simple response; it is an issue and not just a given. Worse than this, on certain moral issues where there is an absence of strong agreement, theories can justify different values and therefore generate conflict. The response of ethicists is often to return to their deeper theories in order to attempt to offer a solution which is consistent and coherent with their theory in the absence of plausible intuitions. And the putative assumption is that moral theory is akin to science or mathematics: when there is no shared agreement or conflict, it is assumed that some of the proposed solutions are in error and ought to be rejected, and along with them their grounding theories. Of course, no one thinks in terms of theories being *better* at specific types of questions or *more appropriate* to certain issues. No one thinks to replace the demand for the one right theory with the most appropriate, or best theory, in this case. That is what we shall propose now.

Let us attempt to put some philosophical meat on the above assertions and attempt to reveal what may well be a central error in moral enquiry: a widespread and subtle transposition of an assumption belonging to the realm of theoretical reason which influences, yet ultimately frustrates, moral reasoning. This assumption is the belief that a well-constructed moral problem can only have one possible solution in the same way that any theoretical question can only have one solution. If more than one solution is available, and it is impossible to decide between the merits of the answers, it is commonly supposed that the question is either badly framed or that it arises as the result of a conceptual error. The problem with pornography, as the preceding pages testify, would seemingly fall into this category.

Not all practical judgements are universal: 'what career ought one to pursue' cannot, for example, be answered definitively for all people, at all times and in all places. (There is, actually, one answer. The principle: do what is appropriate to you and your goals. Such an answer reveals the necessary connection between universality and vacuity which we shall propose below. It tells us nothing about what one should actually do.) There is not one right answer to such questions: there are better and worse answers, and equally valid answers. However, the universality of moral judgements is seemingly necessary to resolve conflicts of value: if I say human sacrifice is wrong and you say human sacrifice is right, either one or both of us are mistaken in our answer, or the question is conceptually confused. Conceptual bewilderment may have arisen from derivations from the more fundamental principle 'killing is wrong'. Even that, in most societies, has exceptions: self-defence, war and, perhaps, euthanasia. In the first two exceptions, the moral stance of the agent is challenged by the situation, whereas in the final example a higher moral principle ('the good life') comes into play. It is easy to see how human sacrifice may be compelled by some belief systems ('we must sacrifice, otherwise it won't rain'), or even determined by a higher moral principle ('the victim will be rewarded in heaven'; 'it is the will of the gods'). Once we have the proper conceptual description before us, then we can ask whether it was a cogent principle or not and whether one or both of us were mistaken in our response to the original question.

The search for universal principles in moral enquiry is however beset by two problems: either they are just not available; or if they are available, they are vacuous and non-substantial. Take, for example, the destruction of the Bamiyan Buddhist idols in Afghanistan in 2001. The Taliban justified the destruction in terms of their faith: if one holds that all false idols are blasphemous, then these idols must be destroyed. Why should we not destroy these statues? The protesters did not have a universal principle with which to trump the relative principle of the Taliban. The answers ranged from: 'because they are beautiful' to some substantial principle of restoration (the past should be preserved for educational purposes). In other words, the supposedly secular principles were themselves relative to a belief system which itself requires justification. The only point of agreement seemed to be the moral principle of respect, but again depending on which tradition or way of life one inhabits, this principle is open to a variety of interpretations and cannot resolve the conflict without substantial interpretation. And that interpretation, one would assume, largely depends on the meanings and values of the particular agent's specific way of life.

However, to reduce standard moral theory to an interpretative enterprise is problematic in that it opens one up to the charge of 'anything goes'. As moral idealism, like epistemological idealism, rests on the initial claim that all 'judgements about' are interpretative, a word or two ought to be said about interpretation and its relation to truth. If you want moral rationality, then you need some standard of judgement which can go beyond the claim that 'I would not have done so' to a more robust 'You should not have done so'. Since interpretations are seemingly ruled by subjectivity, then they tend towards the position of 'anything goes'. Interpretation modelled on monism, whereby the aim of the interpretative process was consensus on the proper or true meaning of a text has largely been undermined by the Marxist attacks on ideology, historicism and Freudian psychoanalytic readings. They all cast doubt on the claim that the author is in the best position to recount the meaning of a text. Meaning is always a meaning *for* a specific time or agent, but just because pluralism gives up on one proper solution or interpretation, it does not entail it cannot identify better or worse readings. There are various meanings or readings of Lawrence's *Lady Chatterley's Lover*, but some are equally valid, and some are better than others. However, not all readings are allowed on to the table. The novel is not, and cannot be about the 1966 World Cup nor the building of the Egyptian pyramids. Something has gone wrong in the procedure of reading the text if the interpretation generates such a reading. Which are best and which are to be discounted as wrong are decided through application of a procedure which conditions possible interpretations (and these procedures will differ from discourse to discourse: moral procedures are different from literary procedures).

Different personal and cultural interpretations, though, even if they deviate from the original situations of a text can often add something to its meaning. In one Dr. Seuss story, *Oh, the places you'll go!*, which introduces children to the course their lives may take, the problems they will face and the successes and disappointments that await them, a British English speaker will find the nonsense lines 'You'll get mixed up/ with many strange birds as you go.' far more meaningful than an American English speaker. ('Birds' is a colloquialism for women in British English.) Neither Dr. Seuss himself, the American public, structuralism, or psychoanalytic readings could have explained such an interpretation, but it is a valid one. And such interpretation is commonplace in our adoption or obedience to moral principles. The moral principle, 'Don't lie', is largely non-controversial, but rarely adhered to in a robustly stringent manner. With children, the principle can be re-interpreted as do not deceive and so Father Christmas is not a deception because there is no malignity or harm intended. And such an interpretation has wider application with adults in many social rituals where out and out Kantianism about truth telling would result in social ostracism: dinner parties; clothes shopping trips; visiting others' houses for the first time; and so on. Interpretation of what is required allows a more nuanced approach allowing one to debate rather than follow imperatives, but not at the cost of allowing all interpretations to stand without justification.

Relativism, as a meta-ethical theory, recognizes the intricate connections that exist between the possibility of making moral judgements and the moral agent's way of life. It would seem that if I am to propose that there is more than one answer to a moral question and this is derived from the interpretative nature of moral inquiry, then I am offering a form of moral relativism. I am not; I wish to distinguish moral relativism from moral pluralism. In the following discussion, I shall try to show how the three main forms of moral pluralism – radical empiricism, ontological pluralism, and hermeneutic pluralism – all rest on shared commitments about moral values whereby morality is understood as an historically situated interpretation of the social existence of the agent using interpersonal values. These values may be revisable, universal yet plural, or the necessary expression of human interests, but in all cases they will be made manifest through social interpretation.

To begin with moral relativism, then: it is most simply understood as the thesis that the agent's moral beliefs, motivations and values are derived from and are dependent on the society he or she inhabits. It is not to be understood as the absurd claim that one has no right to pass judgement on the moral beliefs of others since this itself proposes the value of non-interference as a universal value and, therefore, as a theory of relativism it is self-refuting.[4] One need only hold that moral values are derived from a way of life, which is to say, the ascription of the concepts of good and bad and right and wrong depends on the way of life of the moral agent. This says nothing about the revisability or rejection of these beliefs and it should not be assumed that the beliefs of one's birth remain unchanged.

The most attractive aspect of relativism is quite simply that it explains the variety of moral beliefs and values throughout the world and amongst different societies: there are many diverse and conflicting moral beliefs because they are derived from different societies and are not universally rational or objectively true. Moreover, value systems may exhibit certain features of a limited rationality, that is moral judgements may have logical connections, but only within a context defined by one's way of life. Herein, though, lies the weakness of relativism. Even at its most robust, a theory of moral relativism can merely hold that the rationality of moral judgements is internal to a particular way of life and the attractions of relativism are undermined by one great disadvantage concerning conflicts of beliefs: surely a society with a moral belief, say, that human sacrifice is good should not be left alone to practise what it believes just because values are relative? Other prime examples include female circumcision and the exploitation of children. Relativism is most commonly rejected because it cannot resolve conflicts between ways of life, and for this reason alone moral universalism is a far more attractive theory. However, moral universalism is either vacuous and insubstantial or it, too, leads to conflict. In other words, its supposed advantage is chimerical. If we examine the claim of universality at the heart of most ethical theories, it may be revealed that it is an *ad hoc* and, ultimately, frustrating addition to practical reason.

The rejection of the claim that a moral question has but one solution coupled with the intention to resist a simple relativism overtly commits one to pluralism concerning moral values and motivations. Given that this is the case, it is perhaps wise to say a few words about this thesis. Moral pluralism is firstly a form of moral idealism, or the claim that moral systems are constructions of the human mind. In proposing moral idealism, all I wish to offer is a minimal idealism, or to trace through the moral consequences of taking Kant's Copernican revolution seriously (Kant, 1993: Bxvi). In order for a subject to form judgements at all, certain concepts have to inhere in the subject that set the formal structure and limits of those statements. Following Kant, a theoretical judgement is made possible by the subject's possession of prior and universal concepts belonging to the categories of modality, relation, quality and quantity. To put it simply, I would not be able to experience *x* as the cause of *y*, unless I already possessed the concept of causality and were able to bring it to bear on the content of my experience.

Universality is written into the Kantian epistemological position from the beginning because rational beings necessarily share the same constitutive concepts. If a subject is rational, which is to say if he is a possible knower or maker of judgements, then he must share Kant's twelve concepts and two pure intuitions. Sharing the concepts is not enough, though, because if we are to form the same judgement we must also combine intuitions, that is process them, in the same way in order to talk about the world or ideas at all. The common sense answer is that the 'real' object impinges on our senses and we translate it and filter the data through our concepts. This is not, however, consistent with Kantian idealism. Causality belongs to the concepts of the subject and not to reality, and it is already a speculative step to posit 'objects' in reality outside of experience. Intuitions are given to us as subjects and we form judgements on their basis. So, how do we all form the same judgements? A full response to this question would have to look closely at Kant's description of the schemata and the role of the imagination, but unfortunately we have no space or time to do this. An investigation of these would plausibly lead one from the constitutive concepts of experience to the regulative ideas of reason, and one in particular: the idea of the unity of all knowledge in one mind. The system of knowledge is ideally whole and harmonious (Kant, 1993: 394-466). At the risk of oversimplifying Kant's position, I propose that what he has in mind is the assumption that since theoretical judgements aim at describing *what is*, then they ought to – and here one feels the force of the regulative norm – be the same for me and for you. Our judgements ought to converge. If they do not, we need to rid them of those contingencies (my particular angle to the table, for example) which are insignificant in the formulation of the judgement ('It is rectangular'). Universality is a necessary norm for theoretical judgements since theoretical judgements ideally ought to converge.

Whereas theoretical judgements are determined by modality, relation, quality and quantity, Kant informs us that all moral judgements are determined by the application of one single concept, that is freedom (Kant, 2012: Preface; 1997: 1.i). If the object of the judgement is not understood as a free agent, then, moral judgements are not applicable. The concept of responsibility cannot be applied to tables, chairs, animals, most young children, and the insane simply because they are not free. This is far from being a controversial initial premise because Kant is not stating any metaphysical truth in the traditional sense. He is not saying that morality is possible because agents are free (although, in later writings, he will), he is saying if we make moral statements and hold them to be truth-apt, then we must *assume* that agents are free. According to Kant, if the subject acts freely, then moral judgements can be made in line with the categorical imperative: if the agent is making an exception of himself, or if he uses others as means without their consent, then he is immoral.

Again, here, I would like to avoid specific problems arising from the Kantian account of moral judgements, but it is worthwhile saying something about the possibility of transgression. It is often assumed that, on Kant's account, one is either good or irrational and the agent can never freely commit wrong. However, Kant does reveal two ways in which a human can commit wrongdoing: using others as means without their consent and making oneself an exception to the law of reason. I believe that the latter is merely derived from the former and they both derive from the constitutive concept of freedom: I rely on you to obey conventions, such as promising, which I pretend to do in order to profit from you. This is immoral because I do not give your freedom and your rationality the respect it deserves and I actually contradict the value of freedom. For Kant, other lesser moral constitutive concepts are all derived from the idea of free will (imperatives, autonomy, persons, rational ends), and moral judgements are universal because they are synthetic a priori: they are true for all rational beings. Yet it is not clear that such judgements will not conflict. Kant assumes that they will not due to the fact that there can be one and only one solution to moral problems, but such universality is built into his system due to his assertion that moral judgements are synthetic a priori, and therefore identical to epistemological judgements. However, epistemological judgements are ruled by a regulative concept that there can be one and only one possible true description of objects of experience (unity). Is there any reason to assume that the same norm governs moral judgements?

In fact, one can find a different regulative ideal for the use of practical reason in Kant's thinking: '... its true function must be to produce a *will that is good,* not for other purposes *as a means,* but *good in itself* ...' (2012: 4:396). In his first critique, it is the free will which is regulative, but that becomes constitutive in his later moral works. Hence his movement from agnosticism concerning the freedom of agents in the first critique and the groundwork to a proof of free will in the second. Freedom is the concept which constitutes moral judgements, but if I am free I can form any judgement which is not contradictory to freedom. This interpretation of Kant leads to the criticism that, if the categorical imperative *generates* duties, then absurd maxims will become universal law, such as 'one ought to count to ten every morning'. If we take seriously the idea of the good will, such maxims just do not belong to the moral realm. The good will regulates moral judgements, but on two levels. First, that the reason for action be good in-itself: to be a moral agent one needs to act on a reason which is good and can be recognized as such by others independent of the agent who proposes such reasons implicitly in his or her action. What is rational is good for me, but I can recognize the rationality of the other's intention without endorsing its goodness. The intelligible nature of such reasons, that formal structure with which they explain the action in itself of the agent, is not yet robust enough for Kant. Second, then, the good will recognizes that good in-itself is binding because it is rational, or the right precedes and determines the good. If I form the judgement that a triangle has three sides concomitantly with the judgement that the shape I perceive has four sides, I am rationally compelled to deny that my perception is of a triangle and can assert it only at the cost of my rationality. It is, then, rationally necessary. Kant similarly holds that if a reason is good in itself, that is independently of the particular agent, then it demands to be acted upon by whomever. If he or she does not, he or she acts at the cost of his or her rationality. He wants the fact that they are formally intelligible independent of a particular agent to generate their content as practically necessary for all agents in virtue of the universal nature of such reasons via the presumption of a strong universality: not only need they be intelligible to a possible enquiring agent, but they must bear a practically rational relation to the performance of the action. If I recognize the validity of your reason, then I too must act in the same way. This, though, is a step too far. A good reason is intelligible to both me and you, it is one which makes sense. A good moral reason is one which makes sense and is also freely motivated by reason. Yet, there is nothing in this description which justifies the move from rightness to goodness. Another way to put this might be to talk about agent-relative and agent-neutral reasons for action. Motivating values would have to be agent-relative: there can be no way to conceive of a reason which I recognize as valid but does not affect me as motivating. That Ben Nevis is the tallest mountain in the UK is of interest to the agent who wants to climb the tallest mountain in the UK and I can understand the climber's behaviour given enough information to reconstruct this project in him or her, but for me it is a fact that does not have any effect on my desires. I do not want to climb the highest mountain in the UK. For Kant, though, moral reasons are a special subset of reasons that are agent-neutral but motivating, or agent-relative to all rational agents (and hence agent-universal).

Kant moves from a reason which is recognized as valid by all agents to a reason which must be endorsed by all rational agents: what is right is good. There is no justification for this transposition except the assumption of theoretical wisdom: what is true for me ought to be true for you, but there is no reason why this norm ought to govern the moral realm. For example, I can understand that a Muslim does not eat pork and that it would be wrong to eat pork if I were a Muslim, but I am not and though I can recognize the validity of the reason, that does not make it a universally binding reason. I am however compelled to respect and accommodate the Muslim's interests when offering food to eat. The Kantian would, of course, deny that my specific action is entailed, only under the umbrella of the more general duty, that is to respect the other's personhood which then would be respected through various performances in the particular situation. Yet such a general, abstract requirement can tell us nothing about how to behave unless we have other substantial understandings of how to respect others, which will all be derived from a cultural fabric.

It is possible, given the normative element of the good will, to offer a weaker form of universality. If an agent is free, his reason for action is valid so long as it does not use others as ends without their consent or makes an exception of the agent himself. Strong universality holds that for a reason to be a *moral* reason not only is it required for it to be a formally intelligible reason (in the sense that, if one values rather than just wants X, then I can understand the relationship between your reason and your action independent from you as a particular agent) but it must also be practically necessary (once I recognize the validity of your reason, it is binding on all rational beings, in all places, at all times).[5] Let us here be careful, because Kant's insights are powerful and salient: a requirement of me making moral statements is the assumption that those objects to which the statements will be applicable are free agents. If I did not assume this, then I am not making moral statements at all. If

I assume that I am making statements about free agents, then in order to respect their freedom, I can only offer imperatives for them to endorse or reject. And that means moral reasons are a subset of possible reasons for action: those reasons that all agents, no matter their wants, preferences, gender, cultural background and so on, cannot only endorse but recognize as practically rational, that is, morally binding if thought. If I force them to obey reasons for action that are merely intelligible, if I manipulate or deceive them into obeying, or coerce them with violence, then I am not treating them as a moral agent at all. Participating in moral discussions commits one to procedural limits of possible behaviour: I cannot coerce you, force you against your will, silence you or refuse to offer you reasons for a possible reason for action. Of course, Kant wants these formal limits to be the be all and end all of moral regulation, as though the formal limits of how one can engage in moral discourse can give us substantial moral imperatives.

Kant assumes a strong universality: if a reason is determined in line with the categorical imperative, then it is a moral duty for all subjects, at all times and in all situations. This leads either, on the one hand, to the narrowing of moral duties to abstract universals (respect others, treat others as ends) which are insubstantial and cannot direct action or, on the other, more substantial duties (do not break promises, do not commit suicide) which, although formally binding, may well be too strict and may lead to conflicts. Kant's commitment to the robust or strong universality of moral judgements gives rise to a number of problems (Hegel, 1975: §2; 1971: §§506–512; 1991: §135). First, any agent will at times find themselves torn between possible courses of action, whether these conflicts are between competing moral reasons (keeping a promise and not harming the overall welfare of others), between the demands of duty and personal integrity (keeping one's promise at a significant cost to oneself and one's own valued projects, interests or desires). The procedural approach to moral reasoning will not be able to resolve such conflicts satisfactorily, the agent will always have regrets or feel remorse for courses of action not taken, but this is only a problem when allied to the drive to robust universality: if there is but one answer to a moral problem for all agents, such conflicts are illusory. A weaker type of universality will recognize that there is often more than one course of action that is valid and, yet, the social reality of living requires that choices be made: doing right is never simple or without limitation. To understand the procedural limits strictly, as a specific table of duties, will exacerbate such conflicts, but the Kantian may reply that those are not the true (or well-articulated) duties. True duties are respect others as end-in-themselves in line with the categorical imperative, and keeping promises, telling the truth, developing one's identity. They are all manifestations of this deeper, true account of morality. Conflicts arise from erroneous understandings of the deeper principle.

However, if this is the case, then the advantage of deontology, that is knowing what to do and when to do it, is lost. The specific nature of deontological duties is replaced by vague and abstract principles that require elucidation and since the subject is left to generate determinations of the will out of his reflective understanding, abstractness will enter the picture. If I am to treat others as ends, but I am to decide how to do so, then judgements about how to treat people will remain open to scrutiny and revision. The commitment to universality at the level of procedural requirements determines an oscillation between moral reasons that are too strict and generate conflict, or too abstract to motivate specific actions with any personal conviction or certainty.

The preceding discussion has attempted to show that moral discourse is governed by a norm which is transposed from theoretical discourse without justification: the assumption that there can be but one answer to a problem or but one description of reality. Logically, it would be a poor inference to move from the claim that it has not been justified to one that it cannot be justified, especially without considering alternatives to ethical idealism. In theoretical reason, such an assumption is justified whether one be a realist, coherentist or pragmatist, but there is no reason to suppose it is applicable to moral judgements. In fact, the assumption leads to two undesirable consequences: one, insubstantial moral principles that are vacuous, empty and formal; and two, substantial duties which lead to a conflict that the moral system itself finds contradictory. If one embraces the weaker form of universality and its subsequent normative basis, these two problems are avoided. First, moral principles are substantial because the abstract universal principles generated by the moral will are fleshed out by a particular way of life and its conception of the good. Second, conflicts of duty still occur but they are no longer seen as symptomatic of an error in one's moral reasoning. They are just an inevitable consequence of the recognition of the pluralism of moral values.

Kant's demand for a scientific universality seemingly undermines our very intuitive grasp of the phenomenon of moral action. Agents do have competing motivations and, very often, we find ourselves in situations where we have to sacrifice one principle for the sake of another. The problems with Kant's moral system arise because he chooses to endorse a strong rather than a weak universality. Why does Kant choose to do this? On the one hand, it is because he is a man of the Enlightenment and he wants to avoid the relativism of superstitions and irrational beliefs. On the other, though, it is due to the transposition of the norm of unity from the theoretical realm to the practical realm: we must all form the same judgements. However, in the theoretical realm, this norm was due to the assumption that theoretical judgements describe *what is* but moral judgements describe *what ought to be,* and there is no coherent justification why there should be but one answer to *what ought to be*. And *what ought to be* is determined by the agent's concept of good, not right, so the substantial account of good supplied by a way of life adds the necessary flesh to the abstract bones of Kant's ethical theory. Yet, one can respect the rationality of others and still disagree about the substantial reasons for action.

Weak universalism may commit us to a different norm governing moral judgements, that is the simple recognition of the validity of other agents' motivations or reasons for action even if we do not admit them as binding on ourselves. The problem here, though, is how to replace the criterion of universality which, for Kant, distinguished between reasons for action and moral reasons for action. Like Kant, we can acknowledge the procedural limits on what can stand as a moral reason, so we are able to see that breaking my promise to keep you informed about our winnings is to violate your freedom (because an acknowledgement of your freedom will frustrate me from receiving what I want, that is all the winnings) and that this is an immoral reason for action, even if it is intelligible (that is, stands in a possible explanatory relationship to the action performed). However, we recognize that such procedural limitations of reasons of moral actions still allow for a pluralism of moral principles derived from the agent's social and moral fabric.

Pluralism concerning values and reasons for action in moral discourse is supported by three main theories. First, radical empiricism and agnosticism: in the past, we have been wrong about the most important values and have needed to modify them and even reject some of them, so it would be foolish to invest certainty in our contemporary value set (Rawls, 1993; Mill, 2011). Second, ontological pluralism proposes that values such as liberty, equality, welfare and respect are simply incommensurable and will necessarily come into conflict due to the scarcity of moral and social space in actual existing societies as well as differences in how they are to be substantiated (Berlin & Williams, 1994). Third, hermeneutic pluralism proposes that values are an interpretation of reality made possible by the engagement of historical, knowing minds with the world and hence the historical conditions of knowledge, which are necessary for knowledge at all, will generate different interpretations of value reality (Vattimo, 2004). The discussion of moral idealism above brings together these three understandings of moral pluralism: there will often be more than one answer to moral questions because the reality of moral experience is a construct of an historically situated subject who has no access to moral reality (even if such a thing exists) in virtue of his or her constitution of being a moral agent. Morality is an historically situated interpretation of the social existence of the agent using interpersonal values. The main disadvantage of relativism, that it is impossible to decide between competing ways of life, is, therefore, revealed to be a pseudo-problem. If one cannot decide between them it may be due to pluralism of values and that has to be accepted. Alternatively, it may be that, even given a certain way of life, the reason for action is still invalid (and here one thinks once more about female circumcision or human sacrifice) since it either uses an agent without his or her consent or makes an exception of the subject. So, the procedural limits of possible moral reasons for action still do some minimal work in the new schema. However, they do not do all the work.

As such, we have our first limitation on moral statements, a procedural one. If one is a moral agent, then one must recognize the free autonomy of others, which is to say that they are my equals in discourse. No moral imperatives or answers to the question what should be done must violate the procedural rules of moral discourse, otherwise one is guilty of a performative self-contradiction (Apel, 1998: ch. 1; Habermas, 1984: ch. 1). It seems that the values of autonomy, equality and respect underpin all moral discourse. However, the substantial understanding of equality will differ from culture to culture and the procedural understanding will not be able to overcome conflicts between these historical understandings. If one were to follow Kant, our moral imperatives would be able to fit all actual substantial moral imperatives (be vacuous) or they would be too strict. The actual understanding of morality is situated and historical and the universal values on their own are unable to generate efficacious imperatives or reasons for action. And so, we return to our storehouse of intuitions about what is right and good, as messy and inconsistent as they are, in order to generate actually efficacious moral reasons for action, but now constrained by our procedural norms.

The values of our cultural a priori are for the most part coexistent and plural. One can respect an other's autonomy whilst maximizing overall utility or welfare, but sometimes they will conflict. Sometimes it is impossible to be consistent or even to be faithful to all our values at once, there is only so much 'social space' in our society. Sometimes the values will relate to each other illogically and oddly due to their historical manifestations. Sometimes new moral problems will often bring into stark relief those background values which inform our judgements and force us to re-interrogate them as grounds to our moral judgements. Novel ethical issues will force us to evaluate the substantial manifestations of equality, liberty and other procedural values or even, at a lower level, substantial, historical values. So, for example, abortion is a real moral issue in a society where medical technology (where cost is minimized and safety maximized), religious traditions (the traditional Christian position which places the quickening at conception unlike Islam) and women's material equality (women make decisions for themselves) collide to raise the problem of re-evaluating the concept of the liberty of a specific group in a tradition that has for a long time silenced them. To look at the problem divorced from these understandings is to corrupt what is actually at stake.

Pornography is one such problem: the understanding of obscenity is largely a religious one which has sought to repress the destabilizing or controlling nature of sexual desire. As that metaphysics melts away, we are left with judgements about sexually explicit material that do no sit comfortably with our other judgements about liberty and autonomy, yet we lack a proper and adequate language to discuss the problem. For Hegel, such moral problems – like divine law and deontology, slavery, or the Reformation and equality – are motors of history. Hegel thinks this is what allows us to perfect our moral discourse (the human development alluded to by Mill). If moral pluralism is a plausible version of moral idealism, it faces an obvious challenge: even with procedural limits, it is still a species of relativism: a case of anything goes so long as members of one's culture are in agreement or, even more critically, just need to find one's action intelligible. Many actions and institutions such as human sacrifice could feasibly be consistent with the procedural limits of moral discourse (one can imagine consensual victims) and yet still be intuitively immoral. (I return to this controversial claim below.) It is this challenge which motivates the movement to Hegelian ethics.

To Kant's procedural limits of moral action, Hegel adds objective determinations of the will from one's social and cultural identity. The latter realizes that the abstract nature of the good cannot be created from the abstract thinking of the mind consistent with universal norms. Instead, the moral subject must begin from existing moral values and institutions because his constraint of objectivity involves the idea that the good must be intelligible to the judgements of his cultural peers. Recognition of the rightness of my action is necessary for me to be treated as a free agent.

Those values the agent finds himself thrown into are those that make rational moral thinking possible and are, then, the ground of his own evaluation and the starting point of his own revisionary project. Moral thinking is a socially immanent enterprise. To respect you as a person, I must be able to recognize your identity as a Muslim and know at least a little about what being a Muslim means and requires. The substantial understanding of others as derived from their social identity, and also of oneself, is the objective freedom of the agent. The objective freedom of an agent is the institutions, moral values, social fabric, roles, civil, economic and political structures, and so on that guarantee his or her identification as a subject of his or own deeds and his or her recognition as a moral agent (and not an animal, a very young child, a slave and so on). So, for example, capitalism, the family, and the Christian tradition are all forms of objective freedom: they assign roles and duties that determine how we behave in certain situations and in behaving in accordance with their dictates (or, at times, violating them) we are able to be, and also understood as, a moral agent. Such objective determinations will differ from age to age, area to area and, as it is constituted by various concatenations of class, geography, age and so on, from person to person. As such, we can see how it is possible to recognize the validity of a course of action and to understand it as moral action without the requirement of it being practically necessary for me to act in the same way.

One simplified way to understand Hegelian ethics is as a one-dimensional relativism: a moral assertion is true or false relative to a system and code of values, goods and rules institutionalized in a community. Pornography is morally wrong if the collection of my social peers reasoning in a sound way would assert it to be. Even given the erroneous nature of such an interpretation of Hegel (Hegel is not a relativist), such a position has immediate problematic consequences. First, the reason we are discussing pornography, and why abortion, euthanasia and environmentalism are equally widely discussed, is because there exists no agreed consensus on such issues. They present themselves as problems to be solved because there is no such agreement nor easy way to convince those who would espouse contrary statements (as there is when we talk about the wrongness of breaking promises and of harming people without good reason, even if we disagree on moral theories, metaphysics, politics and religion!). Second, relativism – simply because there is no shared consensus – would have nothing to say about such issues and would be quietist in its approach. 'Wait for a standard consensus to form and then cohere with it', is a rather uninspiring moral philosophy. Third, there would be no way to make inter-cultural (as opposed to intracultural) evaluations: I can criticize those like me, but I cannot criticize those unlike me as they operate under different values, and norms. and are products of a different history.

For these reasons, relativism is hugely unappealing but, as I have already said, Hegel is no relativist. Moral judgements are not transcendental, or products of a priori thinking, nor even laws consistent with the science of human nature. They are contingent, products of an historical tradition and cut across the politics, social values and economics of a particular community. However, there is a further story to be told. Hegel has two axes of evaluation to apply.[6] To the question, 'Is *x* good or right?' the first dimension (the h-axis, if you will, or the *cultural constraint*) is to see whether the statement coheres with the centrally agreed and rational values of the culture to which the statement is presented, the social and moral fabric of the agent's culture. The second (k-axis or the *autonomy constraint*) asks whether the existence of the institution, practice or creed maintains, supports or reproduces a state of affairs that inhibits or supports the procedural requirements of modern moral discussion, that is autonomy, independence and equality. A society with an institution of slavery is worse than one which does not have such an institution on this model. Of course, it rests with the superior culture to explain why this is so, and to bring the other culture into line with its thinking. Such a task is historical and not merely rational: the words require the economic reforms, the aid, the educational system that would support them. And such an enlightenment needs to be self-realized and not achieved through an operation of putative moral force (Hegel, 1991: §57A). So, would a society without an institution of sexually explicit objects be worse than society with such an institution (ours)? If the answer to that is 'Yes', then we can return to the cultural constraint and question to what extent do the historically actual examples of sexually explicit material aid or hinder the autonomy constraint of rational justification.

Hegel expresses these axes in familiar terms: the agent's objective freedom consists in his or her institutional identities, social roles, traditional values and economic, material existence. These roles and values make possible the agent's moral, rational action: they define what is intelligible and what is to be admired or admonished. Subjective freedom is the freedom to act in accordance with, or to break the principles and requirements of, one's objective freedom and to satisfy one's own personal projects, desires, interests and so on. The agent's subjective freedom is the capacity of the agent to achieve what he or she sees as a worthwhile project or a valuable life within the limits of the values and requirements of objective freedom. So, not only does the agent ask whether or not his or her action is appropriate to the expectations of his or her peers, but also whether the expectations of his or her peers are appropriate to him or her. The agent asks himself or herself if he or she feels *at home* in such a culture, whether his or her individuality can be adequately respected in such a culture with all its traditions and values. It is worth noting that Hegel sees this autonomy constrain requirement as a very late historical development, probably in line with the emergence of Mill's own new morality of justice.

The initial, procedural limit to moral rationality is augmented by the substantial requirements of an agent's objective freedom. However, that objective freedom remains conditioned by homeliness or the procedural requirements of Kantian ethics. Morally good reasons are those that are justified by the interpersonal values of a culture, do not violate the procedural limits of moral discourse and those in which the subject can find their own autonomy and equality respected through the expression of their own freely chosen projects and aspirations. Yet, this still may not be enough because human beings immersed in culture can be coerced into believing that they are at home in roles which do not violate the procedural limits of moral discourse, but may still be morally problematic. Human sacrifice, whereby the victim has won the honour of being sacrificed in open competition with all members of the community, seems to be one such case. Therefore, we require one last limit on possible interpretations of the requirements of moral behaviour. There are values which are operative in our practical reason that appeal to one's identity not only as a member of a specific class, nor only as a member of a specific society nor people, but also and above these as a member of the human race.

Some values, such as heroism and honour may appear universal but their actual substantial requirements depend largely on cultural position (so, being heroic in Ancient Rome is different from being heroic in downtown LA). It is fair to say that the values of heroism and honour rely upon a specific society, a specific division of labour in the family and specific social meanings for their requirements to be articulated, but there also exist values which are universal but not procedural. These values reside in a universal account of human nature grounded in naturalism and empirical facts about human beings. It is to return, more or less, to the beginning of moral philosophy and Aristotle's insightful remark that moral requirements cannot be merely natural motivations nor contrary to human inclinations (1980: 1103a33). Modern moral philosophy is often challenged for its attempt to obfuscate the distinction between obligatory or supererogatory actions, or for having requirements that are too demanding, or because of its demand for disinterestedness. Moral requirements must be tempered by the integrity of the agent, his or her own projects and needs, and ultimately his or her nature, that is, interests in self-preservation and a happy life. If one were to interrogate social existence and the historically different ways of life in order to find a commonality between human beings that explains the existence of society and hence the universal aspect of social existence, one does not need to commit oneself to reductive naturalism.

Here we propose a very minimalist naturalism. The commonality of humanity is represented by universal institutions which determine our relationship to our surroundings (religion, science), to one another (economy, class and family) and to what is to be valued above all (secular principles derived from the other two institutions: respect for the dead, the intrinsic value of human life, the taxonomy of who are persons and who are not, and the recognition of the significance of our life as our own). These, in turn, represent the fact that humans *qua* humans will have a basic web of beliefs about creation, purpose and the intelligibility of the universe (religion, science, metaphysics), they will have basic divisions of roles and responsibilities, and an interlaced hierarchy of obligations and duties (family and class structures). They will also see death as, in some sense, intrinsically significant in the life of the community as a whole and to the individuals who constitute that community (rites of death, sanctity of human life, the intrinsic worth of human life, a system of rights, *et cetera*). If one is to imagine what life would be like for a *human* at a specific historical time, one must firstly recognize that, in order to be a human, he or she must be moulded by those institutions necessary for social living (and for moral experience), that is, family, and the rites of death and religion (in its broadest sense), which reflect the natural conditions of human existence. To imagine outside these is to imagine a being that is not human. And to comprehend the particular nature of a culture, one must look at the actual form of its myths, institutions and language in order to understand its view of the world, and the agent's own understanding of his roles, duties and obligations. The creation of societies is an expression of fundamental universal desires in human beings: for security; for the preservation of the family; for protection from meaningless harm and death. These societies then supply and mould the conditions for an agent's moral understanding. Should such categories then violate the natural needs of the human being, the actual meaning of society and association itself comes under strain.

However, we ought to be careful, because such considerations are too minimal to do substantial work (as they would for Hobbes or any other rational naturalist). What constitutes security is always to be understood substantially in social terms and will change from society to society and also change with the progress and mutation of society. Harm and death are permissible for other reasons, 'bloody' good reasons (self-defence, moral sacrifice, protect one's family, to avoid prolonged and inevitable suffering, to bring the seasonal rains), but what constitutes 'bloody' good reasons is a social matter. The good is variable and so a society is a good society if it sets the limits and values that make meaningful lives possible, supplies a given structure of social relations in which the individual can recognize himself as a constitutive part, and satisfies the grounding reasons for the association of individuals. The Italian writer, Vico (1984) knew this better than most and held that the commonality of humanity is found in social existence as constrained by a minimal naturalism. Vico grounds his historical science in the faculty of imagination regulated by basic universal facts about human beings. Hobbes's project, which sought to unite ethics with self-regarding reason to generate political norms, reduced human beings to asocial, atomistic bundles of desires that are too simple to explain the multifaceted variety of social behaviour. For Vico, naturalism constrains the faculty of imagination which produces the foundations for substantive judgements of reason only indirectly: what constitutes good reasons must be in line with human nature but cannot be identical with it. Hobbesian rational naturalism is too restrictive since it begins and ends with human nature alone: all men want welfare, that is the maximal satisfaction of desires. However, this under-determines the possible constitution of welfare and has the consequence of oversimplifying sociology by not supplying the necessary concepts for a full understanding of human behaviour. Humans often sacrifice their own felicity, and that of their families, for other social goods, and unless one can understand the nature of these sacrifices, sociology as a science remains incomplete. The basic needs and desires of humans can be satisfied and manifested in a myriad ways depending on one's worldview.

Vico's sociological method is grounded in a minimal naturalism because the faculty of imagination which generates the theoretical justification of a society's objective freedom is constrained by these naturalistic considerations in the production of possible social worlds. A reflective attitude to one's social practices and mores will disclose their contingent grounding in an imaginative creation of a possible way to exist *humanly*. Such a minimal naturalism when applied to the issue of conflict demands that for a social fabric to fulfil its role, then it must embody the human commitments to the value of life, the significance of death, the goodness of security, the rightness of law, the badness of unnecessary pain, and so on. And, more importantly, the violation, repression or contradiction of any of these requires justification which appeals to central values of the tradition, the grounding myth. Any society which engages in violating practices is either illegitimate or needs to offer a 'bloody good reason' for the violation. 'Bloody good reasons', though, will have to meet the requirements of objective freedom and procedural justice to be morally legitimate. The legitimacy of the institutions of a particular state are to be evaluated along two axes: one, are the institutions legitimated immanently by those historical values and norms understood from the point of view of the agents who belong to that tradition (historical appropriateness or the h-axis from above); and two, is the understanding of the agents corrupted and are their basic needs and interests violated by the social structure (minimal naturalism constraint or the v-axis).

The three axes of normative social ethics are that a culture, obligation, institution, or action is legitimate (or justified or permissible) if: (1) it can justify its institutions and practices to its own members in terms of publicly shared values (the cultural constraint); and (2) these institutions, personal roles and practices do not violate the basic needs which ground the development of all human societies and generate human association (minimal naturalism constraint); and (3) the subject is able to express his or her personal individuality as an ongoing project which has been freely endorsed and chosen and is respected by others – that is, feel at home in a culture where personal integrity as an individual, expressed as my autonomy and recognized via respect from others is possible (the autonomy constraint).[7]

Let me illustrate the approach through three examples, but the reader ought to bear in mind that the following examples are merely indicative of a method and the problems themselves would require a much deeper treatment.

Example 1: Stonehenge. A combination of procedural and naturalistic understandings are not adequate to the task of reconstruction necessary for ethical endeavour. Compare Roman ruins with the edifice of Stonehenge. Metaphorically, procedural requirements are universal in the sense that the laws of applied mathematics and the techniques of civil engineering are universal and will determine what sorts of buildings remain standing and which do not. Naturalistically, we know why human beings build. They do so for shelter, protection and for glory. Substantially, we also know what materials were used and what technology was probably available and how these affected the implementation of the procedural requirements. But, we lack adequate knowledge to make any claim about Stonehenge's use that is not purely conjectural, because there is not enough written down about the way of life of the people who built it. Although, we might quite confidently claim it is not for shelter or protection as it involves too much capital and labour expenditure, we are unable to say what exact glory was expressed in its creation: religious, political, sport-related, and so on. We know an awful lot about Roman life because there exists a documented history. From that history and how they lived – what had value for them, the sorts of leisure pursuits they engaged in, and their religious and moral framework – we are able to understand what the ruins are and what their precise use was. With Stonehenge, the nature of the building cannot be known because there exists no publicly available record of what is valued, how the society is structured and what people in the society believed.

Similarly, a full blown procedural attempt to generate moral laws, even with a minimal nod to the naturalistic requirements of human life (as in Rawls's early re-articulation of the Kantian project) can only be sustained and made intelligible when supported by the assumptions of a shared moral fabric (as Rawls's later work acknowledged) (Rawls, 1999, 1993). Most ethical philosophy rests on a shared consensus of value and intuitions which is very often left in the background. Discussions, though, of female circumcision, human sacrifice and inequality from a Western point of view are grounded in such values but they come apart when confronting the place in which such practices are performed. The procedural requirements of respect and equality are not so easily translated into substantial norms and obligations when ways of life differ. One may say that slavery respects the equality of those who matter (much like Aristotle's metaphysics extended equality to human beings but denied it to the groups which existed above animals but below citizens). Or, human sacrifice may well be justified by bloody good reasons in the same way that self-defence is a bloody good reason and justifies killing in war. The same autonomy of the soldier is present in the consenting participant (to avoid the rhetorical term, victim) in sacrifice. To rule out such practices, as we would in our own culture, through an invocation of the procedural limits with no attempt to understand the sociological, historical reasons that generate these institutions is top–down and ultimately ineffectual. Such discussions will resolve themselves into ones of force of will rather than reason. Procedural and naturalistic limits of moral obligations need always to be tempered by the historical understanding of the values, beliefs and institutions of the way of life with which one has engaged. With members of our own culture, because we share a moral fabric with its meanings and values, we are often led to forget this.

Example 2: human sacrifice. One would think that slavery and the institution whereby human beings are exchanged or owned by others and treated as tools, in short where agents have no ownership of their own body, labour or will, is ruled out by procedural requirements. That it is not, is testimony to the abuse to which metaphysics has been put over the years. When Aristotle demarcates the types of human beings, or when the eighteenth century industrialist affirms that his workers are free to walk away from their jobs, the metaphysics of *anima* and of negative liberty assert themselves at the cost of the fair treatment of others. Procedurally, though, once an entity affirms a choice, no matter how inarticulate, it is to be treated as an equal. But, remember that, for Aristotle, the slave–masters were concerned owners doing the best for the slave who was unable to survive without direction and orders (1912: 1252–1255). Equality is respected in much the same way that the parent respects the autonomy and equality of his or her child: by not letting them do what they would want to do without direction. However, once the assertion that the subject does not know what he or she truly wants is disputed and put to bed, then slavery is one example where procedural requirements rules out an institution. The agent who is enslaved cannot feel at home in his or her moral fabric. Nor can his or her personal individuality as an ongoing project be freely endorsed or respected by others. To feel at home, the slave requires a culture where personal integrity as an individual, expressed as autonomy and recognized via respect from others is possible.

More problematically, one can imagine a society that practices ritual human sacrifice whereby *all* members (no matter their gender or class) of that society participate in sporting games whereby the victor has the honour of being sacrificed to the gods. The sacrifice is required once a year to safeguard the well-being of the civilization. Putting aside considerations about the efficacy or the truth of the metaphysical beliefs, it is clear that the procedural limits of moral discourse have not been violated (the agent freely participated in the games and is prepared to receive the honour for his altruistic action, much the same as a soldier at times of war) and there exists a publicly shared web of meanings that support and maintain the rationality of this institution as part of the society as a whole. (Note that if one denies that the participant is free because his action derives from false beliefs, then the soldier too, for the most part in history, is not free either!) Here, though, one feels the tension of the naturalistic level for the sacrifice of a life, the violation of one's self-preservation, requires bloody good reasons. Bloody good reasons include self-defence, the welfare of a majority of others (however quantifiably measured), or the protection of those to whom one is morally close. Asking that one appease the gods does not share the urgency of these examples, the immediate pull of the either I sacrifice myself or disaster will materialize (and when it is, hermeneutical endeavour will usually show that it is a false superstition peddled in the interests of a controlling class). For the naturalistic needs of an individual, supposedly protected by any society, to be violated requires just such an urgency otherwise the demand is illegitimate. Human sacrifice seems to be one of those very unreasonable demands.[8]

Example 3: female circumcision. There also exist societies in which women are purified and cleansed by the rites of infibulation, whereby the clitoris is removed. As such, any pleasure they would receive from sexual intercourse is made impossible. Mutilation of this sort is again seemingly in violation of a minimal naturalism. However, pleasure is very often conceded for other values: having a tattoo, abstinence due to religious conviction, giving up smoking and so on. Such decisions are made rational through an appeal to a shared moral and social fabric and it is possible that many young women participate freely in such practices as justified by socially held beliefs. Again, it seems that the agent is able to express their individuality through shared practices and the naturalistic limit is violated for good reasons. However, remember that for Hegel, social and moral fabric is an *objective* freedom and not just a rational web of meanings. Here we approach the problem of the procedural limit: either it can freely endorse any obligation or it can arbitrarily reject it. Sometimes the agent wills his or her own domination because, in order to be recognized as a moral agent in a particular society, the procedural requirements of equality and respect bring along substantial requirements which are actually not in the interests of the agent at all. By wanting to participate in a practice and occupy a role in society, I actually repress what is in my interest for what is in the interest of others.

Hegel ties procedural limits directly to objective freedom via the requirement of homeliness: social institutions must be justified in terms of publicly shared values and also be more deeply rational in that they substantially express the individuality of the person through free action and chosen projects. It is obvious that the true justification of female circumcision is the power and control of one group over another, as hermeneutical endeavour would reveal: take away pleasure from sex and you have faithful partners and you are then ensured that your property and name will pass down to your true heir. The social and moral fabric supports only the aims and free projects of a subset of society's members and hence the procedural requirement of equality and autonomy (even if the women may protest otherwise) is not respected. A proper understanding of the transition from procedural requirements to substantial obligations via the criterion of homeliness interrogates the social requirements of the agent. The objectification is negative, that is alienation, rather than a neutral liberation.

6.3 Pornography and social ethics

And so we finally return to pornography. Given the approach briefly outlined above, we are concerned with pornography as a cultural object belonging to late modern industrialized nations which share a liberal and democratic social and moral fabric (very broadly conceived). There is no clumsy attempt to make absolute judgements about the moral implications of sexual representation. It remains a situated debate and not an imaginary transcendental one. Pornography *for us* is morally problematic because, feminists claim, it alienates (not just objectifies) women, it subordinates women and it silences women. In order to make sense of this, let us remind ourselves of our three axes of moral interpretation. A culture, obligation, institution, action is legitimate (or justified or permissible) if

1. It can justify its institutions and practices to its own members in terms of publicly shared values (the cultural constraint)
2. These institutions, personal roles and practices do not violate the basic needs which ground the development of all human societies and generate human association (the minimal naturalism constraint)
3. The subject is able to express his or her personal individuality as an ongoing project which has been freely endorsed and chosen and is respected by others. The subject is able to feel at home in a culture where personal integrity as an individual, expressed as his or her autonomy and recognized via respect from others, is possible (the autonomy constraint).

Let us begin with some very simple observations. The claim that participants would not perform sexual acts for the purpose of recording them unless they were forced by violence, coerced by economic necessity or were subordinated rests upon the claim that no one, except at the cost of their rationality, would participate in the recording of sexual acts. On the surface, that suggests that one would find it hard to justify one's decision to participate in such a recording to one's peers; one would be, in short, ashamed and keep the decision secret. As such, it seems that the making of pornography violates the h-axis of historical reason and hence, like appearing in a snuff movie or an enemy's propaganda film, one assumes that participants must have been forced to do so. Yet, such a claim is riddled with values that are now out of date: the puritanism of Christianity, the nuclear family with monogamous fidelity, small communities with no real possibility for the distinction between private and public behaviour, and, of course, the Christian dualism between the body and the soul. It is also an historically moving standard: in the past, kissing another actor in a film, wearing underwear, being naked and simulating sexual acts would all have enjoyed the honour of distinguishing the moral character from the libertine. The idea that human dignity requires privacy for sexual activity is a remnant of specific puritanical attitudes in our tradition. In a secular society, there is no metaphysical or rational support for an attitude that finds all sexual activity a moral issue. The objectification of the actress who kisses in a romantic comedy is to be morally evaluated on the same terms as the actress in a pornographic scene: they are performing on film for the purposes of individual and freely chosen projects (as much as any of us have freely chosen our paths in life). To assume that to kiss another actor is acceptable, but to have sex with one is not, rests on a background idea that sexual activity itself is bad or should be hidden. Such cultural echoes permeate our moral thinking and support the feminists' arguments without an explicit need to invoke them, and if they were to invoke them, they would be dismissed out of hand as values and world views which are very much out of joint with our society and its objective freedom. We support individuals in pursuing the career that they wish and to limit them without agreed moral values, is to assert that we know better than them what is good for them. Puritanism is an ideology, like the Great Chain of Being before it, which is used to support seemingly rational arguments about what individuals should or should not do, even though we have long since jettisoned the metaphysics which justified such attitudes.[9]

It seems, without a controversial metaphysical picture, we can discount any violation of basic needs (or the minimal naturalism constraint). Pornography need not necessarily involve non-consensual harm or mutilation or overt, serious violence. Some actors will agree to participate freely and most will be happy to do so. If you say that their attitudes are examples of bad faith, or irrational, then you are holding on to outdated world views. If the participation does rest upon force and coercion or harm, then it is not the sexual activity but the dimension of violence which is to be prohibited (as we have seen in the discussion above in Chapter 3). The case then is akin to human sacrifice. Those who participate in extreme violence whereby their basic needs as an organism are damaged and threatened, will do so under descriptions that, under the strain of proper hermeneutic endeavour, will be revealed to be akin to superstition and ideology. There will be a very fine line between what is permissible (in the sense of what one can possibly consent to) and what is not: the extreme limit would have to be the realist portrayal of one's death and there would be a need, for legal reasons if nothing else, to draw a bright line which errs on the conservative side to protect the vulnerable.

Critics of the above comments will quite rightly point out that I am being vague about violent practices in sexual representation. Actors in other films, for artistic reasons, perform in ways that are humiliating and actors participate in scenes in which they are subject to harmful practices (a simulated torture scene may involves some harm for the actor, if not to the extent that is being represented). It is clear from my use of 'serious' violence in pornographic production that I do not rule out *tout court* sadomasochistic representation, nor do I think participants cannot freely consent to be humiliated and harmed within limits. It would also be remiss to sweep under the carpet the very contemporary form of pornography and its representation (or even simulation) of violence to and humiliation of women. There is without doubt a tendency towards ever greater violence and humiliation, most notably of women but also of men, in the content of these materials. Most contemporary pornography available on the internet is not just devoid of a narrative structure and characterization, but is also violent (Dines, 2010). The empirical question must be whether such material is actually arousing, but let us assume it must be otherwise it would not become the prevalent norm. Capital investors, remember, care little about their product, so it matters little whether arousal comes from eroticism or from humiliation as long as it leads to credit card numbers.[10] It is a peculiar aspect of capitalist competition that in a saturated market, a product either needs to have a guaranteed audience or it needs to stand out from its competitors. First, just as the history channels on television are dominated by documentaries on Hitler and the Nazis (without us worrying about how many fascists are being created by their consumption), so a similar psychological compulsion for 'evil' or the 'ab-normal' may fuel the audience's interest in pornographic violence without wanting to practise it. Secondly, one way to sell a product is to concentrate on its quality, but another is to draw attention to oneself through 'shock' (Vattimo, 1992: ch. 4). Such a feature of aesthetic production is inherent in mechanical reproduction: when Duchamp exhibited the *Fountain*, he wanted to open a debate about art by the notoriety he attracted. Since then the idea of 'shock' has been used as a quick way to draw attention to oneself without any deeper aim to justify it. Only the shock quickly becomes banal unless it forever pushes the limits of our expectations. Within pornography, to stand out, to be original, as in art generally, the formal nature of transgression has been adopted without the substantial understanding of why. In pornography, it is simply to make money and, as such, the pain and humiliation is a means to an end, as is the excess and the transgression.

Such violence does not teach us how to treat others at all. In fact, since the days of Andrea Dworkin and MacKinnon, the nature of pornography has actually worsened to a state of not just metaphorical violence and subordination but to the filmic representation of it:

> Men in porn are depicted as soulless, unfeeling, amoral life-support systems for erect penises who are entitled to use women in any way they want. These men demonstrate zero empathy, respect or love for the woman they have sex with, no matter how uncomfortable or in pain these women look ... In a world populated by women who are robotic 'sluts' and men who are robotic studs, the sex is going to be predictably devoid of any intimacy. Porn sex is not about making love, as the feelings and emotions we normally associate with such an act – connection, empathy, tenderness, caring, affection – are replaced by those more connected with hate – fear, disgust, anger, loathing, and contempt. (Dines, 2010: xxiv)

Women actors in these short films are treated as a subject (and not an object) to be humiliated. There is a need for the women to consent to their humiliation, to be the 'dirty whore', they are continually verbally accused of being. Contemporary pornography prefers violence to arousal as though its purpose has changed; but it has not, its purpose remains to make money. One might see in this the last convulsions of a dying masculinity, of an impotent mastery which is now once and for all revealed to be an extension of capital and not natural right, or wit, or strength. It as though males do not want the new world of equality to penetrate their last, hidden shadow of psychic privacy.

However, that is all conjecture without substance. What is true is that the minimal naturalism constraint cannot be violated without bloody good reasons and art or celebrity are not such reasons. We would not let the artist starve to death as some sort of performance, rightly deciding that he is doing so at the cost of his rationality. Participants whose actions are in contravention of their basic needs and physical integrity are, too, rightly doing so at the cost of their rationality. The first thing to ascertain in such films is whether the participants are harmed beyond what is acceptable in employment and whether consent to the practice has been freely given knowing the costs. Factory workers risk harm (mutilation, muscle damage) and shop workers have terrible feet (tears and blisters and so on). I do not intend to be facetious here, but think of the risks and harm that oil workers and miners endure. Let us not be timid here. Much of the material available for consumption in the here and now, down our digital highways, violates the k- and v-axes of ethical judgement and is the result of economic and ideological asymmetry in the relations of power. Would you allow a friend to act in such films? Would you not feel that they have been taken advantage of (to use the colloquial form of the autonomy constraint here)? Could you be persuaded that it was, in some sense a free choice taken to further his or her own interests (to use the colloquial form of the v-axis here)?

There is though a problem beyond that of knowing what degree of humiliation individuals are prepared to consent to in the search for both pleasure and employment. Dines lists these ailments for participants in pornographic production: 'HIV; rectal gonorrhea; tears in the throat, vagina, and anus; chlamydia of the eye; and gonorrhea of the throat' (2010: xxviii). There is a risk that to reduce the problem of pornography to the harm involved in its making is perhaps to reduce the moral problem to one of health and safety and expecting legislation akin to the treatment of animals in research projects. By concentrating on this, the critic may miss the very real cultural damage done by capitalist modes of pornographic production (which we shall discuss below). Should the participants be actually harmed then the k- and v-axes are violated and the production is to be stopped. This is a very strong requirement on the production of film and art: a very bright line is required to rule out those performances which contravene basic human needs of the actors involved, which at the moment in many contemporary productions does not seem to be acknowledged.

Finally, the procedural axis (the autonomy constraint) rules out all those performances which involve coercion, deception and so on. It basically rules out not just harm to individual participants but also the threat of harm. To treat a participant as a moral agent requires their consent to the performance. Again, though, if one believes one cannot consent to sexual performance, reasons in tune with our time must be given and not echoes of religious attitudes. None of this, as yet, touches on the feminist claims and none of this, as yet, adds to our commonly held intuitions as they have been followed through in the preceding pages. As such, we have the position that, if the actors and/or contributors have freely participated in the making of the film or representation, and if there is no risk of undue serious harm to individuals involved in the making, then there is no basis to ban or prohibit pornographic material on the putative assumption that agents would obviously prefer to be earning their money in another way as such an assumption is grounded in an outdated metaphysics no longer appropriate to the cultural conditions of our society. So far, so expected.

Yet, the proper feminist critique of the existence of pornographic materials concerned the fact that it facilitates the alienation of women and makes it easier for men to view them as non- or partial agents who never mean what they say or express what they really want or perhaps even know what they truly want. Thus, the voice of woman is silenced before it speaks and if it does speak it has to say what is expected, otherwise risk rational exclusion, and hence by speaking at all, women participate in a form of ideological oppression. Remember that objectification is a neutral term. Institutions such as pornography allow us a rational way to express our individuality through a shared set of meanings and values. It is rational when it meets the requirements of procedural and naturalistic moral limits via a consideration of the criterion of homeliness. The feminists claim that the techniques available for women to express their individuality and their equality in our culture violates the homeliness criterion. Women, they continue, are left with two choices: one, silence (violating the procedural requirement that agents are respected as autonomous moral agents) or subordination (violating the subjective freedom of the agent more directly because women, to satisfy what they want, have to be understood and understand themselves as what they do not want to be).[11]

Let us look at these claims one by one. First, pornography facilitates the objectification of women as non- or partial agents. This allows others (notably men) to claim to know what women truly want, what their words truly mean. And of course what women really want coincides with what men want. By silencing them, women's interests are suppressed in favour of the interests of others. Second, pornography creates a self-understanding for women and a cultural understanding of women as specific objects that must behave in certain ways and express certain attitudes otherwise they are not actually a proper woman; they are idiosyncratic, erratic, mad and will be rationally excluded. However, by being what is expected of them – what is determined by the discourse of pornography – women actually act in the interests of others rather than themselves. Of course, it is obvious who these others are in both cases: the male. Men use pornography as an institution in order to further their own interests at the expense of women's interests and until this institution is prohibited women's interests will always be subordinated or silenced. The feminist claims rest on this one point: the males in society use pornography as a tool of subordination and repression in order to further their own interests. As such, the procedural requirement and the substantial justification of homeliness are not satisfied for women in our culture because of the existence of pornography.

6.4 Equality for whom

The first two points to be made are about James Bond villains. Their plans for world domination always rest on the minions carrying out their orders to the letter and doing so to the utmost of their ability. None of the underlings can go to the pub on Friday at five pm rather than finish polishing the diamond laser beam gun. The intention of world domination will always be thwarted not by Bond himself, but rather by workers who really do not care that much and would rather do a half-arsed job to get down the pub more quickly. There is a philosophical point to this. The claim that pornography is an intricate part of a plan on the part of males which is maintained, day in day out, for the furtherance of our interests is obviously not a claim about what I am doing now, why I am writing this book, why your partner is watching the footie on the telly, or even the existence of David Beckham himself. Males do not consciously go about furthering their interests (secretly one might add) at the expense of the females. The second point is that Bond has a very easy job of it because the villain is always one person, unlike Al-Qaeda or the IRA, and by killing that person the threat is over. There is a malign agent who plans and creates a system of subordination which is in his interest. Obviously, there is no one origin of the male conspiracy, no one male who has his interests served by subordination. And if there were, the fact that he were male would be contingent: it is his interests that are served, not the interests of the male gender.

The feminist here would obviously point out that the historical and cultural conditions we find ourselves in are not consciously maintained but because men occupy the positions of power, the benefit motivates them to continue to perpetuate the *status quo*. So, we are not talking about individual males, but the male-orientated system. The ur-Father, as it were. Is the ur-Father like a Bond villain? Was there a single intentional act of putting forward his interests at the expense of others and forming a social system? Is it Rousseau's famous man who encloses a piece of land and cons the rest of those around him into acknowledging it as *his* piece of land by right? (Rousseau, 1992). Butler's critique of power here seems salient. Butler's attack on the sovereignty of the subject in the speech-act relocates the whole problem to the concept of power. For her, there is a prior question: what the conditions of possibility of contemporary pornography are. And the answer is the already present subordination of women (and race and class) by the social system of coding that makes meaning possible (Butler, 1997: 65–66, 80). Free speech and silencing as attempts to discuss pornography create a subject (the Male) who subordinates and an object (the Female) who is subordinated by the act of pornography, yet Butler's aim is to show that performative speech acts are interpellations rather than 'acts' in the classical sense of emanating from a transparent, authoritative subject. Interpellation is the way in which ideology addresses the (abstract) pre-ideological individual thus producing him or her as substantial subject: the Male and the Female are constructed in their roles prior to speaking and the blame, if there is blame, is with a system that makes possible this type of speaking and this type of silencing. Pornography acts by undermining the intention of the woman to say no and to say what she wants to say. Yet, if that is the case, then why should the intention of pornography be sovereign and not itself open to misinterpretation?

Butler repeats again and again that feminism is based on a single intentional causal model which identifies a subject who knowingly utters and the agent who is acted upon by such an utterance. Such a model is untenable, although intelligible. It is demanded by a moral view that cites agents as the site of praise and blame, yet our h-axis tempered by the k- and v-axes above implicitly asserts the need to revise our moral categories and framework in light of historically emergent moral problems. Law requires us to blame individuals, but pornography is not a single action or utterance at all, nor is it a conscious and devious subordination by males, nor is the reception of pornography or the acts inspired by it on the site of some imaginary, unified female subject without playful interpretation and deconstruction (otherwise how could Dworkin, MacKinnon and Langton be heard and acknowledged as adversaries or allies in the game of moral discourse). Butler puts this succinctly when she states:

> Such a reduction of the agency of power to the actions of the subject may well seek to compensate for the difficulties and anxieties produced in the course of living in a contemporary cultural predicament in which neither the law nor hate speech are uttered exclusively by a singular subject. The racial slur is always cited from elsewhere, and in the speaking of it, one chimes in with a chorus of racists, producing at that moment the linguistic occasion for an imagined relation to an historically transmitted community of racists. In this sense, racist speech does not originate with the subject, even if it requires the subject for its efficacy, as it surely does. (1997: 80)

Subordination, alienation and silencing of the female does not originate with pornography, nor is the consumer or the producer the origin of inequality. What Butler recognizes is that feminists are seeking the Male (the Father?) who has subordinated them when, in fact, there exists a prior non-chosen origin of the male/female relationship constituted by the system of meanings which has made this subordination possible. The system ought to be the true target of critique rather than some imagined father who originally, historically subordinated women. And that means inequality is a construction of society and a form of cultural existence that requires to be made rational in line with the procedural and naturalistic requirements via the standard of homeliness. Agents cannot feel at home in an unequal society and, an aspect often ignored by feminists, the feeling of unhomeliness is as pertinent for males, females, hermaphrodites, blacks, whites, masters and slaves. Equality is a procedural requirement that is an historical achievement and is required for an agent to be a full moral agent. The feminist critique is not, then, directed at agents who violate the procedural requirements of moral discourse (specific males who deny the autonomy of women, or the autonomy constraint), or at specific males who harm the interests of women (the v-axis), but rather at a social system which supports and maintains unequal relationships between male and females in which pornography plays a constitutive and maintenance role. Wrongdoing in pornography is the historically contingent perpetuation of unequal social and cultural hierarchies.

And that means, if the critique is correct, that it is as significant to the autonomy of males, females, shemales, transgenders and all members of our culture. It is not exclusively a feminist issue. Hegel's master–slave dialectic has been put to a broad range of uses since it was first penned and it is, on one level, although the interpretation does not exhaust its meanings, about how desire is the basis for self-understanding and how that self-understanding cannot be brought about alone (1977: ¶¶178–196). What interests us here is the way in which Hegel uses the master–slave dialectic to articulate how inequality leads to a distortion in the psychological self-understanding of agents, most pertinently *both* the slave and the master. Self-understanding will be supported and maintained much later in the narrative of the *Phenomenology of Spirit* (and also much later in Hegel's writings as a whole) by social institutions (such as marriage, class, gender and so on) and cultural practices (such as education, religion, art and so on). The artistic expressions, meanings and outputs of a culture will also be reciprocally linked to these institutions: as an expression of their 'rationality' but also as an ongoing evaluation of their appropriateness to the world. However, the beginnings of a human being's consciousness of itself as somehow different from other objects in the world begins with its relationship to objects of desire. Most objects of desire are consumed by their possession: objects of hunger, thirst and so on are consumed by us acting upon the desire. Since the human being is conscious of itself as existing beyond the satisfaction of its particular desires, it understands itself as 'not' its desires and free to negate or satisfy them as it wills; the self is independent from the world. And it is that willing over and above the desiring that the human being understands itself as. Yet, through consumption of objects, the self understood as 'I want X' dissolves and ceases to exist. The self over and above desires can then only exist in the positing of another desire in order to negate it as identical with itself. The self is not at home with its desiring aspect (it is more than this) but neither with the negation of the desiring part because that is empty and vacuous.

What self-consciousness requires is the affirmation, or naming of itself, as that which is over and above the desiring aspect and that requires another self-consciousness to understand that it desires what it does because it could choose not to; hence what it desires is not simply a response to instinct but the very affirmation of selfhood. Such naming cannot (in contradiction of both Descartes and Kant) be done alone: the 'I' that is the conditional possibility of being a desiring thing is not an individual affirmation. It requires someone else to understand myself as this, otherwise I could be quite simply mistaken. In the world, amongst the objects I consume with my desires, there are some which resist, deny, affirm or cooperate with my desires. Such things are self-conscious like myself and things like me know me as that which desires, but could choose to desire differently. Self-consciousnesses can name me and give me an identity over and above my desiring activity. Of course, our first engagement is one of conflict because we want to prove to each other that we are above desire and to do so we are prepared to negate desiring itself by risking our life for the sake of recognition, because it matters more to us that we are seen to be not our desires than for us to be obedient to our strongest, most basic desire of self-preservation. Such conflict is resolved unsatisfactorily, either through the death of one of the self-consciousnesses or the enslavement of one of the parties, which gives up its independence from the material world for the dependence on the other. When the victor enslaves the loser, he is left unfulfilled because his willing is translated through the labour of the other and that other is different from other tools because the master knows it is the slave and not him that achieves in the world, that *does*. Thus, the master's own independence, which he believed to have won in the conflict, is hollow and formal.

The relationship of master and slave is unequal and its wrongness resides in the impossibility of either agent being free. The master, who has domination over the slave, fulfils his goals and projects through the use of the slave's will but that will is thereby reduced to a mere tool for him and the slave cannot – given the institutional structure of their relationship – offer his or her consent to the worth of those goals and projects. The master is alienated from the products of his will because they do not arise out of his own labour. The slave, on the other hand, produces the objects of the will of an other and hence is alienated from these products as not his own. The objects of labour both are (the master chooses them, the slave makes them) and are not (the master does not make them, the slave does not choose them) instances of freedom. Social conditions of inequality frustrate individuals' freedom whether or not their interests are served or frustrated by the inequality. Culture, for Hegel, is a medium that makes possible human freedom and so any institutional inequality has to be overcome through the struggle between those that choose and those that are chosen for (who make) (Knowles, 2002; Neuhouser, 2003; Rose, 2007a).

How does this relate to pornography? Well, if, as we have seen, pornography reproduces and maintains unequal relationships, then it frustrates freedom. Pornography, its producers and the discourse as it is determined by contemporary culture, represents the nature of sexual relations. Actors, consumers and groups affected reproduce these relations. A rational, axiomatic principle of our society is equality and the vast majority of pornography is incoherent as regards this principle. The claim, though, differs from the feminist critique by saying that not just a specific group of society but all society and all human relationships will be harmed by the unrestricted production, exchange and consumption of pornography (Mill, 2011; Dyzenhaus, 1992; cf. Skipper, 1993). Yet, this is again no different from other aesthetic objects: film, television, music, literature, and so on, which form the basis of individuals' self-understanding by supplying the basic concepts and forms of social relationships (Gastil, 1976). Pornography as an institution frustrates understanding of others and self-understanding to such an extent that the agent finds it hard to be at home in his or her culture. Rights protection only enforces and empowers the protection of this institution (Dines, 2010: 56). The wrongness of pornography resides not in the harm to one group or individuals (the minimal naturalism constraint), or the subordination of one group or individuals (the autonomy constraint), but in the irrationality of the culture which produces it (the cultural constraint). We see here how the idea of feeling at home is made possible by the objectification of oneself in social practices and it is frustrated by the alienation of oneself in social practices. Alienation results in either silencing and refusal to participate or subordination to what the social practice wants me to be, in spite of myself (as a pre-self of Butler's interpellation). The epistemic bad faith supported by contemporary institutional structures is not in the interest of males and is damaging to all members of society.

For this reason, one can extrapolate from Hegel's insights into the relationship of master and slave and go beyond them to reveal the conventional and artificial nature of unequal social relationships. Hegel allows us to understand how inequality frustrates the appropriate self-understanding and ultimately autonomy of both the master and the slave, but one could go further to disclose the contradictory nature of the social system of meanings. Cultural conditions of inequality are structured around relationships of power, but these relationships require a continued investment of belief for the epistemic bad faith required for objectification to be stabilized. Inequality frustrates the autonomy of the master (he chooses what to make, but does not make it) in the same way that the structures of coercion involved in the socializations arising from female representation in pornography frustrates the supposed interests of men. If pornography creates the possibility of objectifying women and supporting male objectifications, it also harms the interests of the male by making him dependent on the idealized, silent and pliant 'female' and not a real female. The consent he seeks for the worth of his idealizations is made impossible by the autonomy-denial explicit in pornography. If the female chooses to remain silent and accept the male objectifications promoted by the media, then the male is dependent on the consent to her own domination brought about by coercion (so no consent at all). The male's willing is performed, but in the very performance there remains an excess, the consciousness of the other who does what she is told but could have done otherwise. Her autonomy escapes the relationship, it remains in the not saying. The consumption of her objectified self is never complete; it leaves an untouched, inviolable kernel of other free from the willing of the male and it is that small excess which deconstructs the male's certainty in himself in sexual encounters or in his dealings with others. The female other is never wholly and completely exhausted by the subject's consumption of her, and there remains an excess which demands to be understood as an equal and is required for his own interests to be truly satisfied. No amount of objectification or autonomy denial will be able to repress this excess of subjectivity, much like the slave owner who finds it difficult to meet the eyes of the slave brave enough to raise his eyes to him. The excess forms the basis of Butler's ironic deconstruction of the female subject as constructed by society. If pornography is an expression of male domination, it fails and creates the reverse form of dependence: the male's role and identity depends on the continued investment of female compliance. The aim of the male to create a system whereby his interests are privileged fails because he remains dependent on those very things which his system seeks to deny have any will or power.

The real problem with the egalitarian critique is that any hierarchical power relationship which is unjustified and rests solely on power is, as Hegel would tell us, as injurious to the master (men) as it is to the slave (women): the dominator will have a distorted self-understanding because he is uncertain that his supposed understanding of a relationship will be reciprocated. The woman may play the role of the lover, but she may have no sincere interest in the man as a person. The man who treats the woman as an object, as he learnt to do so from his consumption of pornography, cannot possess her or be possessed in that peculiar sexual entanglement of mutual dependence. The pornography consumer is necessarily dependent on her playing her role, but she is only contingently so. Pornography facilitates, if the feminist critique is correct, a failure of the sexual activity:

> Fantasy replaces the real, resistant, objective world with a pliant substitute – and that, indeed, is its purpose. Life in the actual world is difficult and embarrassing. Most of all it is difficult and

> embarrassing in our confrontation with other people, who, by their very existence, make demands that we may be unable or unwilling to meet. It requires a great force, such as the force of sexual desire, to overcome the embarrassment and self-protection that shield us from the most intimate encounters. It is tempting to take refuge in substitutes, which neither embarrass us nor resist the impulse of our spontaneous cravings. The habit grows, in masturbation, of creating a compliant world of desire, in which unreal objects become the focus of real emotions, and the emotions themselves are rendered incompetent to participate in the building of personal relations. The fantasy blocks the passage to reality, which becomes inaccessible to the will. (Scruton, 2006: 344–5)

Without a reciprocal, honest relationship, the pornography consumer is unable to know how he is perceived by her and, hence, how he really exists for others. He alienates himself. The representations of social relationships at the heart of pornography allow neither men nor women (or other sexualities, races and so on) to appreciate or partake in practices and relationships that would be beneficial to their own development and self-understanding (Collins, 1993; Soltenberg, 1993). Such a revelation undermines the feminists' ur-Father or the systematic male conspiracy of pornography.[12] The existence of pornography, if it does maintain and support a male hierarchy, is not in the males' interest. One aspect of the dialectic is to show that inequality is bad because it makes mutual recognition impossible and this, for Hegel, makes personal autonomy impossible (for both the master and the slave).

6.5 Why prohibition and censure of pornographic materials is not a solution

According to the feminist, pornography ought to be negatively evaluated and assigned the category of wrongdoing because it reproduces and maintains unequal relationships between the genders. In the foregoing discussion, this position has been more or less ceded with one caveat: the majority of contemporary sexual representations support a system of inequality, but there is no necessary connection between sexual representation and inequality. It just happens to be the case that most (but not all) of our contemporary pornography incorporates and expresses this inequality. The reason for that, as I hope to show, has nothing to do with pornography, but everything to do with our contemporary economic existence and the feminists' ire which is currently directed at some imagined, originary Male or a set of benefiting contemporary males ought instead to be *our* (male, female, heterosexual, homosexual and all others) ire and directed at the capitalist system of production.

Some (but not all) feminists would go further and demand that, given the moral wrongdoing in the existence of pornography, it ought to be prohibited or the producers, distributors and users of pornography ought to be liable for any harm caused by its existence or display. On the one hand, the prohibition would protect women from harm in its making. There is no need, as we have seen, to see labour conditions as anything specifically to do with sexual products. Workers need to be protected whatever their labour is. On the other, more interesting, hand, the justification for pornography's prohibition or its civil, legal culpability is that its existence harms the equal, moral standing of women in society. It has been shown that the harm of this sort, or the promulgation of inequality is a moral problem for all members of society and not a specific group. It obstructs the sort of rational, human development which separates good cultures from bad ones. And prohibition would do little to remedy that. If pornography were banned, would equality be improved?

The subordination can no longer be understood as a simple denial of the autonomy of one group by another, hence as discrimination commonly conceived. Given this, the MacKinnon move to place the moral problem into a legal frame of discrimination seems problematic. Who is discriminating against whom? It is no longer the case of a ruling group furthering its own interests through the manipulation and coercion of the other group and, since that is the case, the question needs to be asked how such an institution or discourse maintains and supports inequality if it is not in the interests of someone. Obviously, it is not a case of discrimination but more simply a power relationship where the inequality promotes and maintains a state of affairs that benefits someone. So, one needs to say a little more about the relationship between social fabric and individuals and why the framework which generates individuals' feelings of homeliness may be deceptive.

It is clear that in our culture, rights theory is supposed to protect the procedural requirement of moral discourse. However, when such theory – as a translation of the abstract equality into the substantial equality of our culture – is used to protect the interests of the powerful against those of the weak, something is amiss. Women have the right to pursue the career they choose and everyone has the right to their tastes and objects of desire or the things they themselves value. Hegel's criterion of homeliness situates the individual in the role of the arbiter of whether or not the procedural requirements (and also the naturalistic requirements) of morality are met by the social fabric. Such an endeavour is hermeneutical in nature: it involves the interpretation of the substantial values, institutions, meanings and practices which seek to meet the formal requirements. That is, it is an immanent critique of one's contemporary cultural fabric.

Hegel's theory of right outlines three ways in which the cultural constraint is a form of liberation for individuals. It describes how the individual can be an autonomous individual by participating in a social and moral fabric of a specific culture (1991: §149). To feel substantially at home within a culture, that culture has to make possible the integrity required for an agent to be an individual identity and recognized by his or her peers as one; as someone who is not just a child, parent, worker and gender, but as something over and above (and through) these roles. First, the institutions, expectations, meanings and norms of a culture are the objectification and framework of the values which inform the individual's practical reasoning and are a liberation from the dependence on immediate drives. The ability to resist the urgency of the organic drives of the body and to privilege satisfactions is only possible within a cultural environment. Sexual desire and the libido, for example, are channelled into the family (whichever of the many varied forms it might take). The dependence on hunger and thirst and self-preservation in general is repressed by living in a cooperative economic system (again whatever form it might take). Second, the moral fabric liberates the agent from an overt and excessive partiality towards himself or herself (egoism) because we are inculcated in social relationships that make it rational to choose the 'us' over the 'me'. To be a human being requires degrees of self-sacrifice or prioritizing others over oneself and such behaviours are only supported within a social framework of trust. Moral fabric creates the sort of practical reasoning required by social relationships which are necessary for the individual's sense of self. The family makes it intelligible for me not to buy that Aston Martin and instead save up for my kids' college education. Finally, the moral fabric liberates the individual from creating patterns and expectations *ex nihilo* and protects one from the risk of being socially excluded or unintelligible. One's gender, class, sexual orientation, and so on, confer on one a standard of behaviour which is to be engaged with or overcome, but it is only ever the starting point of our action, just as words and the rules of discourse are the beginning point of what we are going to say. Only by first learning the language through repetition and reproduction, can one ever form phrases and sentences which are truly one's own.

Pornography is part of the moral and social fabric of the late industrialized economies. It might even, although I do not yet believe this, be part of some sort of global cultural fabric. Consuming and making pornography can be a liberation. Actors, directors, producers and so on can find meaningful employment in the pornographic industry: this employment allows them to be liberated from immediate desires in the same way that all forms of social labour do. It allows them to form a social group (the pornographers) in the same way one finds solidarity in miners, actors, teachers and so on. Prohibition or legal censure will be an attack on these people's liberation and cultural attitudes which are grounded in outdated puritanism, can limit the choice and affect the value of what these individuals do.

The consumption of pornography frees individuals from the pull of sexual desire in the same way that marriage manages the libido. More significantly, pornography, akin to other aesthetic parts of a culture, is educational: it supplies us with patterns of behaviours in the bedroom: what to do, when to do it and how. This may sound trite, but it is actually an important consideration given the fact that very little in the feminist argument is devoted to non-heterosexual forms of pornography. If one were to learn the practice of being gay from the tittle-tattle and gossip of the workplace, locker room or playground, it would be a long and arduous journey to pleasure (as it still is for many). Pornography, contrary to the feminists claims, actually breaks the silence and gives non-heterosexual sexualities a voice. And it also allows one to reflect upon one's own sexual practices, as even heterosexuals had to learn most of what they initially knew from tittle-tattle and playground gossip. How are we to know what we like, or who we like unless we start experimentation? Experimentation, though, is often clumsy and embarrassing. Pornography offers a way to learn the expectations and norms of a group before blundering in and risking exclusion. It brings a voice to sexual activity in general that, for a long historical period, has been silenced. Romantic comedies teach us how to fall in love and how to behave on dates. Tragedies teach us how to deal with grief and how to behave with those in mourning or nearing death. Shakespeare teaches us what to do if we are too attached to our mother. Pornography teaches us the etiquette of the bedroom and how to transgress and seek consent to transgress with others. Pornography plays a role in a civilized society and the prohibition or legal censure of sexual material will damage the rationality of a specific culture's h-axis.

The critic of pornography might ask why can't such functions be performed by other institutions? And the answer is that they could be, but why should they be? It is not the only way, but it is a way and it has emerged as part of a coherent and (in the main) rational society. One might here want to say that there are other ways to give a voice to sexuality and to educate the individual in the intricacies of sexual behaviour, and surely a monopolized production of such materials by trusted sources and the prohibition of pornography in its current state is a better solution. I very much doubt it. (*The Lover's Guide* (Ludgate, 1991) was mostly bought by adolescents who sought arousal rather than adults who sought education.) Ronald Dworkin thinks we cannot ban trashy pornography because no legal distinction can map out the aesthetic categorization reliant on a high versus low brow basis (1981: 179). However, his objection misses the point: high or quality examples of art cannot exist without the support of the base of the art pyramid. Quality artistic production requires a free market of creation and keeping only the high brow will stagnate the creative process (as does monopolizing funding). Moreover, trash productions materially support high brow art through economic investment and also by conferring a sense of objectivity in aesthetic productions: one can only know what is quality art by measuring it against the trash elsewhere offered. There is also the problem that judgements about what is trash and what has value made contemporaneously with the emergence of art are very often found to be misplaced: one thinks most obviously of unreflective attempts to use the musical distinction between classical and folk as exclusive and normative, rather than a continuum which is descriptive. It often takes the distance of an historical judgement to correctly delineate the distinction.

So, returning to Hegel's three-fold institutional liberation, in what way can the individual find satisfaction in the existence of pornography. First, it can be argued that pornography liberates the individual from the urgency of immediate drives. Labour in the industry confers on one an economic identity and frees one from labouring to supply basic needs much the same as all other forms of labour. As a worker in a specific industry, the individual can find satisfaction in his or her work and wear it as one wears clothes, as a form of identity. Through labour and participation in the industry of pornography, workers will belong to a workplace, a community of workers and a specific class. For consumers, pornography satisfies the economy of libido allowing one to free oneself from the urgency of the sexual drive which when unsatisfied damages individual and personal integrity. It also opens up a free market of personal satisfaction allowing one to choose who one is and what one values though the market shelf of alternatives: hetero, gay, group, couple, role play, non-penetrative and so on. The free choice of which clothes to wear, which ringtone to put on one's phone and which car to drive allows individuals to express their individuality within a structure of meanings. If I drive a SUV, I'm adventurous; an estate, I'm pragmatic; a sports car, I'm having a mid-life crisis. The free choice of sexualities and sexual practices are supported by the multifarious representations of pornography. Pornography is far more varied in terms of objects of desire in terms of sex, gender, body shape and dress. It is far more varied in terms of practices and therefore creates an arena of choice whereby the individual can feel at home with his or her sexuality whereas Hollywood films would just exclude such individuals and create unhappiness and identity problems. Pornography is one way to encourage Mill's experimentation with ways of living through a free market of sexual ideas. Furthermore, pornography is, as we have said, educational: it illustrates new practices, the etiquette of the bedroom and how to treat others.

It is that final comment which rests uneasily in this book. Pornography can be a constituent part of a rational moral fabric, but to say that it is educational and an illustration of how to treat others goes against the very content of *contemporary* pornographic material. Hegel's argument for the rationality of many of our institutions is an apology for capitalism. When there is a monopoly on goods, centralization generally occurs followed by homogeneity. So, if there is only one producer of shoes or mobile phones, then there is a lack of choice and innovation and the individual cannot express his or her difference through the simple act of consuming a product. Hegel's apology for the capitalist system is that it creates the best possibility for the satisfaction of personal freedom and the construction of an individual identity separate and distinct from others (1991). It is thus justified as maintaining and securing freedom and the expression of individuality. Pornography could do this, but like much of capitalist production, the reverse is actually true. Hegel's apology actually fails.[13] There is a weak and a strong form of the problem with capitalism: weakly, it does not encourage diversity and offer choice, but instead generates banality and homogeneity that undermines and makes it difficult for non-standard sexualities and tastes to find expression; and strongly, it encourages the lowest common denominator because it is concerned with an increase in capital and not the value of the product itself and that is the shock, violent form of pornography which has negative normative consequences on social relations by reducing individuals to egoistic atoms.

6.6 The real enemy

The first obvious point to make is that the capitalist mode of production apparently does not support individuality through liberty and heterogeneity. Images of beauty and sexuality are monopolized by centralized media industries that pander to the majority public opinion (viciously constructed by said industries) for fear of offence. The notion of beauty and normalized sexual activity is determined by the latest model or starlet and follows a rather banal pattern. Body shape is wholly determined by the public imagery of films and other media and what we find attractive and what we can do to those objects we find attractive is never seemingly a free choice. For as much as the liberal defenders of the free market ground their arguments in the promotion of liberty, the sad truth is that in a system that levels all values to the notions of desire and taste necessary for exchange and consumption, the machinery of mass production will ensure that majority and conservative forms of desire are always dominant. Contemporary examples of sexually explicit material under capitalism are as banal as the constant images of beauty and desire which bombard agents left, right and centre. What is more, with the advent of individual private screens and the internet, the pretence at narrative has largely been done away with. Pornography's most prevalent form is short titbits for quick satisfaction, as though the one and only aim of sexual activity is orgasm. Larger films and materials are deliberately ripped into just the erotic scene or the sexual activity.

However, most of our consumption is like this: food, television programmes, Hollywood films, cars and mobile phones. One visits an art gallery to 'collect' all the items on display by flitting from one to the other in a predetermined course around the space, spending a minimum of one minute and a maximum of five minutes at each piece. The object is to be consumed and discarded. It is not to remain. If it remains, then there is no longer need and, without need, capitalism does not function. Capitalism is about the reduction of things to transferable and, ideally, disposable goods. It is about excess and never about satisfaction because the satisfied no longer buy. Pornography makes the sexual object a transferable good, but that is no different from making food into a transferable good and not the central ritual of family life, or reducing education into the transferable good of knowledge (Scruton, 2006: 103–107). Like a glass of water, any glass will do and if one is denied, another can replace it. Persons, in the sexual sphere, are reduced by capitalism to the satisfaction of desire and sexual activity to the negotiation between two contracting parties. Sexual arousal, we assume, should not be like this; it must be for a person who is not transferable. Sexual desire, like anger, is aimed at a particular person and not a person with certain characteristics in general. It should be about intimacy and friendship and to represent this pornography would require a narrative. Capitalism undermines this and engineers taste so that the sexual expression of the individual is just another aspect of exchange.

The aim of capitalism is not to make good art. Nor good products. It is not interested in the product *per se* but only in the product as a means to satisfy other desires, as capital in motion. As one insider in the industry astutely observed: 'The product, as well as my job, was anything but transgressive; it was corporate moneymaking at its most cynical, conservative, and tightly controlled. It wasn't even about sex; it was about using sex to separate people from their money' (Rosen, 2010: 28). The aim is to make something which has a monetary value that exceeds the monetary value invested in the sets, actors, writing and so on. And this is as true of the more obvious film world of pornography as it is of the literary world, as the recent success of the quite awful (and anti-feminist) *Fifty Shades of Grey* testifies. There is no point in large capital investment in the product itself when the rules of capital dictate that the ideal is minimum investment for maximum return. Art itself is not immune from such a world, it too is not produced for the inherent or intrinsic value in it, but as a way to make money. Art is just another investment in which capital can grow. This should not be the goal of pornography nor of art. Hegel, like many before him, assumed the particular wills of money-makers would be magically aimed at the universal good of culture, even if, like Mill, he wanted to curb over-democratization of the culture market. The production of pornography is determined by the market and the producer is alienated from the worth of the object which is made by the actors and directors. The capitalist finds no freedom in it since no on recognizes its worth. He sees it as a way to make money, he is indifferent to the product. And the easiest way to make money is seemingly to produce brief snippets of sexual activity without the aid of costly extras such as sets, writers or cohesion. Hollywood, for the most part, buys narratives which have already been constructed. Hollywood films attempt to translate an already existing story into film whilst adding in elements that will sell. For pornography, the elements that sell the film are intrinsic to its production and the aim is to hang a story around that. It is the capitalists' dream product in many respects.[14] And what seems to sell reflects the wishes of the viewing majority: anonymous males (so the viewer can imagine himself in a way that if it were Brad Pitt he could not), banal models (safe choice in order to generate largest possible group of interested viewers) and two-dimensional characterizations (men are wide-boy studs; women are insatiable; plumbers never get the actual job done). Much like the world of high culture, what actually has worth or quality, what involves a very real investment of creative thinking, will always seemingly be a minority taste.

Feminism is not wrong about the fact that contemporary pornography maintains and supports society's already present gender inequality, but it is wrong to seek out some original male conspiracy whereby the intentions of males, whether overt or latent, is to further his interests and those of his biological sex through the subordination of women. It is not about the Male but about the Capitalist who is sexless and genderless; the capitalist who is nameless. If the feminist thinks that pornography is a male-directed conspiracy perpetrated and maintained in his interest, she is wrong. It is about money and the objectification of women, and men, and others, for the sake of profit, for the interests of the capitalist. And we all know what the problem with capitalism is, alienation, in which pornography can play its part.[15]

Peter Singer talks about how the ideology of the Great Chain of Being supports the attitudes by which we distinguish ontologically between humans and animals and, hence, silences our moral conscience on the nature of meat consumption. He asks how a metaphysics so long abandoned can still play such a role in our practical reasoning (Singer, 2002). The ideology on its own, though, does not do the whole work: the forces of capital invested in meat production and exchange ensure that any real moral attempt to interrogate its rightness remains an idiosyncratic and oddball pursuit. Puritanism as an ideology keeps sexual representation off the agenda so the capitalists can go on making poor product since there is no audience which would admit to being consumers and consequently zero demand that the product should change. In a secular society, there is no metaphysical or rational support for an attitude that rejects sexual activity as an area of artistic production or normal labour. Is the objectification of the standard actress who kisses in a romantic comedy to be morally evaluated on the same terms as the actress in a pornographic scene? In whose interest is such an objectification? The actress would be able to find satisfaction in her portrayal, yet the pornographic actress cannot. She is doing her job in silence and as such the capitalist can ensure she does what she is told. Prohibition is actually in the interests of the capitalist because female and minority sexualities want the representation out there so they can deny it. The real interests, like in Singer's story, are the capitalists: cheap, homogeneous art for mass consumption without reflective demands about quality. It is not in the interest of males, but in the interest of the money-makers.

Capitalism leads to alienation, or the impossibility of authentically objectifying myself in my products, actions or expressions. Objectification is a problem when it is alienation, that is, when the product of one's intentional behaviour is nullified by how the other understands it, such that my autonomy in the action is ignored or denied. Objectification is a problem in contemporary pornography not because it is pornography, not because the representation of sexual activity will lead to the subordination and silencing of females, but because that representation is produced in a capitalist economy: what is produced is not produced to make sense of the sexual experience but in order to increase the initial investment. Contemporary pornography alienates because, on the one hand, individuals cannot feel at home or find satisfaction in the models and norms it prescribes for sexual behaviour; and, on the other, it atomizes the relationship between individuals. I see others as competing with me for pleasure, or as a burden, to be compromised and negotiated with if I am going to get my pleasure. And if the relationship between individuals is determined by capitalism and we are alienated from them, then the wish fulfilment represented in the fantasy world of pornography will be where I can be the dominant partner, where my negotiation will enable maximum pleasure for me and I am indifferent to the pleasure of the other. That's what will sell. The last barrier to homeliness is the contemporary form of pornography, from the large productions and literary works right down to the Gonzo approach, its intent is to make money. The anonymous, subjectivized male, (but actually it is the maker, the man with the camera, the producer, the capitalist) and the alienated female (her act is taken away from her) are cost effective representations. Pornography undermines a desirable social bond and egoism in sexual activity (how many and how quickly! Oh, the irony!) becomes dominant, failing the requirements for a way to valuably interact with others. And that means neither men nor woman can find satisfaction in the norms and expectations it promotes if they seek to use pornography as a guide to human sexual relations. There can be no identification between my own world and the world of pornography because it is not what I want to consume nor what we would want to produce if we were asked to make a sexually explicit erotic film. Pornography represents the roles in sexual relations, agents participate in these roles according to these representations yet do not feel that they ought to play these roles.

And so, no doubt some feminists will argue, surely prohibition is required? We say pornography subordinates women, you say it alienates both men and women. Surely you ought to agree that it has to be prohibited or at least be liable for damages?

However, prohibition will not end the inequality brought about by alienation. The actress may see her work as a liberation, she may well take pride in it and see it as a step to future projects and aspirations. By banning or restricting her participation, the feminist makes it impossible for her to assert her own worth. Prohibition also means that the voice of the woman, silenced by pornography, is given the capacity to speak only at the cost of her sexuality. Bataille (1977) uses the sexual transgressive nature of his female characters as a form of liberation. Similarly, imagine an Irish comic who uses the expectations and unconscious associations of his English audience to reveal both its own putative prejudices (and hence liberate their minds) and to affirm his own self-worth and that of his nation (I am the one who mocks you). If Irish jokes were banned (and one wonders whether such a policy is even feasible), the unconscious attitudes enshrined in a shared moral fabric will remain, even if only latently so. The Irish comic brings them to our attention, he reveals to us traditional attitudes which require revision. But he does so because he is in charge of his product, because he owns the means of products and freely creates his product. To prohibit pornography takes away a tool from the armoury of those who wish to overcome alienation.

What is wrong with pornography can be overcome from within by pornographers. And the appropriate representation of sexual relations is a good for society: sex is a part of our lives and how we engage in it and how we view the participants in it determines and realizes our own projects and aspirations. It is a crucial part of freedom. Aesthetic objects increase our own human understanding of both ourselves and others. Just as we should not ban Irish jokes, but positively affirm the Irish as a group in society and simultaneously ban racism, so we should not prohibit pornography. The point is to affirm the countless female producers and directors who are now taking control of large parts of the pornographic industry and state that it is possible that pornography could be a way to address and abolish the unjustified, cultural inequality between the sexes. Deconstruction of the inequality is required and can be brought about by seizing the means of production. Progressive pornography is possible when the class that has been subordinated recognizes its interests separate from the interest of all and represent them through the media available in that society. What stops individuals with creative interests seizing the mantle and producing artistic representations of sexual activity seems to be cultural attitudes concerning the respectability of it all. Puritanism plays into the hand of the faceless capitalist who wishes for the atomization of society to continue. Prohibition or repression of pornographic materials is not just futile but harmful because pornography is the tool to deconstruct inequality. One could make a pornographic film which empowered women and *Baise-moi* seems to attempt this, whether it was successful or not. Pornography may well be an important tool in the deconstruction of social inequality (as the existence of gay porn seems to testify). Any attempt to limit pornography is an attempt to limit possible sexual expression and prohibiting pornography is cutting one's nose off to spite one's face. Prohibition (and even the more minor liability demanded by MacKinnon) is actually an institutional form of silencing, once the practice itself is banned, how do minority groups express their sexuality?

6.7 A problematic case: children

Of course to view pornography as a revolutionary force whereby attitudes which serve the interests not of individuals but of capitalists can be overcome is both fanciful and naïve. It is but one part of an overall strategy. Pornography and sexual activity are but one part of our existence and capitalism is more prevalent than that. However, the evolution (rather than the revolution) of our society to a greater equality and homeliness will be aided by the existence of progressive pornography. And, in its favour, capitalism as an economic model does – as Hegel noted – generate the broadest range of possible objects of desire as well as being the engine behind much of the equal distribution of power in society over the past few hundred years or so. Yet, the relationship between technology, economics and contemporary pornography also raises a more specific moral problem worth briefly discussing.

There is cultural unease with the idea of child sexuality, even if the Victorian, pre-Freudian understanding of children as asexual no longer has much credence. The participation of children in the making of pornographic films is ruled out by the requirement of the k-axis: children are unable to consent to participate in activities they do not understand and are unlikely to enjoy. The problems with the Kantian model of consent, though, as we noticed in an earlier chapter, is that it rules out all child labour (including paper rounds, sticking up, and acting in standard films). Yet there are further problems: it does not touch upon the problem of children consuming pornography in any directly moral way and, also, if there are no participants at all (such as in literary pornography or in animé cartoons), it has no judgement to pass. In short, it cannot pass moral judgement on the subject matter of children 'virtually' represented in such productions. Let us deal with these problems one at a time.

Common sense tells us that children can, if standards are in place and the work is appropriate, be employed to do specific jobs, say delivering newspapers. Such employment is liberating and as long as strict protection is in place will not infringe on childhood's normal development. With acting, as long as child participation in theatre shows or film making does not impact on their normal development, there is no reason for it not to be allowed. Sexual activity at a young age will have an impact on development: Freud has at least taught us that. And that illustrates a crucial point when it comes to childhood consumption of pornography. Children participating and consuming pornography is to be forbidden because, like child labour, they lack the ability to consent because consenting requires moral agency which is not a given but a characteristic acquired by participating in social life. When one is young, one develops one's moral agency, one's autonomy and that requires education and experience. Pornography is the wrong way to achieve this. One can imagine a sexual faculty much like our moral faculty, necessary for social interaction. Such a faculty requires the right sort of context and experiences to develop and learn. Exposure to the wrong material, because it cannot yet be understood, will be damaging (Dines, 2010: xi–xii). This is equally true of violent films and pornographic material. As such, by bolstering the k-axis with the v-axis, the new theory can explain why children should be prohibited from both the production and consumption of pornographic materials. It is then up to the will of the specific culture to set a bright legal line when individuals have, in the opinion of the populace, reached the age of consent, be it sixteen, eighteen or twenty-one.

Yet, the consideration of the effect on children is only part of the limitations of the k-axis for making wholesale judgements about pornography. One of the most explicit sex scenes filmed for mainstream cinemas was for the film *Team America: World Police*. It contained representations of explicit sexual positions, urophilia and coprophilia in a mainstream film which received a normal 15 rating in the UK. (It would be interesting to see whether or not anyone is prosecuted for bringing Crepax or Manara into the UK.) The reason screening was allowed was because there were no participants, only puppets. What, then, of adults consuming animé, or animated pornography which has as its objects children, or, to use another example, participants who pretend to be under age? The h-axis would here play a role as the k- and v-axes struggle (no one is harmed, no one is coerced, the adult has developed autonomy). The result of such representations, if their simulation is an attempt at realism rather than playful role fulfilment (where a 'schoolgirl' is played by a 30 year old woman) is a version of Langton's background lying whereby attitudes are formed towards an object because the material is inappropriate to it. Background beliefs about the sexuality of children will be formed that are wrong and will objectify children such that they cannot feel at home in the culture. The errors involved will have negative normative consequences for all children. The framework of understanding for children though is askew. Most adults wants middle aged women dressed as schoolgirls and not schoolgirls, it is the fantasy of it but also the acknowledgement of what is a proper object of sexual desire. Children should not be understood as such, the h-axis which guarantees equality of treatment (that is, agents can all feel at home, including children) forbids the understanding of children in this way.

6.8 You say tomato, I say tomato

One accusation at the end of this essay may well be that I am being ultimately conservative and repeating ingrained attitudes about sexual history, in the absence of pure, reliable reason. I would answer that history is always a good fall-back guide to what we should and shouldn't do unless there are urgent reasons to doubt it. More significantly, does the wrongdoing at the heart of contemporary pornography justify either prohibition or legal accountability. So long as participants have consented (and this rules out children), so long as the distribution and consumption are regulated such that it is not consumed by inappropriate groups, so long as simulated violence is not a violation of the v-axis and so long as the subject matter does not result in the formation of beliefs that undermine the potential equality of subjects in the culture, then pornography is permissible. If the true problem is alienation, and it seems that the true problem *is* alienation, then the prohibition of pornographic material would be akin to banning industrial production and consumption of products in order to protect factory workers. What would be gained and what would be lost? There is a need for the populace to take control of the industry and the means of production such that pornography is not produced in order to be sold at an increase in value, but it is produced because individuals want to produce it (and not the surplus value).

Interestingly, the means of production are in most people's hands and the big business nature of pornography is already on the slide. We all possess cheap video cameras and have access to sites that exhibit it for free. Amateur porn may well be the seeds of optimism, after all the violent and banal material is nearly always mass produced and marketed. Reciprocally, and one should never be too optimistic, one of the means of production of pornography is the individual's body and since the means of production is so intimately bound with the individual person it is perhaps easy to see why, like athletes and actors, pornographic performers are so easily exploited and so well rewarded.

Would the feminists herein discussed and myself actually agree on good/bad pornography and actually agree on what should be encouraged and what should be frowned upon (perhaps only disagree on the severity of that frowning, whether it is aesthetic, ethical, political or legal)? My answer is, 'No'. Why not? Culture is a multi-layered artefact of a community that involves layers of sophistication, from the simplistic to the abstract. One cannot have high culture without low, and one cannot have complex sex films without the lower regions of simplistic pornography. No matter the objectionable content, if it has not violated the autonomy, minimal naturalism or cultural constraints of moral evaluation, then pornography is permissible.

Interlude 6 Guardami

Within the film, a simple tale is told of a young man from Bosnia who was the best diver from the bridge over the river that joins the two halves of Mostar. When the war has come and gone and the bridge has been destroyed and rebuilt, he no longer throws himself from the bridge. He refuses to risk his death any more because an unsettling fear without an object has entered his thinking about the world. Within the film, the tale – told by a father – operates as a metaphor of the relationship between risk, meanings and death.

The title of the film translates as either the motion specific, 'Watch me!', or the freezing, objectifying, 'Look at me!', as there is no difference in Italian. What is important is that it is an imperative. And it is the order of the protagonist, Nina, who demands that we watch her because her sexuality remains a commodity which she controls. She is an actress in pornographic films: the usual technique for justifying the use of explicit sexual representation, but it is obvious that, to her, sexual activity is nothing but a preference, a taste and a pleasure. Her motivation for participating in the production of pornographic films is explained quite openly and she never shies from responding to inquiries about her work believing it to have equal validity to responses such as 'professor', 'teacher', 'doctor' and so on. The reason why she participates in pornography is stated as 'a question of power' and possession. She believes she possess consumers, that she exerts power over them and she likes to be watched because she enslaves them with her sexuality. She is, in many ways, a prototype example of Sartre's form of bad faith as revelling in transcendence, a form of solipsism whereby she – and she alone – has the subjectifying power of freedom.

Such confidence grounds her autonomy in the face of demands for her labour as product, her body as commodity and her sexuality as property. She continually frustrates the men who would bind her in legal, conventional and literal ties. Her promise is at all times a promise, but always equally a refusal: the power between her and her watcher is asymmetrical because she refuses to exchange or, better, to concede her sexuality to males. She rejects the advances of two predatory males in the opening part of the film, playing them along and then turning the tables on them. She continually rejects the advances of the cruel producer–consumer of pornography, Baroni, (until her penance scene) who wants to restrict her freedom and autonomy, and in her fantasy, she is objectified as an object of desire who possesses her audience for her own ends. The only aspect of existing for an other, a real other, is within the context of her family relationship with her lesbian partner, Christiana, and Christiana's child. The sex between them is quotidian and the inverse of the sex being produced in Nina's films, it is real and sincere, at one point interrupted by the crying of the child.

The opening scene sets so much of the film in context. It is stylized, shot in black and white, with the actors on set aestheticized and rendered perfect, but devoid of emotion. It is about the aestheticism of pornography, about the reduction of the actors to their visual images. The filming of the production of the pornographic material revels in the irreality of the image and continually reminds the viewer of the simulation at its heart, even if the sexual activity is not physically a simulation. The actors are shown as simulating sexual activity even if being physically penetrated (or penetrating). We, the viewer, are reminded that they are playing at being sexual when the camera is turned on; they are never *being* sexual. Emotion only enters the faces of the actors when the shooting is called to stop. Simultaneously, the film reveals the banality and the boredom of the reality of making pornography and how this is very often a flat contradiction of the fantasy aspect of its consumption. We are shown actors shaving off superfluous body hair, joking and working as one would work at any job, the director glancing at his watch and desperate to get away. Actors are even seen in absurd angel costumes vainly trying to keep an erection. In fact, with the exception of Baroni, the producers and directors are indifferent to the value of their product, indifferent to the activity before them, and the participants are indifferent to the final product. Only Nina seems to take pride in her performance, in her talent.

Everything changes when Nina learns she has a tumour and must undergo a course of chemotherapy. The irreality at the heart of pornography, the divorce of the image from the material reality of life is brought to the fore in the dangerous but courageous sexualization of the process of chemotherapy. At that point, the same film techniques, the slow motions, the soundtrack and the music video discourse of the camera work all reveal that what we are consuming truly has nothing to do with what it is meant to be representing. The extent of Nina's bad faith is then fully realized (it is, oddly, Baroni who tells her that sooner or later she will have to depend on someone else). Her initial response is to leave her lover without telling her, to seek solitude, to be on her own as though the reality of cancer will melt away. But, of course, it cannot. And, for the first time, she is aware of the vulnerability of her image, and that it can be taken away from her. Her existence is in the look of the other – 'Watch me', she demands – but she does not want to be seen as suffering or as ill. She sends her fellow patient, Flavio, away but then she invites him to see her perform in a film. Sex is what she uses to be in control, controlling the desires of others, but her illness undermines that, stops her life from being what she wants it to be.

Her mortality begins to stalk her and that is where she begins to realize the importance of the other as more than an object, but also as a reciprocal dependence. She begins with her own family, her mother and father, but it is through her new and old friends, Flavio, a cautious and conservative teacher who refuses to accept her sexualized image of herself, Dario, the nurse, and Christiana, that a new bond of mutual recognition occurs. She is brought face to face with her mortality, like the war for the diver, and thus her actions now have meaning and consequences. Like him, the simple act of being what one wants – of diving – is no longer enough because the other has begun to matter to one.

The film begins to develop a narrative at this point, the camera work changes and pornographic imagery begins to be parodied. The conventional fairground mirrors scene, with its innocent romanticism, between Flavio and Nina is grotesquely reproduced in the pornographic universe as virtual television screens in a Cronenberg-eseque virtual world where Nina's image is fucked on screen. Yet, the hole through the screen which connects the material reality of the two actors results in the penetration of another actress who is not Nina. Her image has become solely an object of consumption. Nina is perturbed that in fact the girl on the other side of the screen is not her, she is no longer the object of desire because her image has been divorced from her body and expropriated by the producers. She can for the first time be substituted by her image, and her image by another.

It is against a background of a burgeoning family and real, mutual existence that death begins to become more and more real for her. Her narrative is from egoism to altruism, to caring more about Flavio's death than her own, to the discovery of meaning in others who recognize her, her postmodern family. Unlike the diver, though, she once more tests her freedom in a very Catholic penance: she submits herself to Baroni with the demand that he can do what he likes, what he has always wanted to do, that he hurt her. Her penance is undertaken as she awaits her test results – her pain and humiliation are to be endured in a divine promise to exchange humiliation for cure. For the first time, the demand to be watched sexually is a torture and a humiliation, but a necessary one (she believes). When she meets Baroni again her power has returned and she sends him back to his wife with his tail between his legs, with the words: 'I used you!' The metaphor of the diver is linked to voluntary humiliation: she fantasizes about him once more diving from the bridge as she suffers at the hands of the Male.

Her penance is successful, she is cured, but Flavio is not. Just as pornography undermines real sexual relationships, so the final scene undermines pornography. On Flavio's deathbed, they finally make love. It is erotic and painful; sad and very real. The sex is significant and meaningful and the director eschews shots of organs, instead concentrating on the faces of the actors. ('In true erotic art it is usually the face and not the sexual organ that provides the focus of attention' (Scruton, 2006: 154).) The eroticism of the final scene resides in their attire, they are clothed and it is non-explicit, especially as contrasted with much of the irreality of the pornographic scenes and the capitalistic view of sex. The nature of her sincere sexual gift to Flavio contrasts most notably with the penitential exchange where Nina is humiliated and fisted by Baroni. Both are voluntary, but only one is a true gift and as a gift she takes pleasure in the giving, not just the possessing. Her narrative is a narrative to understand what sex is.

Guardami is a real attempt to make an adult film about the modern context of sexual relations. The explicitness is necessary to the adequate telling of the tale and yet, the content of these scenes, would be subject to legal redress under MacKinnon's conceptual understanding of pornography and her normative aims. Given the aesthetic interest the film demands (and I shall not argue it is perfect, it is not), that would be a shame. The film is about sex, death and people. It is a modern day tragedy, about how we, as individuals, need to depend on others when faced with tragedy and how the atomism and consumerism of contemporary society is a form of general repression of our humanity. We need pornographic films to understand ourselves and to take control of our own sexuality. Otherwise we will remain in silence and immature.

7
Money-makers and Shadows

The preceding pages were not truly about pornography. I do not mean that in any ground-breaking Magritte sense, nor even in the playful Foucauldian repetition of what Magritte meant (Foucault, 1983). All I mean is that pornography was revealed more and more progressively to be a symptom or a communication of a deeper disease. Pornography is a pseudo-problem. All of the accusations laid at the door of pornography are ultimately broad cultural misgivings about our way of life and how we understand others.

Let us summarize the content of the discussion in order to reveal what was actually at issue in the foregoing pages. First, it began with an attempt at a definition of what pornography is, but the aim of that, much like the aim of this work as a whole, was not what it appeared on the surface. It is difficult to define aesthetic objects in general, let alone subsets of them, but what is important is to offer a descriptive and not a normative definition of them. If one were to define pornography as the representation of the violent subordination of women, it is a short logical step to its wrongness. Such an argument would be banal (even if it remains important given contemporary cultural conditions) because there remains a large set of sexual representations that do not involve the violent subordination of women, and there is seemingly nothing wrong with these representations unless one believes that there is something wrong with sexual activity *per se*. If one demands that snuff movies be prohibited (rather sensibly one might add), it is because killing human beings, all things being equal, is wrong. The representation of it is macabre, but the wrongness is located in the act itself, not the recording of it. The violent subordination of women is wrong, whether it is recorded or not, but if the demand that prohibition of pornography amounts to the demand that all exploitation, harming, and subordination of actors in the production process be criminalized for moral reasons, then it is a banal demand.

The moral problem with pornography, if there is such a problem, must then be located not in the production process but in its consumption, or more generally in its existence. But even if the content of pornography is morally objectionable, it might be the case that, like other material, it is a medium through which ideas are expressed and, thus, such opinions and ideas are protected in a liberal democracy by the right to free expression. If no direct harm is related to the consumption of pornography in an uncontroversial causal and probabilistic story, such as the connection between the consumption of alcohol and driving, then to censor or restrict access to it is a decision on the part of one agent on behalf of another agent violating the liberty of that agent to choose how to spend his or her time. However, as feminists are keen to emphasize, the protection of free speech as an unlimited right protects the interests of the powerful over and above the weak. We are all free to say what we want, but those in positions of putative authority, privilege, and economic power have voices which are heeded, whereas others do not. An unlimited right to free expression is a tool for the interests of the powerful, not the precondition for an equal free market of ideas.

Yet, the powerful is not, contrary to the grounding claim of feminist theory, the male. The unholy triangle of objectification-silencing-subordination at the heart of the feminist critique of pornography is grounded in the rhetorically negative connotation of the word objectification. Objectification, though, is not always bad. Bad objectification is better understood through the Marxist–Hegelian concept of alienation. Objectification is bad when the agent cannot recognize himself or herself in the image which conditions the other's apprehension of his or her actions and projects. Alienation occurs when the agent cannot recognize his or her conscious willing in the products of his or her intentions. And alienation is not a male conspiracy, but a capitalist one.

The feminist critique and the liberal defence of the value of pornography both fail because they are so thoroughly modern: they both seek an agent who has committed wrong, but if there is wrongdoing in the existence of pornography it resides in a state of affairs which is maintained and supported by the system of capital investment and private property. And if that is the case, then modern moral theories that seek to identify an agent who has done wrong and an agent who has been wronged – a preoccupation with agents grounded in a fixed, real subject – are redundant. There is a need for an ethics which can evaluate the systems of meaning which make possible moral discourse, the identification of subjects and actions. The final chapter was an attempt to offer the beginning of such a theory, although it is admittedly very incomplete at the moment.

The practical issue at the heart of the debate is whether or not access to pornographic materials should be prohibited and restricted, or whether the consumption of the materials should be protected by the right of individuals to pass their time as they wish. As has been stated, the unconditional right to freedom of expression privileges the powerful and thus representations of sexual activity should not be put into a box marked '18' and then left to the discernment of individuals in the same way that passing one's Saturday, watching football or jogging, is left up to individuals. Representations of sexual activity are not just a matter of taste and they should be reflected upon. And so, reciprocally, their prohibition and censure would have a detrimental effect on the aims of feminism. If to be rational, a woman must give up her sexual identity, then her voice is once more silenced. To engage with the aesthetic representations of sexual activity, to find oneself at home, or not, in their images, requires that they are, like other aesthetic objects, out in the open and not merely tolerated or overtly prohibited. Capitalism and the interests of money-makers are actually furthered by the shadowy domain in which sexual representation contemporarily exists: a domain viewed as a matter of taste, tolerated by a moral majority and hence a liberation for those in the know, but a domain in which cultural critics and commentators are loath to engage. With such conditions, minimal investment can generate maximum returns and the quality or value (and, one might add, the nature) of the product is irrelevant to the production process. Pornography is kept immature by its critics and by its liberal defenders.

And that means we can return to the two utopian views already cited. MacKinnon, on the one hand, tells us, 'In a society in which equality is a fact, not merely a word, words of racial or sexual assault and humiliation will be nonsense syllables. Sex between people and things, human beings and pieces of paper, real men and unreal women, will be a turn-off' (1993: 109-110). On the other hand, Nussbaum affirms that: 'It may therefore be not too utopian to imagine a culture in which men's sexual desire for women will not commonly be associated with projects of possession and control, and in which female sexual agency will not inspire fear and suspicion' (1999: 12). Both writers emphatically assert that the problem is not pornography, but the absence of equality between the sexes. Pornography is a pseduo-problem. The aim then is equality and yet the way to equality, and proper sexual relationships, where – one should note and underline – the alien concepts of possession and power are excluded is through, as MacKinnon (not Nussbaum!) continues, a 'context of repose into which thought can expand, an invitation that gives speech its shape, an opening to a new conversation'. Such a conversation requires representations of the human condition, that is aesthetic renderings of what it is to be human, how it is to be human, and reflection on the form of open questioning; not closed systems of meaning in which individuals are arbitrarily enclosed. To reach such a utopia requires sexual representation by and for individuals, intimately involved in the production process and seeing the product of their activity as having value. In short, it requires a *progressive* pornographic production which makes possible homeliness in the cultural conditions of understanding. It is capitalism that restricts such democratic access to production (although things may well be changing).

Then, should we go for revolution? The answer is, 'Nes, or so', or in Italian, 'Nì or son', in German, 'Na and Jein'. One must always remember that the author of the present work is English and not French and, as a nation, we had our fill of revolutions in the seventeenth century. Capitalism has many, many disadvantages as the economic basis of a cultural life but it would be remiss not to recognize the impact industrialization and the free markets have had on public sanitation, health, social mobility, and education. Capitalism has actually sown the seeds of overcoming alienation through the empowerment of whole classes through education and democracy. However, at its heart, the relationships between intentions and actions, activities and productions, creations and value, are skewed by the overriding aim to increase the capital invested and not (as was the case in the building of the pyramids, or the writing of the *Inferno*) the aim of creating something of value (whether that be an action or an object). Just as the prohibition of pornography would undermine the aims of liberation and equality sought by the feminists, so too would the abolition of our whole economic system and the basis of our material reality be detrimental to the aims of the critique itself.

Probably. And here I look with envy at the collection of books written by Karl Marx which sit on my shelves. Such conjectures and offhand comments are, more than probably, indiscreet. A thoroughgoing critique of our economic reality requires many more pages and much more thinking. It is rarely ever an either/or decision. Capitalism has reached its limits. Whether we need a revolution or an evolution is hard to say, but there is always a time when the material conditions of life, which initially responded to the concrete and abstract needs of humans, frustrates those very needs. Especially equality. The aim is to remember our end – equality – and how we are going to get there. Ensuring that pornography belongs to the mainstream of aesthetic culture is one way of achieving equality in sexual desire, rather than through its prohibition or restriction.

So, the conclusion to the discussion is that there are no moral or political grounds for the prohibition or restriction of pornography and there are moral and political grounds for its existence. Pornography can play a rational role in the deconstruction of inequality and in the creation of expectations that can ground meaningful, sexual existence. Not all pornographic materials will do this, very few will, in fact, do so, especially in the contemporary climate where, due to the existence of pornography in the tolerated shadows, it remains immature and unreflective, alienated from the majority of those who would see a value in it, if it were produced for its own sake rather than for capital accumulation. There are some examples of high art in the pornographic realm, a few of which have been discussed here, but just as in other aesthetic forms, the good can only be produced at the top of a pyramid of free and unrestricted creation, so must we also have the low, the irrelevant and the failures.

And that leads me on to one last observation. A recurring theme in good pornography (and even in the bad) is the centrality of existentialism: anxiety, embodiment, limitations, social expectations, transgression and freedom. And, of course, much existentialist literature in its heyday was scandalous due to its sexual content. It was also very aware of the fragility of the human condition and how social conventions are a shield that, when faced with mortality or the compulsive power of sexual desire, very quickly fall away (Camus, 1988; Trocchi, 1996). At present such indications are merely observations and nothing more, but existentialism, for all its philosophical faults, was about putting the human condition right back at the heart of philosophy. It was about remembering we are bodies, that we exist in a constant struggle with the other's apprehension of us, and we are free to do what we want to the point of absurdity. Pornography may well be one more wake-up call to the conventional and assumed natural status of human behaviour and, if nothing else, a reminder that we act as we do because of unquestioned, inherited codes of meaning. Pornography may well, then, in its existence, reproduction and consumption, be the very tool to open that new conversation which MacKinnon wanted, or be the aesthetic equivalent of retrieving 'the body from rationalist disdain' (Herman, 2002: 53). It won't be, though, if it is kept in the shadows in the interests of the money-makers.

Notes

2 The Mull of Kintyre Is Not in Naples: The Definition of Pornography

1. Can pornography be shared? Have I overstated this private element? I think not, it can only be shared as pornography in couples (constituting a person) or small orgy groups (again constituting a person). The public at an adult cinema or at a strip show (so long as they do not constitute a stag party or some other prior group) are lonely. Loneliness itself, one may argue, negates or *nihilates*, to use an apt Sartrean term of art, any bond between the self and the other.
2. Heidegger traces modernity back to Socrates. I do not agree.
3. Justice Stewart in *Jacobellis* v. *Ohio* 378 US 184, 1964, cited in Longino (1980).
4. In fairness, the definition of this report was to a large extent set by the terms of the governmental inquiry.
5. Cake could be a possible taboo object in some cultures where luxury and excess are seen as offensive and to be prohibited. In such a culture, one could imagine the object as being desired because it is taboo, much as fetishism in our own culture works. I maintain that, even in that culture, the psychology of the desire for such a cake could not be sexual even if some subjects would be unable to distinguish between taboo desire from one culture to the next, due to the necessary subjective element in their constitution. A sexual desire must have a sexual object and a cake cannot be that unless the subjective constitution of the agent has, in some sense, gone very wrong indeed. There must be a relationship between the object of sexual desire and some sort of evolutionary story about the purpose of sexual desire. Bestiality, for example, is at the very limit of sexual desire because it involves the anthropomorphizing of a non-human animal. To anthropomorphize a cake is quite frankly weird.
6. Rea's article offers, in my opinion, the best definition of pornography to date in the literature. I do however still find it problematic for a variety of reasons, as discussed in the article Rose (2012). The existence of this article is the reason why this chapter makes no direct attempt to engage with Rea's definition. Note that the difference between shoes and cakes as discussed in the previous endnote is that shoes are a sexual object because humans wear them. If one has a sexual fetish about cakes because people eat them, then I suppose that is less weird.
7. The aesthetic tradition, one may feel, owes much to Kant here (1991). However, as pointed out by a very helpful anonymous reviewer, 'disinterest' for Kant is one of the criteria of an experience of beauty in general and not a condition of whether an object is art or not. Levinson (2005) offers something similar when he distinguishes between the erotic as 'sexually stimulating' and the pornographic as 'sexually arousing'.

8. Bartel (2010) discusses the relationship between the aesthetic interest and the pornographic interest one can take in a work. His conclusion is that a pornographic work can have artistic value, but pornographic interest is solely directed at content and not at formal qualities. He may well be correct, although his thesis does demand better discussion. In this argument, though, all that is required is that pornographic works can have artistic value and he agrees with this.
9. And here, one should make a nod to Aristotle's *Poetics*, which binds the structural, narrative and substantive view of genre with the emotional function and its carthasis.
10. The full uncensored entry in Pepy's diary is cited in Tang (1999: 90).
11. We shall ignore the grammatical error that seems to suggest that the guide is intended for a single would-be Casanova rather than a couple.

3 Oblique Suggestions, Polarized Pumpkin Eaters and Women Haters: The Morality of Pornography

1. One objection here is, of course, that some exchanges which are legal may not actually be moral. For example, the British Museum selling the Elgin Marbles to the City of New York. Although not legally wrong, many might feel it to be morally wrong. However, I feel that any wrongness in exchange must be premised on or derived from a wrongness either in production (buying a snuff film), or in ownership (buying stolen goods), or in consumption (legally buying kitchen knives to use in street violence). This is only an intuition at this stage and requires more discussion, but it seems more than plausible that the Elgin marbles were possessed in a less than moral way (as many Greek friends have told me).
2. Attitudes towards artists, at least in the West, seem to be determined by not just the tolerance of moral failings, but the actual celebration of them; as though artistic production requires some sort of moral transgression. There are a long list of types who fit this bill with Lord Byron as the original and paradigmatic example. Moreover, not just the artist but the process of artistic production is seemingly a special moral case: the treatment of animals in Damien Hirst's art is bracketed off because the meaning and the expression of that meaning is considered more significant; more so, one feels, than in the hobbyist taxidermist.
3. One thing to dismiss immediately is the claim that the two arguments differ because pornography is not art. The working definition of pornography holds that it is a 'cultural' object and we have more broadly described it as an aesthetic object in the previous chapter. Should it be denied that it is an instance of art, then we must revisit the definition already formulated. We shall say something about the value of pornographic art below and whether or not it can ever rise above banality or the level of the trite.
4. Of course, this quotation has been heavily doctored, but it does give a flavour of MacKinnon's rhetoric. Her argument is far more subtle than her rhetoric at times seems to suggest and I shall give it proper consideration below.
5. In defence of MacKinnon, she has a possible answer about intimacy. What is a special case about sex is that it is an invasion of intimacy in a way that racial

harassment is not. It is individual through and through and the agent cannot either deny the representation of their sexuality nor distance themselves from it once it has been recorded. One can say that being identified as 'black' is a universal, a generalization that can be negated, 'I am more than my blackness and not identical to it', but harassment about sexuality is intimately individual. It is about *me* and *my* body through and through (MacKinnon, 1993: 60–61). However, method acting would seemingly be very individual when the actor uses emotions that relate to his or her own personal history. How can the pornography actress not deny that the sexual acts were simulated and yet the method actor deny that the emotions were simulated (when they were not)? But one can use one's own skills in film making, method acting and bringing one's own experiences out through the character's emotions.

6. MacKinnon's political target is the use of free-speech statutes because, according to her, the institutional tolerance of pornography is akin to the institutional support of slavery. The legal prohibition must follow the moral revelation of pornography's role in the reproduction of cultural conventions of inequality and power relations. Again, though, pornography does not necessarily have to reproduce cultural conventions and can often challenge them, a point we shall return to. For a possible example, see Despentes and Coraliè (2000).
7. There are three main forms of pluralism: hermeneutic pluralism, whereby an object is partially constituted by the conditions that make it possible, and as such the same object can differ for different agents depending on their conditions of experience (Vattimo, 1992); radical empiricism, whereby one acknowledges that agents have historically been mistaken about values and so, more than probably, are still mistaken, so it is best to put questions of value into debates about reasonableness rather than rationality (Rawls, 1993); and, finally, ontological pluralism, or the rejection of monism as concerns metaphysical accounts of value (Berlin & Williams, 1994).
8. Dines (2010) makes an empirical and not a conceptual point about violence, harm and pornography. MacKinnon's identification of pornography as harm is empirically true in the contemporary milieu, if not a conceptual point about pornography in general and she supports this with some very telling data. Thinkers such as Ronald Dworkin have an outdated idea of what pornography actually is, believing it still to be akin to the images produced in the seventies. I agree with her claims, although oddly I feel it is a very American problem (and that is a problem which will be exported because America still sets the cultural agenda). The question of violence will be touched upon in this chapter and then returned to in the last chapter. Basically, if non-consensual violence is perpetrated in the production process, then the object produced is immoral.
9. This is not to say that Kantianism is truer or a better ethical theory than its rivals, only that it is more appropriate to the matter in hand. To balance it out, concerns with the global distribution of wealth and the problem of famine are much more appropriately dealt with from a utilitarian point of view. See for example the wealth of Singer (1972) as opposed to the poverty of O'Neill (2007) on these questions.
10. Apologies to advocates of the two moral theories so far discussed who will take rightful umbrage at my rather dismissive approach. The point is not to

dismiss these theories but just to show that it is better to talk about these problems in a different idiom. Pluralism means one cannot dismiss the truthfulness of such theories since, without revision, the idea of truth and ethical theory is problematic.

11. Again, this is another reason that the explicitly moral use of utilitarian theory resolves itself into rights talk. (Mill, 1962: ch. 5). Utilitarianism functions best as a social theory interested in statistics, not as a theory concerned with individuals.
12. Herman (2002: 61) makes this point about Andrea Dworkin and especially her book *Intercourse*.
13. For an interesting account of the problems of being scientific in this area, Rosen gives a good, narrative account of how human and political interests often determine knowledge in studying pornographic phenomena (2010: ch. 10).
14. Two caveats needs to be added to this point. One, to assume that pornographic material is not institutionally structured to incite violence may well be the very point of contention with critics such as MacKinnon and Russell, but that involves a more subtle discussion of power and socialization, which we will carry out in the next two chapters. Consequently, it is not a critique of individual film-makers and individual consumers, but social conventions and values as a whole. In fact, by silencing pornography, the possibility of bringing to light such cultural attitudes may be lost. Two, the above point seems to suggest that there is no connection between arousal and violence, or that they are distinct psychological states. This is obviously empirically contentious and very much more needs to be said in the succeeding chapters.

4 Otherwise We'll Have Words: The Politics of Pornography

1. Both Dworkin's argument and Langton's (2009: chs. 1–2, 6–7) response, which we shall look at below, rely too heavily on the utilitarian policy argument. The disagreement and the resolution seem to rest on this point of interpretation, yet utilitarianism is just not appropriate to the discussion; it is a red herring as we have seen in the previous chapter. The question is always already one of principle and equality. Does the existence of pornography and its consumption have an effect on equality? And they both agree that this is the main question. They both play with the idea of external preferences which seem to be a new offering as a way to allay Mill's fears about the intensity problem in utilitarian act-theory, that is mere intensity as a measure of value. Mill was, at times, just too faithful, never quite able to admit the paucity of his initial favoured theory when most of his intuitions would have lead him in another direction. If someone likes killing, it seems absurd to consider his preferences at the outset only to discount them later on because they are 'external preferences' or as Mill might say 'ignoble'.
2. The question is then posed whether or not the current discussion is bounded by the requirements of liberal democracies. What would the status of pornography be in non-liberal states? With reference to my initial claim in the second chapter about the emergence of pornography in the industrial age, I should

add that, democracy, liberalism and capitalism are intimately bound up with industrialization. A cultural theorist could plausibly claim that pornography, and especially morally problematic pornography, is only possible in a liberal society. There is an immediate plausibility to such a suggestion, if no argument is yet forthcoming. I would not dream of making such a suggestion without an argument, though.

3. It cannot be as simple as this, though, because there is a very real question of moral as against legal responsibility in play. Whose is the will that instigates the processes of discrimination? Is it the boss who consumes pornography? Is it the boss because of conventional, misogynist attitudes and, therefore, not pornography? Is it the producers of pornography, hence reducing the boss to the level of a simpleton with a very weak will? Such considerations constitute the origin of Butler's (1997) critique of radical feminism to which we turn later in the text.
4. Butler, following Foucault, believes the liberal discussion of pornography is flawed by its insistence on power as emanating from a central institution (the state) when, in contemporary culture, it is much more nebulous and distributed. I shall consider this below when we get on to the concept of power proper.
5. If her exaggerated claims about the nature of intention are taken seriously, then the question is a broader one about our whole conception of moral agency. Such a critique has already been voiced by Nietzsche and determinism alike. It is not the place here to consider it in depth.
6. Langton is making a claim consistent with an earlier understanding of the specific nature of films, whereby the industry is one of illusion such that 'the outside world is the straightforward continuation of that presented on the screen' (Adorno & Horkheimer, 1997: 126).
7. Dworkin tells us: 'The British Race Relations Act, for example, forbids speech of racial hatred, not only when it is likely to lead to violence, but generally, on the grounds that members of minority races should be protected from racial insults. In America, however, it is a fixed principle of constitutional law that regulation is unconstitutional unless some compelling necessity, not just official or majority disapproval of the message, requires it. Pornography is often grotesquely offensive; it is insulting, not only to women but men as well. But we cannot consider that a sufficient reason for banning it without destroying the principle that the speech we hate is as much entitled to protection as any other. The essence of negative liberty is freedom to offend, and that applies to the tawdry as well as the heroic' (1991: 104). Langton argues: 'To permit incitement to racial hatred would be to give weight to racist preferences of a kind that egalitarian governments have a duty to ignore, so such speech should not be permitted. Or: to prohibit such speech would be to make progress toward an important social goal, namely, equality, so such speech should be prohibited. If this were the case, then the United Kingdom policy would not conflict with a principle of equal concern and respect. It would, on the contrary, be in harmony with it' (2009: 163). MacKinnon's Indianapolis ordinance is very similar to UK law. Dworkin fails again and again to confront the radical feminist argument because liberty according to him is sovereign over equality. It is what empowers it, he is a true liberal (R. Dworkin, 1991). He is a monist and not a pluralist (like Williams) or now it seems MacKinnon.

5 Rae Langton's Photo: Domination, Subordination, Equality

1. A history of the use of 'objectification', when it was first applied to human relationships in this normative sense would help to resolve this curiosity. Intuitively, I feel it must have appeared most definitely after the apex of German idealism and more than probably sometime in the twentieth century. One feels it may have been born with radical feminism itself and that would tell us something of importance. My conjecture would be that the post-Kantians developed the moral theory in a way that was concomitant with the concept of alienation in Marx, as we shall see.
2. One wonders whether subjectification has a parallel cluster of meanings. I subjectify an object (my computer) when: I see it as ... having interests of its own which may or may not coincide with my own, possessing autonomy and a will, being an agent and doing, being individual and unique (it is after all *my* computer which has wronged me, not just computers), as having physical integrity (otherwise my striking it with the racquet would make little sense) and so on.
3. This is not always the case for Langton: objectification sometimes depends on affirmation of autonomy (as applied to persons and not objects). She uses the example of sadistic rape where the rapist wants to hear the victim's 'No!', to affirm that she does not want it as that is part of his desire. I am not sure that this is even an instance of objectification. I would reiterate that it is about power and the third dimension, one is complicit in one's own domination: you are not normal unless you like a little bit of being tied up and so on. This may well be closer to the Sartrean model we consider below and will show the clear lines of development from Kant to Sartre. Very simply, though, this may not be a case of objectification.
4. One wonders whether the Kantian model commits one to the Sartrean self and antagonistic Other conflict (described below) because it is an either/or, either self or object but never self-as-object-for other. For a more rounded, and quite exemplary discussion of Kantian ethics and sexual relations, I urge the reader to look at Herman (2002). Of course, her Kant is a very soft, Hegelian Kant, see my comments on this in Rose (2007a: ch. 6, 145).
5. What does it mean for knowledge to be made? Vico (1984), as one example, divides knowledge into divine knowledge and artificial knowledge: God has made the universe so only He can know everything, whereas the limits of men's reason stretch to know only those things man has made (mathematics, social laws, and so on). One might be tempted to restate the Vichian thesis along the lines of description and construction or direction of fit. One can discover facts about natural items, but one can construct understandings of moral systems because they have to do with how the desires of human beings are made to fit the world. Vico's principle applies to the realm of behavioural or human sciences when the consciousness of human beings seeks to enframe the world and to fit not only desires but imaginative ideas.
6. What follows is rather brief and I hope to be forgiven for this. I am merely showing that Langton's evil male father theory can be replaced by a more

common philosophical theory and that this can help us to better understand the operation involved in objectifying.

7. Other thinkers include Vico (1984) who sees all knowledge as the elaboration of imaginative, expressivist confrontation with danger. See Rose (2008). Vico is worth mentioning because he is an important element in the reconstruction of Hegelian thought in the next chapter. Here, though, he remains in the background.
8. Herman (2002) offers a far more subtle reading of Kant on this point, though, as I have already mentioned.
9. I resist the urge to continually capitalize the word 'other' as one would normally do when discussing Sartre just to be consistent with my use of it elsewhere in this book.
10. Sartre seeks to remedy this somewhat in his later works, see for example his *Critique of Dialectical Reason* (2004).
11. For a more rounded account of Hegel's theory of action, please refer to the articles collected in Laitinen & Sandis (2010).
12. Such a claim is far from controversial and remains consistent with feminism, which is the discourse that demands coherence in this chapter. For example, 'The capabilities approach insists that a woman's affiliation with a certain group or culture should not be taken as normative for her unless, on due consideration, with all the capabilities at her disposal, she makes that norm her own' (Nussbaum, 1999: 46). Nussbaum implicitly embodies a version of homeliness.
13. There is a direct connection to sexuality here according to Scruton: 'The experience of arousal may then be explained on the analogy with linguistic *understanding*: just as I understand your utterance by latching on to the intentions with which you thereby acquaint me, so do I respond to your glance or caress by recognising the desire behind them, and seeing, through the desire, the possibility which might otherwise have remained concealed. A caress may be either accepted or rejected: in either case, it is because it has been "read" as conveying the message that "we might surely make love"' (2006: 25).
14. Something I too am guilty off up to this point. Hopefully, the final chapter will at least open the possibility of a discussion of different sexualities and their representation, but unfortunately because the debate is dominated by feminists and their opponents, I too have had to approach the problem through this avenue.

Interlude 5 The Devil in Miss Jones

1. When I talk about the remake, I refer to the 2005 Vivid production directed by Paul Thomas and starring Savanna Samson released on DVD under the title of *The New Devil in Miss Jones* rather than the numerous sequels and spin-offs.
2. The translation I have before me of the play translates the title as 'In Camera'. It has also been translated as 'No Exit'.
3. If it does fail, it is in the gratuitous lesbian scene. The scene may be viewer rather than character led, but I am not convinced. One possible defence is

that the film does not shy away from homosexuality as a form of both self and other pleasure as is obvious from the double penetration scene.

6 'I Can't Do It by Myself!': Social Ethics and Pornography

1. If one reads the report and its abridged cousin, there are times when the voice of Bernard Williams cuts through to deliver a philosophical caveat or a reflective comment on commonsensical claims (Williams, 1981).
2. I would suggest that if one is interested in the groundwork for such a position (and I hope one day to offer a better argument for it), it can be found in various articles (Rose, 2007b, 2008, 2009a, 2009b, 2010, 2011, 2013), even if at that time I did not envisage any attempt at a coherent project. Hindsight seems to contradict this.
3. The above discussion of values and motivations is, in part, derived from Frankfurt's (1982) idea of second-order desires.
4. Williams (1972) divides relativism into cultural relativism and what he calls 'interesting relativism'. Needless to say, we shall be concerned with the latter form of the thesis.
5. Skorupski (1999) asserts that proper value pluralists are committed to situations in which the choice between the courses of action A and B is characterized by an inescapable and inarbitrable choice. Value pluralism derived from the strong universalist roots of Kant would take such a form and is then either vacuous or not convincing, as Skorupski shows. He would argue that the weak universalism I offer here is nothing but a relativism or an historically-tuned ethics consistent with nineteenth century writers. If it is, then that is enough because we seem to have forgotten to be historically sensitive in our ethical thinking, 'plumping' more for seemingly objective and universal principles. A rose by any other name ... However, I believe there is a substantial difference in that Skorupski (at least my intuition tells me this) when pushed would be a realist about moral value whereas, as I have argued above, I have identified the artificial, irreal nature of moral values.
6. Hegel himself has another solution to this problem which I shall here ignore. He believes that historical progress will perfect the categories of moral knowing justified by his broader metaphysics. I ignore it because to discuss it would again involve a digression from which we may not return.
7. The position advocated here has much in common with the thought of Hampshire: 'The two elements in procedural justice – a universal rational requirement of two-sidedness and respect for locally established and familiar rules of procedure – are linked as two natural needs in our minds in their practical and political workings. If either the rational requirement or the respect for custom breaks down and ceases to operate, we should expect catastrophe. Conflict will then no longer be resolved within the political domain but will be resolved by violence or the threat of violence, and life will become nasty, brutish, and short. Whatever one's conception of the good, such anarchy will generally be reckoned a great evil, alongside starvation and near-starvation, disease, imprisonment, slavery, and humiliation' (1999, 91–92).

8. These comments may have import for a theory of just war and also the autonomy of soldiers who execute political aims. Considerations of going to war do not, *prima facie*, constitute an objection to what I have said.
9. Compare how Singer (2002) deconstructs the distinction between 'human' and 'animal' in his essay on equality; basically, it is a residue of early modern thinking that supports non-rational attitudes in contemporary society.
10. Please note that I am not asking whether sadomasochistic activities or representations are arousing. The history of pornographic production and the free participation in these activities testifies to the affirmative. There is something about the images of violence devoid of narrative context that is peculiarly contemporary and is questionably arousing. A good discussion of this aspect of contemporary pornography is to be found in Dines (2010). And to be completely conjectural, it strikes me as a plausible sociological thesis that violence and pornography is empirically more prevalent in American-produced films. Whether this is because America produces the most films, or has the widest distribution, or sets the cultural language for the rest of us to follow, I do not know. It might be because of a very real religious zeal for Protestant Christianity in America (which in Northern Europe quickly became the absence of faith or outright atheism) as opposed to Catholicism. The latter's image of the sacred woman surviving from pagan beliefs, or just Catholicism's very aesthetic demission which Protestantism has always lacked. It may just be the consequence of self-hate of the body and its desires in Protestantism which needs to be annihilated in the resurrection rather than be reborn, purified. One would need to be a sociologist or cultural theorist to justify such claims and I am most certainly not that. I just make stuff up.
11. What is more significant is the consent to one's own humiliation implicit in the violent films described above and the effect that has on our culture. If one were to watch contemporary pornography, what sort of sexuality would develop and what sort of fellow-feeling? If we learn from these films about how to act in the bedroom and in the intimate one-on-one with a stranger at the end of the evening, neither participant in such actions would feel at home in such practices. The woman cannot seemingly find satisfaction in humiliation and pain (especially not in an openly consensual or playful context and these films are not) and the man would not satisfy the intimate reciprocity required by the giving inherent in sexual activity.
12. Perhaps this book will be bought by Hollywood and made into a film. I imagine a series of figurines of which my favourite would be the ur-Father. He would look like W. G. Grace. I also expect him to carry a cricket bat.
13. And Hegel knew this. For all his celebration of individual freedom and substantial Kantianism, he knew that capitalism will always produce a disenfranchised class. His solution? To ship them off to the colonies before they destabilize the social fabric because they cannot feel at home. Their individuality counts for nothing (1991: §§244–249).
14. Conjecturally, technology and the emergence of pornography very early on in the history of the internet may have determined the viewers' expectations. With slow bandwidth, films had to be small files and that meant poor quality of short duration. The 'plot' structure that made that possible may have become a norm which needs to be overcome now technology has advanced. This is akin to the effect that the 'money shot' has had on sexuality. It seems

obvious to me that the meaning of the money shot was originally 'this is real and not simulated sex you are watching' and acted as a closure on a stag film. But now, it seems, such practices are objects of desire themselves since the feedback loop of the films has determined practices.

15. Some feminists seem to be aware of the role capitalism plays in inequality: 'One needs no crystal ball to guess that the forces of global capitalism will be around for a while, and with them a tendency to treat people not only as consumers but as commodities, items for use and consumption, and that this is likely to have a continuing effect on women's lives, as the ever-burgeoning sex industry illustrates' (Langton, 2009: 244).

References

Adorno, T. & Horkheimer, M. (1997) *Dialectic of Enlightenment*, trans. J. Cumming, London: Verso.

Anscombe, G. (1958) 'Modern Moral Philosophy', *Philosophy*, 33.124: 1–19.

Apel, K.-O. (1998) *From a Transcendental-semiotic Point of View*, ed. M. Papastephanou, Manchester: Manchester University Press.

Aristotle (1912) *Politics: A Treatise on Government*, trans. W. Ellis, London: J. M. Dent.

Aristotle (1968) *Poetics*, trans. D. Lucas, Oxford: Oxford University Press.

Aristotle (1980) *The Nicomachean Ethics*, trans. D. Ross, Oxford: Oxford University Press.

Attorney General's Commission on Pornography: Final Report (AGCP) (1986), 2 vols, U.S. Department of Justice, Washington, D.C.

Austin, J. (1962) *How to Do Things with Words*, Oxford: Oxford University Press.

Baron, L. (1990) 'Pornography and Gender Equality: An Empirical Analysis', *The Journal of Sex Research*, 27.3: 363–380.

Bartel, C. (2010) 'The "Fine Art" of Pornography? The Conflict between Artistic Value and Pornographic Value', in D. Monore (ed.), *Porn: How to Think with Kink*, Oxford: Wiley-Blackwell.

Beauvoir, S. (1969) *The Second Sex*, trans. H. Parshley, London: Verso.

Benjamin, W. (2008) *The Work of Art in the Age of Mechanical Reproduction*, trans. A. Underwood, London: Penguin.

Berger, F. (1977) 'Pornography, Sex, and Censorship', *Social Theory and Practice*, 4: 183–209.

Berlin, I. (1958) *Two Concepts of Liberty*, Oxford: Oxford University Press.

Berlin, I. & Williams, B. (1994) 'Pluralism and Liberalism: A Reply', *Political Studies*, XLI: 306–9.

Butler, J. (1997) Excitable Speech: A Politics of the Performative, London: Routledge.

Collins, P. (1993) 'Pornography and Black Women's Bodies', in D. Russell (ed.), *Making Violence Sexy: Feminist Views on Pornography*, Buckingham: Open University Press.

Debord, G. (1983) *Society of the Spectacle*, Detroit, USA: Black & Red.

Dines, G. (2010) Pornland: How Porn Has Hijacked Our Sexuality, Boston, USA: Beacon Press.

Dworkin, A. (1981) *Pornography: Men Possessing Women*, London: The Women's Press Ltd.

Dworkin, A. (1987) *Intercourse*, London: Arrow Books..

Dworkin, R. (1981) 'Is There a Right to Pornography?' *Oxford Journal of Legal Studies*, 30.3: 177–212.

Dworkin, R. (1991) 'Two Concepts of Liberty', in E. & A. Margalit (eds), *Isaiah Berlin: A Celebration*, London: Hogarth Press.

Dyzenhaus, D. (1992) 'John Stuart Mill and the Harm of Pornography', *Ethics*, 102.3: 534–551.

Eaton, A. (2007) 'A Sensible Antiporn Feminism', *Ethics*, 117: 674–715.

Eliot, T. S. (1997) 'Hamlet and His Problems', in *The Sacred Wood: Essays on Poetry and Criticism*, London: Faber and Faber.

Ewing, A. (1967) *A Short Commentary on Kant's Critique of Pure Reason*, London: University of Chicago Press.

Flynn, T. (1984) Sartre and Marxist Existentialism: The Test Case of Collective Responsibility, London: University of Chicago Press.

Foucault, M. (1983) *This Is Not a Pipe*, trans. J. Harkness, Berkeley: University of California Press.

Frankfurt, H. (1982), 'Freedom of the Will and the Concept of a Person', in G. Watson (ed.), *Free Will*, Oxford: Oxford University Press.

Frankfurt, H. (1988) 'Coercion and Moral Responsibility', in *The Importance of What We Care About*, Cambridge, Cambridge University Press.

Gastil, R. (1976) 'The Moral Right of the Majority to Restrict Obscenity and Pornography through Law', *Ethics*, 86.3: 231–240.

Habermas, J. (1984) *Communication and the Evolution of Society*, trans. T. McCarthy, Cambridge: Polity Press.

Hampshire, S. (1999) *Justice is Conflict*, London: Duckworth.

Hegel, G. (1971) 'Philosophy of Mind': Part 3 of the *Encyclopaedia of Philosophical Sciences with the Zusatz*, trans. W. Wallace & A. Miller, Oxford: Oxford University Press.

Hegel, G. (1975) *Natural Law: The Scientific Ways of Treating Natural Law, Its Place in Moral Philosophy, and Its Relation to the Positive Sciences of Law*, trans. T. M. Knox, Philadelphia: University of Pennsylvania Press.

Hegel, G. (1977) *The Phenomenology of Spirit*, trans. A. Miller, Oxford: Oxford University Press.

Hegel, G. (1991) *Elements of the Philosophy of Right*, trans. H. Nisbet, Cambridge: Cambridge University Press.

Heidegger, M. (1993) 'The Question Concerning Technology', in D. Farrell Krell (ed.), *Basic Writings: Martin Heidegger*, London: Routledge.

Herman, B. (2002) 'Could it be Worth Thinking about Kant on Sex and Marriage?' In L. Anthony & C. Witt (eds), *A Mind of One's Own: Feminist Essays on Reason and Objectivity*, Cambridge, USA: Westview Press.

Huer, J. (1987) *Art, Beauty and Pornography: A Journey through American Culture*, London: Prometheus Books.

Kant, I. (1963) *Lectures on Ethics*, trans. L. Infield, New York, USA: Harper Torchbooks.

Kant, I. (1991) *The Critique of Judgment*, trans. J. C. Meredith, Oxford: Clarendon Press.

Kant, I. (1993) *Critique of Pure Reason*, trans. J. Meiklejohn, revised V. Politis, London: Everyman.

Kant, I. (1997) *Critique of Practical Reason*, trans. M. Gregor, Cambridge: Cambridge University Press.

Kant, I. (2012) *Groundwork of the Metaphysics of Morals*, ed. M. Gregor & J. Timmerman, Cambridge: Cambridge University Press.

Kendrick, W. (1987) *The Secret Museum: Pornography in Modern Culture*, Berkely: University of California Press.

Kieran, M. (2001) 'Pornographic Art', *Philosophy and Literature*, 25.1: 31–45.

Knowles, D. (2002) *Hegel and the Philosophy of Right*, London: Routledge.

Kojève, A. (1969) *Introduction to the Reading of Hegel,* 2nd edition, trans. J. Nichols, London, Basic Books Inc.

Laitinen, A. & Sandis, C. (eds) (2010) *Hegel on Action,* Basingstoke, UK: Palgrave MacMillan.

Langton, R. (2009) Sexual Solipsism: Philosophical Essays on Pornography and Objectification, Oxford: Oxford University Press.

Levinson, J. (2005) 'Erotic Art and Pornographic Pictures', *Philosophy and Literature,* 29.1: 228–240.

Longino, H. (1980) 'Pornography, Oppression and Freedom: A Closer Look', in L. Leder (ed.), *Take Back the Night: Women on Pornography,* New York: William Morrow.

Lovelace, L. (2006) *Ordeal,* Sacramento, USA: Citadel Press Incorporated.

Lukes, S. (2005) *Power: A Radical View,* London: Palgrave MacMillan.

MacIntyre, A. (2007) *After Virtue: A Study in Moral Theory,* 3rd edition, London: Duckworth.

MacKinnon, C. (1993) *Only Words,* Cambridge, USA: Harvard University Press.

MacKinnon, C. & Dworkin, A. (1997) *In Harm's Way: The Pornography Civil Rights Hearings,* Cambridge, USA: Harvard University Press.

Marx, K. (1993) *Grundrisse,* trans. M. Nicolaus, London: Penguin.

McElroy, W. (1997) *XXX: A Woman's Right to Pornography,* New York: St Martin's Press.

Mill, J. S. (1869) *The Subjection of Women,* London: Longmans, Green, Reader & Dyer.

Mill, J. S. (1962) *Utilitarianism,* ed. M. Warnock, Glasgow: Fontana Press.

Mill, J. S. (2011) *On Liberty,* London: Walter Scott Publishing Company.

Monroe, D. (2010) 'Ruminations of a Dominatrix: An Interview with Mz. Berlin', in D. Monore (ed.), *Porn: How to Think with Kink,* Oxford: Wiley-Blackwell.

Narveson, J. (1993) *Moral Matters,* Ontario: Broadview Press.

Neuhouser, F. (2003) *Foundations of Hegel's Social Theory: Actualizing Freedom,* Cambridge, USA: Harvard University Press.

Nussbaum, M. (1999) *Sex and Social Justice,* Oxford: Oxford University Press.

O'Neill, O. (2007) 'Kantian Approaches to Some Famine Problems', in R. Shafer-Landau (ed.), *Ethical Theory: An Anthology,* Oxford: Blackwell, 258–270.

Parent, W. (1990) 'A Second Look at Pornography and the Subordination of Women', *The Journal of Philosophy,* 87.4: 205–211.

Pepys, S. (1893) *The Diary of Samuel Pepys,* ed. H. Wheatley, London: George Bell and Sons.

Rawls, J. (1993) *Political Liberalism,* New York: Columbia University Press.

Rawls, J. (1999) *A Theory of Justice,* 2nd edition, Oxford: Oxford University Press.

Rea, M. (2001) 'What is Pornography?' *Noûs,* 35.1: 118–145.

Report of the Committee on Obscenity and Film Censorship (RCOFC) (1979) U.K. Home Office, London: Her Majesty's Stationery Office.

Rose, D. (2007a) *Hegel's Philosophy of Right,* London: Continuum.

Rose, D. (2007b) 'Imagination and Reason: An Ethics of Interpretation for a Cosmopolitan Age', in D. Morgan & G. Banham (eds), *Cosmopolitics and the Emergence of a Future,* London: Palgrave.

Rose, D. (2008) 'Vichian Normative Political Theory: History and Human Nature', *New Vico Studies,* 26, 75–102.

Rose, D. (2009a) *Free Will and Continental Philosophy,* London: Continuum.

Rose, D. (2009b) 'Hegel's Theory of Moral Action, Its Place in His System and the "Highest" Right of the Subject', in D. Knowles (ed.), *G. W. F. Hegel, International Library of Essays in the History of Social and Political Thought*, Surrey: Ashgate.

Rose, D. (2010) 'Hermeneutics and the Rational Resolution of Conflict', in C. Chakrabarti & L. Grimes (eds), *Religion, Pluralism and Politics*, Cambridge: Scholars Press.

Rose, D. (2011) 'The Relevance of Hegel's Social Thought to Contemporary Conservatism', in D. Ozsel (ed.), *Reflections of Conservatism*, Vol. 1, Cambridge: Scholars Press.

Rose, D. (2012) 'The Definition of Pornography and Avoiding Normative Silliness: A Commentary Adjunct to Rea's Definition', *Philosophy Study*, 2.8: 547–559.

Rose, D. (2013) 'Society and the Origin of Moral Law: Giambattista Vico and Non-reductive Naturalism', in B. Musschenga & A. van Harskamp (eds), *What Makes Us Moral: On the Capacities and Conditions for Being Moral*, Amsterdam, Netherlands: Springer.

Rosen, R. (2010) *Beaver Street: A History of Modern Pornography*, London: Headpress.

Rousseau, J-J. (1992) *Discourse on the Origin and the Foundation of the Inequality*, trans. D. Cress, Cambridge: Hackett Publishing Company.

Russell, D. (1988) 'Pornography and Rape: A Causal Model', *Political Psychology*, 9.1: 41–73.

Russell, D. (1993) *Making Violence Sexy: Feminist Views on Pornography*, Buckingham: Open University Press.

Sartre, J-P. (1991) *Being and Nothingness: An Essay on Phenomenological Ontology*, trans. H. Barnes, London: Routledge.

Sartre, J-P. (1992) *Notebooks for an Ethics*, trans. D. Pellauer, London: University of Chicago Press.

Sartre, J-P. (2004) *The Critique of Dialectical Reason*, Vol. 1, trans. A. Sheridan-Smith, London: Verso.

Scruton, R. (2006) *Sexual Desire: A Philosophical Investigation*, London: Continuum.

Seuss, Dr. (2011) *Oh, the Places You'll Go!* London: HarperCollins Publishers Ltd.

Singer, P. (1972) 'Famine, Affluence, Morality', *Philosophy and Public Affairs*, 1.3: 229–243.

Singer, P. (2002) 'All Animals are Equal', in H. Kuhse (ed.), *Unsanctifying Human Life*, Oxford: Blackwell.

Skipper, R. (1993) 'Mill and Pornography', *Ethics*, 103.4: 726–730.

Skorupski, J. (1999) 'Value-Pluralism', *Ethical Explorations*, Oxford: Oxford University Press.

Soltenberg, P. (1993) 'Pornography and Freedom', in D. Russell (ed.), *Making Violence Sexy: Feminist Views on Pornography*, Buckingham: Open University Press.

Spink, A., Wolfram, D., Jansen, M., & Saracevic, T. (2000) 'Searching the Web: The Public and their Queries', *Journal of the American Society for Information Science and Technology*, 52.3: 226–234.

Tang, I. (1999) *Pornography: The Secret History of Civilization*, Basingstoke: Channel 4 Books.

Thomson, J. (1971) 'A Defense of Abortion', *Philosophy and Public Affairs*, 1.1: 47–66.

Traeen, B., Nilsen, T., & Stigum, H., (2010) 'Use of Pornography in Traditional Media and on the Internet in Norway', *Journal of Sex Research*, 43.3: 245–254.

Vadas, M. (1987) 'A First Look at the Pornography/Civil Rights Ordinance: Could Pornography be the Subordination of Women?' *Journal of Philosophy*, 84.9: 487–511.

Vattimo, G. (1992) *The Transparent Society*, trans. D. Webb, Cambridge: Polity Press.

Vattimo, G. (2004) *Nihilism and Emancipation: Ethics, Politics and Law*, trans. W. McCuaig, New York: Columbia University Press.

Velleman, D. (2002) *The Possibility of Practical Reason*, Oxford: Oxford University Press.

Vico, G. (1984) *The New Science: Principles of New Science of Giambattista Vico Concerning the Common Nature of the Nations*, 3rd edition of 1744, trans. T. Bergin & M. Fisch, New York: John Hopkins University Press.

Williams, B. (1972) *Morality: An Introduction to Ethics*, Cambridge: Cambridge University Press.

Williams, B. (1976) 'Moral Luck', *Proceedings of the Aristotelian Society*, Supplementary Volumes, Vol. 50: 115–135.

Williams, B. (ed.) (1981) *Obscenity and Film Censorship: An Abridgement of the Williams Report*, Cambridge: Cambridge University Press.

Williams, R. (1997) *Hegel's Ethics of Recognition*, London: University of California Press.

Wolf, S. (1990) *Freedom within Reason*, Oxford: Oxford University Press.

Literature

Arsan, E. (1980) *The Best of Emmanuelle*, trans. L. Blair & A. Hollo, Suffolk: Chaucer Press.

Bataille, G. (1977) *Story of the Eye*, trans. J. Neugroschal, London: Penguin.

Camus, A. (1988) *The Stranger*, trans. P. McCarthy, Cambridge: Cambridge University Press.

Carroll, L. (2011) *Alice in Wonderland*, Public Domain Books. Kindle edition.

Crepax, G. (1992) *Emmanuelle*, Rome: Blue Press.

Crepax, G. (1994) *Valentina*, Vol. 5, Rome: Blue Press.

Crowley, A. (2008) *White Stains*, USA: Createspace.

James, E. (2012) *Fifty Shades Darker*, London: Arrow Books. Kindle edition.

Lawrence, D. H. (1997) *Lady Chatterley's Lover*, London: Penguin.

Manara, M. (2001) *Gulliveriana, e Ballata in Si Bemolle*, Milan: Mondadori.

Manara, M. (2002) *Il Gioco*, Milan: Mondadori.

Réage, P. (1972) *The Story of O*, London: Corgi Books.

Sade, D. (1990) *The One Hundred and Twenty Days of Sodom and Other Writings*, trans. A. Wainhouse & R. Seaver, London: Arrow Books.

Sartre, J.-P. (1990) 'In Camera', *In Camera and Other Plays*, trans. S. Gilbert, London: Penguin.

Stoker, B. (1911) *Lair of the White Worm*, Slough: W. Foulsham & Co. Ltd.

Trocchi, A. (1996) *Young Adam*, Edinburgh: Rebel Inc.

Filmography

Admason, A. (2001) *Shrek*, Dreamworks: 90 mins.
Beineix, J.-F. (1986) *Betty Blue 37° 2 Le Matin,* Director's cut, Cargo Films: 185 mins.
Bertolucci, B. (1973) *Last Tango in Paris*, Produzioni Europee Associati: 250 mins.
Bertolucci, B. (2003) *The Dreamers*, Recorded Picture Company: 115 mins.
Brooks, M. (1968) *The Producers,* Embassy Pictures: 88 mins.
Clark, J. (1978) *Debbie Does Dallas,* School Day Films: 80 mins.
Damiano, G. (1973) *Devil in Miss Jones*, Pierre Productions: 67 mins.
Despentes, V. & Coralie, T. (2000) *Baise-moi*, Canal+: 77 mins.
Dugan, D. (2011) *Just Go with It*, Columbia Pictures: 117 mins.
Ferrario, D. (1999) *Guardami*, Trio Films: 91 mins.
Hodges, M. (1980) *Flash Gordon*, Dino De Laurentiis Company: 111 mins.
Kubrick, S. (1999) *Eyes Wide Shut*, Hobby Films: 159 mins.
Ludgate, S. (1991) *The Lover's Guide*, ITV Studios: 63 mins.
Luna, B. (1990) *The Ages of Lulu*, Apricot: 95 mins.
Medem, J. (2001) *Lucía y el Sexo*, Alicia Produce: 128 mins.
Moretti, N. (2008) *Caos Calmo*, Fandango: 105 mins.
Thomas, P. (2005) *The Devil in Miss Jones*, Vivid: 120 mins.
Trey, P. (2004) *Team America: World Police*, Paramount Pictures: 98 mins.
Winterbottom, M. (2005) *9 Songs*, Revolution Films: 71 mins.

Music video

50 Cent (2005) 'P.I.M.P.', Snoop Dogg Remix, *Get Rich or Die Tryin'*: 5 mins 01.

Index

Printed and bound by CPI Group (UK) Ltd, Croydon, CR0 4YY